Women and Poverty in Britain

Also by Caroline Glendinning

Unshared Care: Parents and their Disabled Children (Routledge and Kegan Paul, 1983)
A Single Door: Social Work with the Families of Disabled Children (Allen and Unwin, 1985)

by Jane Millar

For Richer, for Poorer: DHSS Cohort Study of Unemployed Men (with S. Moylan and B. Davies) (HMSO, 1984)

Women and Poverty in Britain

edited by

Caroline Glendinning

Research Fellow
Social Policy Research Unit
University of York

and

Jane Millar

Lecturer in Social Administration
and Policy
University of Ulster

WHEATSHEAF BOOKS

First published in Great Britain in 1987 by
WHEATSHEAF BOOKS LTD
A MEMBER OF THE HARVESTER PRESS PUBLISHING GROUP
Publisher: John Spiers
16 Ship Street, Brighton, Sussex

© Caroline Glendinning and Jane Millar, 1987

British Library Cataloguing in Publication Data

Women and poverty in Britain.
1. Women, Poor—Great Britain
I. Glendinning, Caroline II. Millar, Jane
305.5′69′088042   HQ1593

ISBN 0–7450–0307–9
ISBN 0–7450–0308–7 Pbk

Phototypeset in 11 on 12 Linotron Times by
Input Typesetting Ltd, London SW19 8DR

Printed in Great Britain by
Antony Rowe Ltd, Chippenham, Wiltshire

THE HARVESTER PRESS PUBLISHING GROUP
The Harvester Group comprises Harvester Press Ltd (chiefly
publishing literature, fiction, philosophy, psychology, and science
and trade books); Harvester Press Microform Publications Ltd
(publishing in microform previously unpublished archives, scarce
printed sources, and indexes to these collections) and Wheatsheaf
Books Ltd (chiefly publishing in economics, international politics,
sociology, women's studies and related social sciences).

273155

Contents

List of Contributors

CAROL BUSWELL is Senior Lecturer in Sociology at Newcastle Polytechnic. For the past three years she has been doing research on Youth Training Schemes especially with regard to the training of girls. In the past she has done research in comprehensive schools and has published articles on gender, aspects of curricula development and changes in the sixth form.

CLAIRE CALLENDER is Lecturer in Social Policy at the University of Bradford; prior to this she taught at the University of Leeds and at University College, Cardiff. Her research on women in the labour market has focused on women, redundancy and unemployment and related social policy issues. She has recently completed some research evaluating a workshop training unemployed women in new technology, which she also helped to set up.

JULIET COOK was born in Oxford and was educated at the London School of Economics. She has researched and taught in a variety of places, for example, the University of the West Indies, the Open University, the University of Oxford and Coventry Polytechnic. She lives in Southport and has two children and two step-children.

CAROLINE GLENDINNING has been Research Fellow in the Social Policy Research Unit, University of York since 1974. Her current research is on the financial consequences of informal care of elderly and disabled people. In order to be involved in her young daughter's life she has recently begun to experience at first hand some of the disadvantage typically associated with part-time employment.

HILARY GRAHAM is Head of the Department of Applied Social Studies at Coventry Polytechnic. She writes and researches in the area of parenthood and poverty. She is the author of *Women, Health and the Family* (Wheatsheaf Books, 1984) and of various articles on caring and coping.

DULCIE GROVES teaches at Lancaster University, mainly on income maintenance and social policy in a women's studies context, with major research interests in women's incomes. She recently added a London PhD on women and occupational pensions to her rather older degrees from Nottingham University and Bryn Mawr College, USA.

HEATHER JOSHI is concerned with motherhood as practitioner and social scientist. She was born in 1946 and her children in 1982 and 1985. She works at the Centre for Population Studies, London School of Hygiene, and is also a Fellow of the Centre for Economic Policy Research.

JANE LEWIS teaches in the Department of Social Administration at the London School of Economics. Her main research interest is in women and social policy, past and present, and her most recent book is *Women in England: Sexual Divisions and Social Change, 1870–1950* (Wheatsheaf Books, 1984).

SUSAN LONSDALE is a Senior Lecturer in Social Policy at the Polytechnic of the South Bank in London. She is the author of *Work and Inequality* (Longman, 1985), and is currently writing a book on women and disability.

JANE MILLAR is a Lecturer in Social Administration and Policy at the University of Ulster, Coleraine. She has previously worked in the Social Policy Research Unit, University of York and the Social Research Branch of the Department of Health and Social Security. Her research has been into the financial consequences of unemployment and the living standards of lone parents.

GILLIAN PARKER is a Research Fellow in the Social Policy Research Unit at the University of York. Before taking up her post at York she was engaged in research on consumer debt in the Department of Social Administration and Social Work, University of Birmingham. She is the author of several articles on consumer credit and debt and has recently edited (with R. Walker) *Money Matters* (Sage, forthcoming).

DAVID PIACHAUD is Reader in Social Administration at the London School of Economics. He worked at the Department of Health and Social Security (1968–70) and in the Prime Minister's Policy Unit (1974–79). He is the author of books and articles on the causes of poverty, the costs of children, the re-distribution of incomes and international comparisons of social security.

ALAN WALKER is Professor of Social Policy at the University of Sheffield. He has written widely on poverty and old age, and has recently completed a major research project on the family care of elderly people. His books include *Community Care* (ed., Basil Blackwell/Martin Robertson, 1982), *Social Planning* (Basil Blackwell/Martin Robertson, 1984) and *Ageing and Social Policy* (ed. with Chris Phillipson, Gower, 1986).

SHANTU WATT was born in Kenya and, after coming to Britain, worked in the youth and community work field before qualifying in social work. She is now lecturing in youth and community development; is married with two daughters, aged fourteen and four years; and recently completed an MSc in Community Studies and Race Relations at the University of Bradford.

Acknowledgements

A number of people have made important contributions to the production of this book. Edward Elgar, former Managing Director at Wheatsheaf Books, gave us enthusiastic encouragement during its early stages. We also wish to thank Mary Maynard for her helpful comments on an earlier draft of Chapter 1; Geoff Hardman for assistance with computing; Steve Johnson for preparing the figures; Sara Perren for compiling the index; Lesley Warren for help with the bibliography; and, in particular, Anna Wyn-Jones and Christine Petch for the massive task of preparing the manuscript. Our colleagues in the Social Policy Research Unit, University of York and the Department of Social Administration and Policy, University of Ulster, gave us encouragement and practical advice. Finally we would like to thank our contributors for their patience and goodwill in coping with the demands we have made on them.

'How Five and Twenty Shillings were Expended in a Week'*

It's of a tradesman and his wife I heard the other day,
And they kicked up a glorious row – they live across the
    way.
The husband proved himself a fool when his money was
    all spent;
He called upon his wife, my boys, to know which way it
    went.

Chorus
She reckoned up and showed him, she showed him quite
    complete,
How five and twenty shillings were expended in a week.

There's two and threepence for house rent – attend to me,
    she said;
Four shillings always goes for meat and three and
    ninepence bread;
To wash your nasty, dirty shirt there's sixpence halfpenny
    soap;
There's one and eightpence goes for coals and tenpence
    wood and coke.

Now fourpence goes for milk and cream and one and
    twopence, malt;
There's threepence goes for vinegar and twopence
    halfpenny, salt;
A penny goes for mustard; three halfpence goes for thread;

*From *A Touch on the Times, Songs of Social Change 1770–1914* ed. Roy Palmer
(Penguin, 1974).

You gave me threepence the other night for half a baked
sheep's head.

Red herrings every morning's fivepence farthing in a week;
Sometimes you send me out for fish – you say you can't
eat meat.
Last Monday night when you got drunk there was
ninepence went for capers;
You'd a penny box of congreves and a halfpenny baked
potato.

A penny goes for pepper, too, as you must understand;
Twopence halfpenny soda, starch and blue, and a farthing's
worth of sand;
Fourpence halfpenny goes for candles; three farthings goes
for matches,
And a penn'orth o' pieces o' corduroy you had to mend
your breeches.

A shilling potatoes, herbs and greens; tenpence butter,
now you see,
And sixpence coffee, eightpence sugar, and one and
fourpence tea.
There's twopence goes for this thing and a penny for that
and t'other;
Last night you broke the chamber pot and I had to buy
another.

There's eightpence for tobacco and seven farthings swipes;
Threepence halfpenny goes for snuff and twopence
halfpenny, tripe.
A penny you owed for shoe strings, down at the cobbler's
shop;
You know last Sunday morning you'd a bottle of ginger
pop.

Now twopence goes for blacking and eightpence
halfpenny, cheese;

Three farthing rushlight every night to watch the bugs and
fleas.
It cost me threepence to mend your coat when you tore it
on a nail,
And twopence halfpenny calico to mend your old shirt tail.

'Well now,' he said, 'I've reckoned up and find without a
doubt,
One pound four and sevenpence halfpenny exactly you've
laid out.'
She said, 'To call me to account you never should begin;
With the fourpence halfpenny that was left I'd a quartern
of gin.'

*   *   *

capers scented tea.
congreves a friction match (after its inventor, Sir W.
Congreve).
swipes weak beer.
shoe strings shoe laces.
rushlight thin candle with a rush wick, made by dipping
dried rushes in tallow.
quartern a quarter.

'The wage of an urban semi-skilled worker in regular
employment in mid-century was around 15s. to £1 a
week. . . . The "comfort line" came at something over £1
a week, depending on the size of family' (John Burnett, *A
History of the Cost of Living*, 1969, p.263). The ballad
therefore probably gives the budget of a skilled worker,
whose earnings (with the addition, possibly, of those of his
wife and children) totalled at least thirty shillings a week.
(The items listed add up not to 25s., but to 27s., and several
purchases are mentioned without prices being given.)

The ballad appears to have been enormously popular. It
was issued by a least four different London printers and
also by others in provincial centres, including Leeds,
Nottingham, Birmingham, Bristol, Preston and Manchester.
There are numerous, earlier versions in which the budgets

total 15s., 16s., 18s., £1.1s. and £1.2s., so apparently the ballad was updated periodically to keep abreast of the rising cost of living.

Part 1
The Sexual Division of Poverty

1 Invisible Women, Invisible Poverty

Jane Millar and Caroline Glendinning

INTRODUCTION

This book is about what has hitherto been a largely invisible subject—the extent and causes of women's poverty in Great Britain. Most studies of poverty, whether carried out by governments or by independent researchers, have largely focused on the financial circumstances of families or household units. They therefore fail to recognise the extent of the poverty which is experienced by women, and the particular dimensions and causes of that poverty. But poverty is not gender-neutral. Whether they are young or old, living with or without men, caring for children or other dependants, women are more likely than men to be poor, as the contributions to this book demonstrate. Drawing on a range of recent research studies, they describe women's experiences in a variety of different contexts—training schemes, employment, redundancy, retirement—and in different roles—as breadwinners, single parents, wives, mothers and carers. These accounts illustrate the extent of women's poverty and economic disadvantage in the labour market, within the welfare state, and within the family.

However, this book is more than simply a description of the extent of poverty among women in Britain today. It also explores the causes of that poverty. It locates those causes firmly in a sexual division of labour which marginalises women's involvement in the labour market while at the same time assigning little or no value to their caring and domestic work within the family. Central to this division of labour is a widespread assumption that women are—and should be—financially dependent on men. Significant too is the fact that the economic inequalities which women experience in the external, public worlds of work and welfare are mirrored in the internal, private world of the home and family. Indeed, the fact that these inequalities are experienced as much in the private domain as in the public, coupled with the widespread failure to acknowledge and value the economic contribution which women make through their unpaid work in the home, together help to account for the traditional invisibility of women's poverty. Women's own economic circumstances are obscured under assumptions about their dependence on men. The focus of both research and policy is therefore generally on the ability of *men* to provide, through waged labour or welfare, for women and other dependants. We shall argue that, as a consquence, women experience considerable economic disadvantage in the labour market and in the private and public systems of welfare, both of which are fashioned to and dependent on male-oriented patterns of employment.

However, these assumptions are increasingly being subjected to vigorous challenge. In this first chapter we hope to take that challenge further by discussing three broad issues. First, why women's poverty has been invisible for so long and why, even in recent studies by eminent researchers and in the latest government statistics, does it remain so. Secondly, we shall suggest some reasons why women's poverty is at last becoming more visible. Finally, we shall examine the complex interplay of economic and ideological factors which historically have combined to structure the material disadvantage experienced by women and which continue to maintain that disadvantage.

In discussing these three issues we shall adopt a broad concept of poverty which takes into account a wide range of material (and some non-material) resources. We shall be concerned not simply with the fact that in general women have access to less money than do men in similar circumstances, but also with the methods by which women obtain that money; through their own waged labour, through public dependence on the state or through private dependence on men. We shall be concerned with the costs and constraints which are typically experienced by women, but not by men, in the course of achieving access to these various financial resources. We shall also be concerned with the degree of freedom which women have over their own resources or the resources which are made available to them. This freedom is likely to be determined by a number of factors including the level of available resources, the demands on those resources, and whether the resources are obtained in the form of wages for a paid job or as a housekeeping allowance given to an unpaid worker within the home. In other words we shall be concerned both with women's unequal access to material resources and also with inequalities in their power to determine how those resources are consumed.

It should be clear that we consider it as important to examine the nexus of economic and power relationships within the household and the positions which women hold in those relationships as it is to examine the external occupational and welfare systems which also shape women's experiences of poverty. Indeed, we shall argue that these two dimensions of women's economic lives, the internal domestic and the external public, are inextricably linked in a number of complex ways. Interweaving back and forth and linking the two worlds is the all-pervasive theme of women's financial dependency.

Our focus on the private as well as the public dimensions of this dependency leads us to consider a further unique feature of women's experience of poverty: the fact that through their own impoverishment women help to prevent poverty for others in a number of ways; or at least reduce its effects. First, women's unpaid labour in the home helps to free their male partners (and, historically, other male relatives too) from the time-consuming constraints of domestic and caring activities, thereby enabling men to engage in paid employment and maintain or enhance their earning power relatively unfettered by home responsibilities. Nor are these male earnings reduced by having to employ somebody to undertake essential household services. Secondly, as (low) wage-earners themselves, women help to cushion their families from the impoverishing impact of male low pay; data from the late 1970s shows that without the earnings contributed to the household budget by married women, the number of families living in poverty would quadruple (CSO, 1980: quoted Land, 1983b). Thirdly, women play a vitally important role in managing scarce resources *within* families, often to their own cost, so that their children and partners are protected from some of the harsher effects of living in poverty.

It will therefore be clear that this book does not simply map out in a purely descriptive fashion the extent and depth of the material poverty experienced by women in Britain today. Throughout, we have also endeavoured to explore and explain the causes of women's poverty by drawing attention to the various power relationships, structures and institutions—the labour market, the welfare state, the family—which perpetuate the likelihood that women will be poorer than men.

We have chosen to concentrate on women's poverty in Britain, although much of the analysis (though not necessarily the empirical data) clearly has parallels with other developed industrialised nations. (See for example, Leira (ed.) (1983); Skrede (1986) for Norway; Scott (1984) for the USA; Baldock and Cass (eds) (1983) for Australia.) However, it is arguable that the need for a book about women's poverty in Britain is especially acute in view of the long and internationally respected tradition of empirical studies of poverty in this country which, as we shall describe below, have nevertheless overlooked the extent and causes of the poverty experienced by women. In addition, our focus on the situation of women in Britain has enabled us to adopt a specific policy orientation. Past and current legislation, regulations and administrative systems are therefore included in all our contributors' analyses of women's poverty, not just in relation to the welfare state but also in relation to the labour market and domestic financial arrangements.

Nevertheless we are aware that this book contains some important limitations. In the first place our primary focus on material resources—in particular on remuneration which is received for work or in place of earnings—means that we have been able to give less attention than we should to the vast amount of indispensable work which is done by women with no material reward whatsoever. In conventional economic analyses such work is assigned no value at all. However if this *unpaid* work is added into an equation which relates the amount of work done to the level of material reward, it vastly increases the extent and depth of women's poverty.

Secondly, this book does not fully reflect the diversity of women's experiences and the very different life-chances of women with different class or ethnic backgrounds, or with different physical or mental abilities. If women's poverty generally has largely been invisible, then the poverty and other forms of disadvantage experienced by Afro-Caribbean and Asian women, by women with chronic health problems and disabilities, or by women whose own childhoods were materially greatly impoverished has remained even more invisible. Similarly we know very little about the material resources which are actually available to, or controlled by, women who live in very wealthy households. However, it would be inappropriate simply to add together various sources of advantage or disadvantage into a single cumulative index. Race, disability and class are, like gender, powerful factors which shape women's lives, but they do so in different ways. For example, the institutional and ideological mechanisms which create and reinforce racial disadvantage are different from those which impoverish women with disabilities (Glendinning, 1980; Campling, 1981a and b; Carby, 1982).

We have drawn particular attention to the important dimension of race; in Chapter 3, Juliet Cook and Shantu Watt describe how racism shapes the different experiences of poverty for black women. But more work clearly needs

to be done to trace the effects of other major social and
political variables, in order to understand better how life-
chances and subjective experiences of poverty differ
between women as well as the ways in which, as a whole,
they differ from those of men. More immediately, however,
we need to show how even these common experiences of
poverty have remained relatively hidden for so long.

THE DEFINITION AND MEASUREMENT OF POVERTY: RENDERING WOMEN INVISIBLE

Poverty is a situation in which resources are insufficient to
meet needs. Both resources and needs can be defined and
measured in different ways. 'Absolute' definitions of
poverty define needs in terms of a set of basic essentials
assumed to be necessary for subsistence. 'Relative' definitions argue that needs are socially determined; poverty
therefore means exclusion from the customary ways of life
in society. A third group of studies use a poverty line set in
relation to supplementary benefit levels and thus define
poverty as being below 'officially' recognised minimum
income levels. However, when we try to examine the extent
of poverty among women it is clear that, despite these
differences, in all empirical studies of poverty the poverty
of women is largely invisible. There are certain aspects of
the way poverty is measured which are common to all
poverty research, and which have the effect of obscuring
gender differences in the causes, extent and experience of
poverty.
    Central to these conventional studies of poverty is the fact
that, whether carried out by government or independent
investigators, they are focused on the resources of *collective*
units—families, households or tax units. The resources and
needs of the individuals within these collective units are not
considered separately. There are three main reasons why
researchers have concentrated on families and households
rather than on individuals. First, in studies which use income
as the measure of resources, it is argued that to measure

individual income would vastly overestimate the extent of poverty because:

[S]ome people do not enjoy incomes in their own right and, since these are mainly dependent children or married women not in employment, information about individuals' incomes tells us little about the extent of poverty. . . . In brief, most persons without any income, and many with only a little income, benefit in some way or another from the incomes of other individuals with whom they live and it would be misleading to ignore such income sharing. (Fiegehen *et al.*, 1977, p.43)

Secondly, many of the items which contribute to any individual's standard of living are items of joint consumption. They are enjoyed by the household as a whole and contribute to the living standards of all its members. Such items include housing conditions and amenities, heating and consumer assets such as cars, washing machines and fridges. Attempts to assign these items of joint consumption to individuals would, it is argued, be meaningless and therefore people living together are assumed to share a common standard of living. Household consumption and, by extension, the income which is used to purchase those goods and services for consumption are therefore assumed to be shared more or less equally among the various household members. Thirdly, as well as being assumed to lead to a pooling of resources, sharing a home is also assumed to result in proportionately lower levels of need. Two people sharing can live more cheaply than two people living in separate households. These assumed 'economies of scale' are reflected in the supplementary benefit scale rates where the rate for a single person is equivalent to about 60 per cent of the rate for a married couple.

Thus poverty researchers have concentrated on measuring the poverty of aggregate units and have largely ignored the distribution of resources and needs within those units. The particular circumstances of women are therefore obscured in several ways. First, women are included in the numbers of people in poverty only if the family or household income is below the poverty line; they are not counted among the poor if household resources are above that line, regardless of whether they actually have equal access to that income. Yet what evidence there is on the distribution of resources within households shows clearly that it is perfectly possible for women to experience substantial poverty and deprivation in families whose family income brings them above the poverty line (Pahl, 1980; Edwards, 1981; Land, 1983b; and see Hilary Graham's chapter below).

Secondly, the use of a household or family measure means that, within poor households, all members are assumed to be equally poor. But again (as both Hilary Graham and Gillian Parker show in Chapters 11 and 12) the burden of poverty—of doing without and trying to make ends meet—falls mainly upon women. Furthermore this self-sacrifice on the part of women is viewed as a legitimate result of their altruistic and care-giving 'nature'. In effect, the needs of women are assumed to be, if not less than those of men, certainly of less importance; 'self-denial is still seen as women's special share of poverty' (Land and Rose, 1985, p. 86). Moreover, the assumption that items of 'joint' consumption contribute equally to the standard of living of all family members is also problematic. The purchase and use of many consumer goods is clearly related to gender. As Hilary Graham describes in Chapter 11, cars in particular can be a drain on household resources, contributing to the living standards of men at the expense of the needs of women and children. In contrast, women's unlimited access to washing machines scarcely seems to be an adequate compensation. Thus the disproportionate degree to which women suffer the consequences of poverty in terms of reduced consumption is also obscured by the assumption that all household members share the same standard of living.

Thirdly, the financial dependency of women within marriage—the fact that some married women have little or no income in their own right but 'share' in their husband's income—is assumed to *protect* women against poverty. For example, Layard *et al.*(1978, p. 24) explain that poverty and low pay are not correlated because 'most of those on low pay are married women, and married women are not usually poor'. The extent of low pay among women is therefore considered irrelevant to the extent of poverty among women because 'really' women are dependent upon men for their standard of living. This assumption is not only inaccurate but is actually damaging to women because it uses the financial dependence of *some* women to justify ignoring the lower resources of *most* women. As we shall show below, less than one-fifth of all adult women in Britain today are in fact wholly dependent financially on a male breadwinner.

The measurement of poverty in terms of families or households therefore means that women's poverty within families remains hidden; that the extent to which women bear the burden of poverty also remains hidden; and that the question of women's independent access to resources is considered unimportant. Furthermore and perhaps surprisingly, the incorporation into relative definitions of poverty of important social dimensions such as powerlessness and social exclusion has not been extended to any examination of the relative positions of women and men. Instead, existing research tends to focus on the measurement of resources in terms of outcomes (income levels, expenditure, assets, and so on) and takes no account of how these outcomes are arrived at. Thus simple measures of cash income do not take into account differences in the method or ease with which that income is obtained; nor the differential time and effort which may be expended in order to achieve a given standard of living. In particular the value of time—both in the generation of resources and in their use—has hitherto been largely ignored in poverty studies. (But see Piachaud's (forthcoming) discussion.) If time were included it would almost certainly point up substantial differences between women and men. First, there is the substantial amount of time and effort expended by women on unpaid domestic labour which is entirely ignored and given no value. Thus when Scott (1984, p.x) adopted 'a redefinition of work that included unpaid work and assumed that all income was payment for work done, [she] realised that men were getting paid at a rate eighteen times that of women.' Secondly men, being on the whole better paid than women (and married men being more favourably taxed than married women), can obtain a given level of income through fewer hours of employment than women. Each may have the same amount of cash at the end of the week but it will have taken a women longer than a man to earn it. Nor is account taken of the psychological benefits of obtaining income from employment and hence having an independent income rather than being dependent on another person. As Cragg and Dawson (1984, p. 71) found in their study of unemployed women:

[T]he prospect of supplementary income [from employment] is prized not only for its simple purchasing power, but for the measure of independence it grants to the wife in personal and household decision-making. Wives often voiced some unease about the supplicatory aspect of their position and placed great value on money earned rather than given.

Both government and independent studies of poverty also generally fail to take systematic account of transfers 'in kind' both from employment and the state. The 'perks' of employment—occupational pensions and benefits, company cars, and so on—generally go to the higher paid and more often therefore to men than to women (as Claire Callender shows in Chapter 7 with reference to redundancy payments; and Dulcie Groves with regard to occupational pensions in Chapter 10). So far as transfers from the state are concerned, women obtain less than men from the education system (Deem, 1978; Arnot, 1986) and have more difficulty in getting access to state housing (Brion and Tinker, 1980; Austerberry and Watson, 1981); but there has been little systematic analysis of the extent to which, overall, women and men receive equal levels of fiscal and cash benefits from the state, relative to their needs. If the information were available to compare fully the access of women and men to both material and non-material resources and the conditions under which this access is obtained then it seems likely that the gap between women and men would be even wider than is found simply by comparing income levels.

Conventional poverty research therefore tells us little specifically about the poverty experienced by women and, in particular, about the poverty experienced by the vast majority of women who are married or living with a male partner. Nevertheless it can—and does—show that in terms of *income poverty* there is a substantial gap between lone (i.e. not currently married or cohabiting) women and comparable men. The evidence that is available from the various British poverty studies over the past 20 years does consistently show that lone women tend to be over-represented among the poor and that lone women are more likely to experience poverty than lone men. In Abel-Smith and Townsend's (1965) analysis of poverty in 1953/54, according to their measure of poverty 10 per cent of all households were poor but this was the case for 42 per cent of women living alone without dependants compared with 29 per cent of men in the same situation, and for 24 per cent of lone mothers. Similarly Fiegehen *et al.* (1977), in their analysis of poverty in 1971, found that 52 per cent of poor households were 'headed' by a woman compared with only 21 per cent of all households; and that households 'headed' by a women were four times more likely to be poor than households 'headed' by a man (18 per cent compared with 4 per cent). The analysis by Layard *et al.* (1978) showed that in 1975 while 71 per cent of lone women pensioners were living in poverty this was the case for 61 per cent of lone men pensioners; for 64 per cent of lone mothers but only 23 per cent of lone fathers; and for 25 per cent of single working-age women but only 14 per cent of single working-age men. Looking at the individuals in poor households rather than simply at the sex of the 'head' of the household, Townsend (1979) found that, at all ages except under 15, women were more likely than men to be living in households with incomes below supplementary benefit levels.

Our own analysis, based on the 1983 *Family Expenditure Survey*,[1] also shows that, overall, lone women are more at risk of poverty than lone men (Table 1.1). Using a poverty line of 140 per cent of ordinary rates of supplementary benefit we found that the two types of household most likely

Table 1.1: The Extent and Risk of Poverty¹ by Household Type: Great Britain, 1983

	All households %	Poor households %	Risk of poverty (% in each group in poverty)
Pensioners			
Couple	9.7	14.7	42%
Woman	10.9	23.6	61%
Man	2.7	4.9	51%
Non-pensioners			
Single woman	3.9	4.6	33%
Single man	5.1	5.5	30%
Couple, no children	17.2	7.3	12%
Couple, children	28.2	20.7	20%
Lone mother	3.6	7.7	61%
Lone father	0.4	0.6	43%
Others²	18.4	10.3	15%
Total	100	100	28%
Base	6973	1938	

Notes:
1. Net normal *household* weekly income minus net housing costs below 140 per cent of ordinary rates of supplementary benefit. 'Normal' income refers to current income for all except those unemployed or sick for less than three months, in which case 'usual' income when in employment is used. Calculated from the 1938 Family Expenditure Survey.
2. These include all the 'multi-unit' households, i.e. households containing more than one family or 'tax-unit'.

to be poor are elderly women living alone (61 per cent) and lone mothers (61 per cent). Together these two groups of women accounted for 32 per cent of poor households but only 15 per cent of all households. However, unlike the results of the analysis by Layard *et al.* quoted above, our analysis suggests that the risk of poverty is very similar for lone women and men of working age without dependants.² Thus the evidence from this and other studies shows that women living alone are at a much higher risk of poverty than men living alone. The increase in the numbers of women in such situations is one of the major factors behind the increasing recognition being given to the 'feminisation of poverty', and it is to this that we turn in the next section.

BECOMING VISIBLE: THE 'FEMINISATION OF POVERTY'

In recent years there has developed a thesis that poverty is a phenomenon which increasingly affects women more than men. This notion of the 'feminisation of poverty' implies a *shift* in the burden of poverty from men to women, with women now being at greater risk of poverty than men. For example, Scott (1984, p. 3) writes: 'women are becoming a more visible part of the poor because in fact a process of "feminization of poverty" is taking place.' The thesis is supported by two main arguments: first, that the rate of poverty amongst woman-headed households is on the increase; and secondly, that households headed by women now constitute an increasing proportion of the poor.

It is difficult adequately to judge the truth of the 'feminisation of poverty' thesis because of the lack of adequate data with which to compare past and present—in part a reflection of the fact that, as we have already shown, studies of poverty have tended to obscure the real extent of women's poverty. However, Jane Lewis and David Piachaud's comparison (in Chapter 2) of the current situation with that at the turn of the century shows that, then as now, women made up the majority of the poor. Indeed, the whole notion of the 'feminisation of poverty' 'is problematic if it is taken to mean that the over-representation of women amongst the poor is a *new* phenomenon rather than a *recently recognised* phenomenon' (Cass, 1985, p. 5). It is not so much that women are now more likely than before to be poor, but that their previously invisible poverty is becoming increasingly visible. We suggest that there are two main reasons for this development.

The Myth of Women's Financial Dependence on Men
One set of reasons for the emerging visibility of women's
poverty focuses on the fact that fewer women nowadays
have lives which fit the conventional assumptions on which
both poverty research and social policy have traditionally
been based.

First, important demographic changes have taken place
in recent years which have resulted in increasing numbers
of women becoming 'heads of households' or forming single
adult households and thereby becoming visible in house-
hold-based poverty studies. Perhaps the most dramatic of
these changes has resulted from the explosion in the population of elderly and very elderly people. Between 1901 and
1981 the number of people aged over 65 rose from 1.7
million to more than 8 million, an increase as a proportion
of the total population from almost 5 per cent to 15 per
cent. Such increases have been even more marked for the
very elderly; during the same period the numbers aged 75
plus increased by more than 500 per cent to over 3 million
(Henwood and Wicks, 1984). Women form a much higher
proportion of the elderly population than their male
counterparts, and are also more likely at all ages over retirement not to be married (i.e. single, widowed or divorced).
The gender difference in marital status actually increases
with advancing age, so that amongst those over 75 years old
80 per cent of women are not married compared with just
over a third of men (Peace, 1986). The numbers of non-
married elderly women who now constitute 'heads' of household units therefore form an increasing proportion of the
population. As Alan Walker and Dulcie Groves show in
Chapters 9 and 10, such women are particularly likely to be
poor.

A second major demographic change has occurred as a
consequence of increasing rates of marital breakdown. Over
the past 25 years the number of families headed by a lone
parent has approximately doubled, mainly as a result of
rising divorce rates. As Jane Millar demonstrates in Chapter
8, lone-parent families are overwhelmingly headed by
women and they are also at particular risk of being poor.

Female lone parents therefore constitute a second group of women who, as household 'heads', are increasingly visible in studies of poverty.

A further demographic factor which is helping to increase the visibility of women's poverty is their increasing participation in the labour market. In the last 35 years the economic activity rate of women (i.e. the percentage of women in work or seeking work at any one point in time) has more than doubled. This increase is particularly true of married women. The presence of children (particularly young children) does have a marked effect on women's employment opportunites, as Heather Joshi demonstrates in Chapter 6. Nevertheless the trend of increased economic activity is still very clear among women with children, helped by a reduction in average family size and therefore in the number of years spent bearing and caring for young children. This picture was confirmed by the major survey of women's employment carried out by the Department of Employment in 1980. Using a broad definition of economic activity, it was concluded that 69 per cent of women of working age had full-time, part-time or occasional paid employment (Martin and Roberts, 1984, p. 19). The survey also found that 'women increasingly tend to return to work between births and to return to work sooner after childbearing is finished, particularly if they have worked between births' (p. 137).

As well as recognising the increasing presence of women in the labour force, attention has also to some extent been directed towards the circumstances and conditions under which they work. A major impetus for this focus has come from evaluations of the equal pay and equal opportunities legislation of the 1970s. As Susan Lonsdale describes in Chapter 5, this legislation has largely failed to make any impact on the widespread segregation of women and men workers into different types of jobs with different hours, conditions and prospects, those of women invariably being inferior. Even where jobs are broadly comparable, women's hourly rates of pay tend to be lower than those of men. Paradoxically, therefore, as married women have moved in increasing numbers into low paid and part-time jobs, their poverty has become more visible than when it was locked away out of sight within the family. Women's poverty is therefore becoming increasingly visible as the result of major demographic and socio-economic changes. Increasing numbers of women are living at some point during their lives without male partners on whom they might depend financially; this is most apparent during periods of single parenthood and in old age. In addition women are spending an increasing proportion of their adult lives in paid employment. As paid workers they are therefore more visible, but are concentrated disproportionately in low-paid employment.

Consequently only a small proportion of women in Britain are now not economically active and are wholly dependent on the earnings of a male breadwinning partner. According to the 1981 Census (OPCS, 1983, Table 12) there are 21.7 million women aged 16 and over in Great Britain. Of these, 6.3 million are over retirement age; 4.9 million are single, widowed or divorced women of working age (almost one million of whom are lone mothers); 5.7 million are married women in full-time or part-time employment; and 0.3 million are married women either seeking paid work or currently unable to work because of ill-health. This leaves only 4.5 million married women of working age who are neither in nor seeking employment. Yet not even all of these women are financially dependent on their husbands as about half a million are married to unemployed men, in effect making them dependent on the state rather than on male earnings. The traditional picture of the financially dependent woman therefore now applies only to a very small minority—about 18 per cent—of all women. Even if we include as financially dependent those married women in part-time jobs and elderly married women (although most of the latter will derive the majority of their income from the state) this still gives a total of less than half (47 per cent) of all adult women partially or fully dependent on their husbands. A similar pattern exists in other developed societies. For example, in Norway in 1981 only one quarter of all families were dependent on one income alone (Skrede, 1986). Similarly, evidence from Australia suggests that only one in three of all women over the age of 14 could be presumed to be fully and privately supported by a male partner (Baldock and Cass, 1983, p. xiii).

It can hardly be realistic, therefore, to ignore any longer the issue of women's *independent* access to resources (as conventional studies of poverty have done) on the grounds that this does not reflect their real, total access. Quite clearly for many women nowadays those independent resources are all the resources they have—there are no male partners whose higher incomes might enhance their standard of living.

The Challenge of Feminism

A second factor which has led to the gradual uncovering of women's poverty is the growing body of feminist critiques of social and economic structures, social policy and social research. One of the central themes of these critiques has been the breaking-down of the conventional dichotomy between the public world of paid work and the private world of the home and family. Conventionally the former is the domain of men, the latter the domain of women. The public world of paid work is the focus of public and economic policy; the private world, certainly according to functionalist sociological theory, is a haven of expressive warmth and emotional support (Parsons and Bales, 1956). This clear dichotomy is not so outdated as it may seem; on the contrary it has recently re-emerged in the speeches of conservative politicians and in the philosophical writings of New Right moralists both in Britain and the United States (David, 1983; Levitas, 1986).

Over the past 15 years feminists have continually tried to breach the divisions between these private and public worlds. They have argued that the two are inextricably related and that it is therefore as important to investigate the political and economic dimensions of the personal, domestic worlds of women (and men) as it is to examine the more public aspects of their lives. Equally important, feminist

critiques have endeavoured to identify and make explicit
the public causes of women's private experiences and argued
that these are issues which need to be addressed by public
policy.

One of the most persistent themes which has emerged
from this critique is the argument that the unpaid work
which women do in the home must no longer remain invisible. Its historical invisibility, it is universally agreed, is the
result of the fact that it is performed without remuneration,
'which is why recognising it as work was not automatic,
but rather constituted a great step forward and a scientific
discovery' (Delphy, 1984, p. 78). We have already indicated
some of the ways in which women's unpaid work in the
home contributes to the creation of female poverty (and,
conversely, to the comparative comfort of others). This
theme will be taken up over and over again by the contributors to this book, who will illustrate how women's (actual or
presumed) domestic responsibilities structure their material
disadvantage in the labour market and welfare systems,
thereby rendering them vulnerable to poverty. Meanwhile
the fact that this unpaid work has been (and continues to
be) invisible in both government and independent research
on poverty helps to contribute to maintaining the invisibility
of women's poverty.

A second stream of analysis which has emerged from the
feminist perspectives of the last 15 years has focused on the
internal organisation of hitherto 'private' relations between
men and women, and has sought to make explicit both the
political and the economic dimensions of those relationships. It has thus been possible to see how men and women
occupy unequal positions of power within the home as well
as in the world outside:

The interpersonal relationship of a man and a women is not an island. . . .
Even if a husband and wife . . . do not work together, their respective
situations in the labour market, as members of differently treated groups
in this market, are part of their overall situation—and therefore of their
relationship. (Delphy, 1984, p. 115)

So far as the uncovering of women's poverty is concerned,

this focus on the structuring of relationships within the home and family has begun to reveal how women can—and often are—poor *within* marriage, regardless of the level of income received by their male partners. It is increasingly clear that men and women do not always have equal power and control over the material resources of the household and that, for women, financial dependency does not necessarily provide any safeguard against poverty. These issues are discussed in more detail by Hilary Graham in Chapter 11.

Feminism has therefore presented a major contribution to our understanding of poverty and inequality by challenging the assumptions which have hitherto formed the basis for both research and policy on these issues. Specifically, feminist critiques have sought to breach the divisions between the public and private domains. In doing so they have helped us to understand first, the enormous significance which women's unpaid work plays in the creation of their own poverty and other people's wealth; and secondly, the economic inequalities which women experience within the home and family. Both of these themes have contributed enormously to increasing the visibility of women's poverty. In the final section of this chapter we shall pursue this analysis by exploring the causes of women's poverty and their roots in the sexual division of labour.

THE GENDER DIVISION OF POVERTY

In the final part of this chapter we shall discuss the reasons why, at whatever age and whatever their employment and domestic circumstances, women are more likely than men to be poor. In doing so, we must break down the distinctions between home and work, public and private worlds, to show how gender-related patterns of advantage and disadvantage in each are interdependent and mutually reinforcing. We shall also draw attention to some of the ideological and cultural factors which are involved in the creation of women's poverty and to the roles of the state and social policy in creating and perpetuating the poverty experienced by women.

The roots of women's poverty are clearly embedded firmly in the sexual division of labour—in the different tasks and roles which are adopted by men and women. This division places on men a primary responsibility to fulfil the role of economic provider through employment in the public sphere outside the home, while women are responsible for child-bearing, child-rearing and domestic work within the private sphere. Women's participation in the labour market as wage-earners and breadwinners is therefore secondary to their domestic role. It is the restrictions imposed by women's domestic responsibilities which, as many of the contributors to this book demonstrate, place women in a secondary and marginal position in the labour market, disadvantaged and far less well paid than men.

However, the sexual division of labour does far more than simply define women's responsibilities and roles, for the *nature* of the work from which women's primary domestic responsibilities are constructed clearly affects their experiences in the public world of the labour market. The most salient features of women's domestic work and child-care are, first, that they are private activities performed without the company or collaboration of others; and secondly, that they are unpaid. Both of these features—but especially the latter—help to structure women's experience in the labour market and contribute to the poverty women experience in paid work. For example, the types of work which are done at home *without* pay are reflected in the types of work which women typically do in the labour market for *low* pay—work which essentially involves caring for or servicing others in some way. Effectively, women's gender-related roles are transferred from the home to the workplace. And because domestic and child-care work done in the home is taken for granted and unpaid, when similar *types* of work are performed in the labour market they are accorded low value and attract poor remuneration:

The deeply ingrained ideology of motherhood which asserts that women's prime responsibility is to the care of children, provides a 'natural' justific-ation for women's low status in paid work. (Baldock, 1983, p. 23)

These two features of the gender division of labour—women's primary responsibility for domestic work and child-care and their low status and marginal position in the labour market—are complementary and mutually reinforcing. The consequences for women's ability to compete in the labour market and command status, pay and other material rewards from paid work on an equal basis with men are described in detail by Susan Lonsdale and Heather Joshi in Chapters 5 and 6. In addition, as both these contributors and Claire Callender in Chapter 7 point out, women are less likely than men to benefit from protective and regulatory legislation in the labour market. Indeed, there is evidence (discussed by Susan Lonsdale and by Carol Buswell in Chapter 4) that a low-paid, low-status and largely unprotected secondary labour market is emerging, in which women are increasingly being confined. Not only do women receive fewer material rewards from paid work, therefore; they are also likely to be working in harsher conditions and, as Claire Callender shows in Chapter 7, at greater risk of being pushed out of the labour market into (invisible) unemployment.

Out of the labour market too, women are disadvantaged by the gender division of labour. Assumptions about their primary domestic responsibilities have historically denied women access to the same types and levels of income replacement benefits as men when they are unemployed, sick, caring for disabled relatives or in old age (Dale and Foster, 1986, Chapter 6; and see Dulcie Groves' account in Chapter 10 of the development of occupational pensions). Since the implementation of the 1978 EEC Directive on Equal Treatment for Men and Women in Social Security, this direct discrimination has largely been removed. However both state and occupational welfare systems still heavily discriminate *indirectly* against women because the rules governing eligibility and levels of benefits are geared to male patterns of employment and earnings. Women who have limited or discontinuous employment histories, or whose withdrawal from the labour market is because of a contingency (such as the care of young children) not typically experienced by men can therefore expect to receive lower levels of benefits—or none at all—from social security or occupational welfare schemes. Consequently women are more likely to find themselves dependent on means-tested or minimum benefit levels than are men in similar circumstances. The effects of this indirect discrimination on women's experience of poverty in unemployment, single parenthood and old age are explored in Chapters 7 to 10.

The gender division of labour also contributes to the structuring of relationships between men and women within the family. As Brittan and Maynard (1984, p. 143) point out: 'the various activities women perform for their families . . . define for them an asymmetrical power relationship with men.' Part of this asymmetrical power relationship is represented by the fact that because of their 'breadwinner' status and generally higher incomes, men are able to legitimate (for themselves at any rate) a claim to greater control over household resources and a right to appropriate or retain for their own personal use income which might otherwise be shared between all household members. In Chapter 11 Hilary Graham shows clearly how even scarce financial resources may be appropriated by male partners for their own use. Men's greater control over household resources and how these are spent is also apparently regarded as legitimate by many women—though as both Pahl (1985a) and McKee and Bell (1985) indicate, such issues may create considerable tension and play some part in the eventual breakdown of a marriage.

The gender division of labour also contributes to the construction of a specifically feminine role and consciousness which is organised around the twin themes of 'caring' and 'altruism'; the servicing and supporting of others without economic reward, even if this entails considerable personal sacrifice (Graham, 1983; Land and Rose, 1985). Unpaid, unvalued and invisible labour in the home helps to create clear expectations that women will, as a matter of course, do things for others, whether this involves caring for children, providing emotional support or washing socks. If the labour is invisible, so too is the sacrifice which is involved; and this leads to the final dimension of women's relationship to poverty which is discussed in Chapters 11 and 12 of this book—their role in *managing* scarce domestic resources in order to protect children and, especially, men from the full impact of financial hardship. Moreover, as Gillian Parker shows in Chapter 12, such strategies can involve considerable subterfuge and anxiety lest they are discovered by male partners whose status as economic provider would consequently be threatened.

We have argued that in a number of complex and inter-locking ways the sexual division of labour is related to the poverty women experience in the labour market, in relation to systems of welfare and in the home. However, behind this patterning of gender roles lies a powerful ideological force—the notion of women's financial dependency on men. This notion does more than simply describe the reality of the economic circumstances of very many women; it also creates and legitimates those inequalities. For example, the ideology of female dependency helped in the latter half of the last century to exclude women from the labour market and enhance men's negotiations for a larger 'family' wage (Land, 1980). Similarly Lewis (1984) has shown how the concept of women's economic dependency has been a powerful factor in maintaining male work incentives (particularly among working-class men). In Chapter 4 of this book, Carol Buswell illustrates the powerful subtle pressures on female school-leavers which create expectations of future participation in a secondary labour market and very limited earning power which are entirely consistent with assumptions about their future financial dependency.

The ideology of dependency essentially legitimates women's poverty, whether that poverty is earned through low-paid employment or assigned by subsistence-level benefits. Nowhere perhaps is this stated more clearly than in relation to the welfare state and the assumptions and conditions which, historically and currently, regulate entitlement to income maintenance benefits. Women's financial dependency as reflected in welfare state legislation both legitimates and creates women's poverty. Perhaps the clearest statements about the *desirability* of women's economic dependency were made in the Beveridge Report (see Dale and Foster, 1986, pp.16–17). Although these arguments seem quaintly old-fashioned today it is salutory to remember that as recently as 1974 the government was justifying its refusal to compensate married women carers for their loss of earnings on the grounds that they 'would be at home in any case' (Groves and Finch, 1983), and only in July 1986 that invalid care allowance was finally extended to married and cohabiting women.

Far from protecting women from poverty, as generations of employers, civil servants, politicians and even trades unionists would have us believe, women's assumed and actual financial dependence on men is in fact the major cause of their poverty. Women's assumed dependence legitimates low pay and benefit systems which are indirectly discriminatory; their actual dependence contributes to material inequality and poverty within the home. In the following chapter Jane Lewis and David Piachaud explore how this notion of dependency has affected women's experience of poverty over the last century; and in Chapter 3 Juliet Cook and Shantu Watt analyse the ways in which the additional dimension of racism structures the experience of poverty for black women.

NOTES

1. The authors acknowledge the use of the Family Expenditure Survey data from the ESRC Data Archive, though the authors alone bear responsibility for the analysis and interpretation reported in this chapter.

   It would have been useful to be able to use the actual 'official' estimates of the numbers of families with incomes below 140 per cent of supplementary benefit in 1983 as published by the DHSS (1986a). However, these published tables are an extreme example of 'gender-blindness' in poverty research in that no breakdown of the statistics is given by sex. Our figures are not comparable to the DHSS figures because of a number of differences in the calculations: we measure total *household* income whereas they measure family ('tax-unit') income; for pensioners they use the long-term rates of supplementary benefit whereas we have used the ordinary rate of all households; and in addition DHSS figures are based in part on supplementary benefit administrative statistics.

2. This could indicate an improvement in the relative situation of lone women and/or a deterioration in the relative situation of lone men (perhaps as a result of increased levels of unemployment). It may also in part be a consequence of the fact that we used a lower poverty line (140 per cent of the *ordinary* rate of supplementary benefit as opposed to 140 per cent of the long-term rate). Because in general women have lower incomes than men, a higher poverty line would include more women.

2 Women and Poverty in the Twentieth Century

Jane Lewis and David Piachaud

The number of eldery people, predominantly women, living on their own, is rising. One-parent families are increasing. Unemployment among women is growing. Not surprisingly, therefore, there has been a recent spate of literature on 'the feminisation of poverty' by among others, Hilda Scott (1984) and Martin Rein and Steve Erie (forthcoming). Yet the assumption that the feminisation of poverty is recent is misplaced. The simple fact is that throughout the last century women have always been much poorer than men. At the start of this century 61 per cent of adults on all forms of poor relief were women (GB 1909, p. 16). Today 60 per cent of adults for whom supplementary benefit is paid are women. One hundred years ago women constituted a minority of the paid labour force, they were paid far less than men, they did most of the cleaning, cooking, child-care and other unpaid household tasks, they lacked economic and political power . . . *plus ça change.*

In looking at poverty among women from an historical perspective, which is here confined to Britain over the last century, we have concentrated on the ways in which women's dependencies on the family, labour market and state have been and are interlocking, and how the relative importance of each has increased or diminished. We review how the command over resources has been differentially distributed between men and women and consider how the poverty experienced by women has changed. What we cannot do is to present a complete analysis of all the factors affecting poverty among women over the last century. When we discuss women's marginal position in the labour market or dependent children as causes of poverty, we are not implying that the solutions to female poverty lie in full employment for women and avoiding motherhood. We would argue that women's material poverty reflects the way in which society has persisted in undervaluing so much of the work that they do. Only a radical rethinking of our social and economic policies, such as that suggested by Anna Coote (1981), who suggested we start by thinking how best to provide for our children rather than how best to achieve full employment, will improve women's position in the long term.

It is impossible to draw direct comparisons between women's poverty in the late nineteenth and twentieth centuries. Maud Pember Reeves (1913) described the Edwardian working-class wife with five or six children living in a couple of rooms with no domestic water supply nor a cooker that turned on and off, struggling to balance an irregular income of 'round about a pound a week', undergoing frequent childbirth and more frequent pregnancy, standing at the wash-tub and mangle for long hours to earn an extra 1/6d a week (which would feed the family for a couple of days), or resorting to the pawnshop and, in final desperation, to the Poor Law Guardians for relief. Beatrix Campbell (1984) recently described life for a working-class wife whose family is on supplementary benefit: income may be regular, but an equivalent and largely unrecognised skill is still required to administer it; housing may now have 'mod cons', but how can we compare a tower block with running damp to an Edwardian walk-up with one tap per floor and shared lavatories? Elizabeth Roberts (1984) has suggested that despite the harshness of their environment and their desperate mutual poverty, many working-class wives in the period before World War I looked back on their lives with satisfaction—they took pride in what they had accomplished for their families. The mothers described by Campbell take little pride in their existence. The sense of social exclusion must necessarily be more complete in late twentieth-century society where there is so much more, so much closer, to aspire to. The overall improvements in living standards serve to emphasise the relative deprivation of the poor.

Comparing the circumstances of women over a long period clearly presents difficulties. The problems of definition that arise in assessing poverty at any one time—the poverty level to be used, the appropriate income unit, the measure of income, the work involved in paid and unpaid activities—are enormously magnified when we try to look at poverty historically. Nevertheless, the continuity of women experiencing an inferior economic position to men does stand out, whatever the definitions used. Over the past century women's command over resources has been lower than men's. It has also been to a large extent indirect, being a result of dependence on a father or husband.

Before examining this in more detail we first consider some of the demographic factors affecting the poverty of women. There have been marked improvements in female life expectancy at birth, from 51.6 years in 1901 to 76.2 years in 1981, although women's life expectancy at age 21 has not increased as much (CSO, 1986). This, together with the falling fertility rate, has produced a growth in the proportion of elderly women from 7 per cent of those over school-age in 1891 to 22 per cent in 1981, as shown in Table 2.1. At the same time child-bearing patterns have altered markedly. Titmuss (1958) drew attention to the contrast between the average working-class woman of the 1890s marrying in her teens or early twenties, who experienced ten pregnancies and spent 15 years of her adult life in either pregnancy or nursing, and her post-war counterpart, who spent four years either pregnant or nursing. The decrease in family size has meant not only that women have more time to engage in other pursuits, but has also resulted in improvements in their health status and arguably, therefore, in higher energy levels. The Women's Co-operative Guild Collection, *Maternity: Letters From Working Women*, (Llewellyn Davies, 1915), testified to the high levels of

Table 2.1: Composition of Female Population (Excluding Girls) by Age and Marital Status: Great Britain, 1891–1981

			Age				
			Under 20	20–24	25–44	45–64	65 and above	All
1891	(a)	%	27.0	12.2	34.8	19.2	6.8	100
1921	(b)	%	18.5	10.9	38.0	24.2	8.4	100
1951	(c)	%	7.8	8.4	36.8	31.3	15.7	100
1981	(d)	%	8.1	9.0	32.4	28.2	22.3	100

			Marital Status			
			Single	Married	Widowed and divorced	All
1891	(a)	%	47.8	42.3	9.9	100
1921	(b)	%	41.9	47.7	10.4	100
1951	(c)	%	25.5	61.0	13.5	100
1981	(d)	%	20.4	61.4	18.2	100

Notes: (a) Aged 10 and over; (b) Aged 12 and over; (c) Aged 15 and over; (d) Aged 16 and over.

Sources:
Census of England and Wales 1891, Vol III, HMSO, London, 1893; Census of Scotland 1891, Vol II, HMSO, Edinburgh, 1893; Census of England and Wales 1921, Occupations, HMSO, London, 1924; Census of Scotland 1921, Vol III, HMSO, Edinburgh, 1924; Census 1951 England and Wales, Occupation Tables, HMSO, Edinburgh, 1956; Census 1951 Scotland, Vol IV, HMSO, Edinburgh, 1956; Census 1981 Economic Activity, Great Britain, HMSO, London, 1984.

morbidity experienced by many women as a result of childbirth, an issue that received medical recognition during the 1930s when one eminent obstetrician estimated that 10 per cent of all pregnant women were disabled by the experience of childbirth (Blair-Bell, 1931).

In terms of marital status the most marked change, shown in Table 2.1, is the decline in the proportion of single, never-married women and the growth in the proportion of divorced and separated women, many of whom have children—although it should be noted that nineteenth-century marriages were as likely to be broken through death (usually of the husband and father) as are contemporary families by divorce (Anderson, 1985). The growth in 'female-headed' households has been even greater than

Table 2.1 suggests, since most single women in the past were dependent on their parental household or were 'in service'. (The proportion of women in the labour market working as indoor domestic servants was 36 per cent in 1881 and 27 per cent in 1911; not until the post-war period did the proportion of indoor servants fall substantially, to 11 per cent in 1951 (James, 1962)). Changes in the age structure and marital status of women affect in turn their position in the family and labour market, to which we turn.

DEPENDENCY ON FAMILY, LABOUR MARKET AND STATE

This section describes the relationship between these dependencies, the next analyses the circumstances of each. Proceeding in this order needs explanation but does, we believe, make sense. To analyse, say, the labour market as a separate entity is to ignore the fact that women's opportunities within it are often shaped by family commitments. The experiences of Francie Nicol, a working-class woman from South Shields, at the beginning of the century provides an example of what we mean. She began her adult life by marrying, having children and relying on her husband for support, but his drunkenness and failure to provide forced her into the labour market. Here, by dint of Herculean effort, she managed to run a fish and chip shop and keep her family going, building the business up from scratch again after her husband returned to drink away the profits (Robinson, 1975). Many other women in such circumstances would have found themselves applying to the state for relief.

The gradual development of state benefits provided a means for some women of escaping from humiliating private dependency on the family (in the case of unmarried mothers, for example), as well as a more adequate level of income. But state benefits also served to structure and support female dependency in the family (as will be made clear in the next section). What is important here is to understand the way in which access to all resources in our society has been and is gendered, with the consequence that women found and find themselves enmeshed in a web of different dependencies. Dependency on the family, in effect on male relatives, whether father or husband, was more complete in the early twentieth century than it is today. This is because fewer women were active in the labour market; because what earnings they had fell below subsistence needs; and because state provision was less generous and access to it more restricted.

We shall examine first the nature of the options open to working- and middle-class women seeking to depend on the labour market for support rather than on men; and then look at the position of women, often with children, who became widowed or divorced, and of unmarried mothers. Single working-class women were as likely to work at the turn of the century as today, but marriage was for most an economic necessity. Social investigators of the Edwardian period calculated that a single woman needed 14–16 shillings a week to subsist in 1906. The average wage of female textile workers was 15/5d and of women in non-textile industries, 12/11d (Cadbury *et. al.*, 1906; Drake, 1920). Thus a majority of women could not afford an independent existence. Contemporary observers remarked on the matter of fact nature of early twentieth-century working-class weddings. As Ellen Ross (1982) has remarked, marriage was not so much a matter of emotional and sexual intimacy as a contract between a husband who would bring home a wage and a wife who would manage household and children.

Thus it seems wrong to draw too stark a contrast between dependency on the family and dependency on the labour market. Marriage was to a large extent a labour 'contract'. Many forms of paid labour, such as the major occupation of domestic service, also involved a housing 'contract'. Most working-class women lived with their families of origin until marriage, because the cost of housing proved an intolerable strain on their budgets (Higgs, 1910). As long as employment possibilities were limited and wages provided little or no surplus over and above subsistence needs, employers in the retail trade found it easy to require their largely female employees to 'live in'. Similarly many working-class women continued to enter domestic service, despite its low status, because it did at least provide board and lodgings and a measure of respectability, even if the fate of domestic servants in old age depended very much on the whims of their employers and on personal thrift. Marriage provided working-class women with the means, or hope, of escape.

In the case of the middle classes before World War I, single women were not expected to earn their own living at any point in the life-cycle, which rendered them dependent on the good offices of their male relatives. Beatrice Webb recorded in her diary the misery that a 'surplus' (i.e. unmarried) daughter could experience, confined in later life to the meaningless rituals of her family home and, in the end, to the care of her ageing parents (Caine, 1982). Marriage was a means of livelihood for all classes of women, but a middle-class daughter who did not find a husband was more likely to be deemed to have 'failed in business'. The minority of single middle-class women for whom relatives failed to provide faced an extremely narrow range of options in the late nineteenth century, the most acceptable of which was that of governess. Such women often led as isolated a life as any working-class domestic servant and would usually look forward to an old age of privation, as the many benevolent societies for the relief of genteel female poverty bore witness to. The expansion of semi-professional employment for women during the early twentieth century and its growing acceptability for single middle-class women in the inter-war years, marked a real advance for this group of women in terms of their income levels (both during their working lives and in old age), and in the degree of autonomy they were able to exercise over their lives.

Dependence on the family was thus reinforced for married women of all social classes by the lack of any alternative. Access to employment, especially in the professions, was largely controlled by men and women's earnings could not in any case support a family. Nor was the state any comfort. Married women had no separate personality in the eyes of the Poor Law and until World War I it was not uncommon for the authorities taking an able-bodied man claiming relief into the workhouse to require his wife and children to go too (Thane, 1978). Beveridge's National Insurance scheme reinforced the practice of making social benefits contingent in large part on labour market participation so that, for example, married women were dependent on their husbands for pension contributions. Feminists at the time criticised Beveridge for 'denying the married woman, rich or poor, housewife or paid worker an individual personal status' (Abbott and Bompass, 1943). It is still the case that public law treats the couple as a unit for benefit purposes and aggregates their needs and resources. This contrasts with married women's position in private law (for example, in relation to marital property and divorce), which treats them as economic individuals (O'Donovan, 1985).

Changes in the relationship between dependency on the family, the labour market and the state have however been significantly different for particular groups of single women, namely widows, divorcees and single mothers. The history of their experiences highlights the way in which women's dependency is due both to childbearing and rearing and to their lack of leverage on the labour market; how these reinforce one another; and how state policy plays its part in structuring the precise nature of women's dependency.

The 1909 Royal Commission on the Poor Laws showed that while more men received indoor relief (in the work-house) than women, more women received outdoor relief than men. This was largely because of the numbers of widows with children drawing relief. However women's relief payments were usually somewhat lower. Widows fared somewhat better than other lone mothers, but they were all regarded with suspicion and treated harshly; in 1871 for example, the Local Government Board issued a circular to the effect that outdoor relief should not be granted to the able-bodied widow—undoubtedly considered to be the most 'deserving' of the three groups—if she had only one child or none. In cases involving more than one child, the circular advised that it might be better for the local Board of Guardians to test the widow's need by offering to take her children into the workhouse rather than offering her outdoor relief. In practice, Guardians varied considerably in their treatment of widows, especially in regard to their willingness to grant outdoor relief and in the rates of relief they were prepared to pay. Deserted wives were regarded with more suspicion and the local Guardians were advised to deny them outdoor relief for twelve months to ensure that they were not colluding with their husbands to defraud the authorities. Unmarried mothers were invariably forced to enter the workhouse and, despite the insistence of the central Poor Law authorities that the function of the Poor Law was to relieve destitution and not to correct morals, they were often treated punitively (Thane, 1978).

The central issue for the state was whether to treat these groups of women as workers or as mothers. The early twentieth-century state proved reluctant to step in and play the role of breadwinner, preferring, at least in theory, to take the children into the workhouse and force the mother to work. There is evidence that large numbers of widows and deserted wives undertook sweated homework to make ends meet (Lewis, 1984). Those who were employed full-time rarely worked in insured trades and even in the inter-war years, when coverage under National Insurance expanded, women's needs were assessed as being less than those of men and they received lower benefits.

The pendulum swung in favour of treating women with dependent children and no husbands as mothers rather than workers at different times for different groups of women. As the most 'deserving', widows were granted pensions in 1925. Eleanor Rathbone (1925, p.11) welcomed this as follows:

When I think of its [the Widows, Orphans and Old Age Contributory Pensions Act] provisions, the faces which float before my mind are those of women whom I used to know 20–30 years ago, when running an Association of Homeworkers and The Association of Trained Charwomen, both under Liverpool's Women's Industrial Council . . . the lives they led were harder and drearier than anything we comfortable people have ever experienced for a week. Some had their children, others seemed to have nothing . . . nor hope of anything but to be able to go on stitching or scrubbing till they died.

Despite Beveridge's desire not to treat this group of women as automatically deserving of state support, widows' pensions have proved resistant to erosion. After World War II the attention given to maternal bonding theory contributed to all women with children, including deserted wives and unmarried mothers, being treated as mothers first and workers second. Widows, divorcees and single mothers have clearly increased their share of state benefits, and in turn their dependency on the state since World War II. However this does not mean that the pendulum could not swing in the opposite direction again. In some 22 states in the USA single mothers drawing 'workfare' must now put their children in day-care and work for their benefits (Nathan, 1986). Similar thinking has informed family legislation of 1984 in Britain which seeks to treat divorcees equally and encourage them to enter the workforce rather than be dependent on men's alimony payments. But when women's leverage on the labour market is poor, this is blatantly unequal treatment. Even if the state does not treat single mothers as workers plain and simple, it may try to return responsibility for their welfare to the family. Thus some Canadian provinces have decided not to give welfare to single mothers under nineteen, forcing them to rely on their family's generosity. The changes contained in the British government's 1986 social security legislation have been described as an attempt to re-privatise women's welfare (Land, 1986). In a male-dominated society in which access to resources is gendered, inequality between the sexes is likely to flourish if unregulated.

Thus women over the past century, and still to a great extent today, have found themselves faced with a dilemma of dependence on either the family, the labour market, or the state—none of which offers much choice, control or a route to independence. Having briefly described the overall dilemma, next we shall analyse the different dependencies in more detail.

HISTORY OF DEPENDENCY

The Family

In terms of women's economic status, the family has imposed both costs and benefits: costs in the form of work that had to be performed and opportunities that were forgone; and benefits in the form of a share in family resources. Historically, being single did not mean that there were no family responsibilities. At the start of the century the Fabian Women's Group estimated that half of all single women workers were wholly or partly responsible for someone else's maintenance, although Rowntree put the figure at only 12 per cent (Smith, 1915; Rowntree and Stuart, 1921). Eldest girls were least likely to marry, primarily because their labour was needed by their parents or other elderly relatives.

It was marriage, however, that brought the greatest family burdens with, in most cases, only a short period before the birth of the first child and then many years of child-rearing. The fact that families were much larger than now did not necessarily mean that proportionately more time was needed, since older children could and did care for younger children. But washing, cooking and cleaning in particular expanded with family size. In terms of overall workload, child-rearing must have been a greater burden to women in the past.

By contrast, the burdens carried by women caring for the growing number of elderly dependants is probably greater now than in the early part of the century. It is estimated today that there are one and a quarter million informal carers in Britain (EOC, 1982) and that about 90 per cent of them are married women. Because life expectancy at the turn of the century was shorter, it was less likely than now that daughters would face a prolonged period of caring for a frail parent. However, Jill Quadagno (1982) found that in the ribbon-weaving village of Chilvers Cotton in 1901, 84 per cent of those over 60 years old were living with a family member. Elderly women were more likely to find a place with relatives than were elderly men for, as the Royal

Commission on the Poor Laws commented, women were more use to their children by contributing babysitting, sewing, etc. A much larger proportion of those caring for the elderly in the early twentieth century were single women, in large part a reflection of the fact that there were considerably more unmarried women in the population.

While it is difficult to come to decisive conclusions about shifts in the burden of caring, it is clear that domestic technology has changed dramatically and has certainly eased the drudgery and hard labour that characterised early twentieth century housework. Clothes must no longer be pounded in a dolly tub and mangled, nor floors scrubbed on hands and knees with minimal help from machinery and myriad cleansers. Nevertheless, it is not clear how far the time spent on housework has significantly changed. For example, when washing clothes or floors became easier, it was not only possible to do such tasks more quickly, but it also became expected that they would be done more frequently. In the case of a substantial number of middle-class women, it is likely that the burden and the number of hours spent doing housework increased after World War II. These women would have employed one general servant even during the inter-war period. After the war not only was this no longer the case but, increasingly, middle-class women went out to work as well. While a growing number of 'career' women married to professional men today hire nannies during their children's early years, if they still bear primary responsibility for home and family, their leisure-time may well be much more restricted than it was earlier this century.

In return for the burdens imposed by the family, there was the hope of an adequate income. This depended first on the husband receiving a 'family wage', which was an ideal rather than a reality for many (Land, 1980). As early as 1889, Booth's survey of London showed one third of the population to be in poverty and hence incapable of earning a family wage. Rowntree's second survey of York in the 1930s showed that even in class E (the top third earning 63/6d or more a week) one-fifth did not earn enough to keep himself, his wife and three children out of poverty

(Rowntree, 1941, p. 161). Yet even if the husband's wage was adequate the problem for all married women, especially those in low-income households, was (and is) that they are in large measure financially dependent on their husbands. In her pioneering analysis of the family wage system, Eleanor Rathbone (1924) described women and children's status as that of 'male luxuries'. The contract whereby the husband brought home a wage and the wife managed home and children was by no means always kept. But whereas if women failed to do their part men could (and often did) enforce compliance by the use of violence (Ayers and Lambertz, 1986), women had no such recourse. Evidence throughout the twentieth century—Rowntree's study of York (1902), Caradog Jones' (1934) of Liverpool in the 1930s, Jan Pahl's (1980) recent research—shows that a large number of married women have not even known what their husbands earned. Housekeeping money tends to remain constant regardless of increases in prices, family size or husband's earnings. The well-documented result is that women, as the domestic chancellors of the family exchequer, put the needs of husband and children first and their own last. Working-class budgets of the Edwardian period show that even in respectable working-class households where the husband kept back only a small sum for personal items (chiefly tobacco and drink) his diet tended to differ significantly from that of the other family members. The worker expected and received 'a relish to his tea'. Furthermore, working-class women's struggles to make ends meet relied both on what Rowntree (1902, p. 43) called 'the mutual helpfulness of the poor' as well as a whole network of neighbourhood credit that varied in its degree of respectability. The closeness of many early twentieth-century working-class communities was, as Abrams has remarked (Bulmer, 1986), sustained largely by the mutual interdependency born of poverty. Women often ran up credit in the local shops, resorted to the pawnbroker or worse still to a moneylender without telling their husbands. (As Gillian Parker's chapter in this volume shows, this situation has changed little today.)

The Labour Market
Women's role in the labour market and the labour market's role in determining women's income levels will be considered in two stages; first, who has been economically active: and second, how have women's earnings altered relative to men's?

Table 2.2: Economic Activity Rate by Age, Sex and Marital Status, 1891–1981

		All women %	Married women %	All men %
Under 20	1891	43.7	na	59.0
	1921	48.4	14.6	63.2
	1951	78.9	38.1	83.8
	1981	56.4	45.5	64.5
20–24	1891	58.4	na	98.1
	1921	62.4	12.5	97.0
	1951	65.4	36.5	94.9
	1981	69.3	54.6	89.1
25–44	1891	29.5	na	97.9
	1921	28.4	9.1	97.9
	1951	36.1	25.1	98.3
	1981	59.4	55.7	97.5
45–64	1891	24.6	na	93.7
	1921	20.1	8.0	94.9
	1951	28.7	19.0	95.2
	1981	51.9	51.7	90.3
65 and over	1891	15.9	na	65.4
	1921	10.0	4.2	58.9
	1951	5.3	2.7	31.1
	1981	3.7	4.2	10.7

		All women %	Single women %	Married women %	Widowed/ divorced women %	All men %
All ages	1891	35.0	na	na	na	83.9
	1921	32.3	60.8	8.7	25.6	87.1
	1951	34.7	73.1	21.7	21.1	87.6
	1981	45.5	60.8	47.2	22.9	77.8

Sources: See Table 2.1.

The trends of economic activity rates are shown in Table 2.2. Overall, women's activity rates rose between 1891 and 1981 from 35 to 45.5 per cent, but this total conceals important variations. Among married women, the activity rate rose from less than one in ten in 1921 to over half of those aged 20–64 in 1981. Among single women, activity rates have remained around three-quarters of those of men.

Table 2.3: Composition of Economically Active Women by Age and Marital Status, Great Britain, 1891–1981

	Age					
	Under 20	20–24	25–44	45–64	65 and over	All
1891 %	33.8	20.3	29.3	13.5	3.1	100
1921 %	27.7	21.1	33.5	15.1	2.6	100
1951 %	17.7	15.9	38.2	25.9	2.4	100
1981 %	10.0	13.7	42.3	32.2	1.8	100

	Marital Status		
	Single	Married	Widowed and divorced	All
1921 %	78.9	12.9	8.2	100
1951 %	53.6	38.2	8.2	100
1981 %	27.2	63.6	9.2	100

Sources: See Table 2.1.

By 1981 women had become 39 per cent of the economically active population and most of these women were married. By contrast, in 1891 only 4 per cent of the economically active population consisted of married women—indeed, 54 per cent of economically active women were then aged under 25 compared with 24 per cent in 1981, as shown in Table 2.3. The proportion of married women in the workforce has dramatically increased and the participation rate of married women aged 25–44 is now higher than that of younger married women. This reflects women's greater attachment to the labour force throughout their adult lives. They no longer tend to leave the workforce permanently on marriage as they did prior to World War II, nor to leave on the birth of their first child and return only when their children were grown up—the characteristic pattern of women's labour market behaviour during the late 1950s and 1960s. These economic activity figures from the Census are subject to two limitations. First, casual employment undertaken by married women in the past was largely ignored, as officials were often not sure how to categorise it. Married working-class women undertook casual work to supplement the family income—charring, sewing, hawking fruit, etc.—especially when the wage-earner was ill, unemployed or otherwise unable or unwilling to provide. Little of this highly irregular work was recorded in the Census and few of its rewards were consumed directly by women themselves. Secondly, most of the recent increased economic activity by women has been in part-time work and women remain unequal participants in the labour market.

Table 2.4: Women's Wages as Percentage of Men's Wages: Average of Manual Workers

	1886	1906	1984
Woollen and worsted	57.2	51.6	65.2
Hosiery	47.1	45.4	65.8
Footwear	51.5	45.6	68.3
Textiles	na	54.9	66.3
Clothing	na	44.8	68.9
Food, drink and tobacco	na	43.4	63.1
Paper and printing	na	35.4	58.1
Metals, engineering and shipbuilding	na	37.3	65.0
All industries	51.5	na	58.7

Sources: British Labour Statistics, Historical Abstract 1886–1968, Department of Employment and Productivity (London: HMSO, 1971), Tables 35 and 37; *New Earnings Survey, 1984* (Part C), Department of Employment (London: HMSO, 1984).

Next we turn to women's earnings relative to men's. Ideally we should like to look at hourly earnings, but historical data on this are limited. Therefore we compare in Table 2.4 the average wages of full-time workers in a number of industries in 1886, 1906 and 1984. It will be seen that women's wages remain far below (in most cases around two-thirds) men's, although there have been some relative increases over the last century.

In 1886 the average wage of male manual workers was 25 shillings a week; only one in a thousand women earned over the men's average (Department of Employment and Productivity, 1971). In 1984 the comparable proportion had risen—but still only 4 per cent of women manual workers earned over the male manual average (Department of Employment, 1984a). In both 1886 and 1984 less than 5 per cent of men earned less than half the male average, but over one-third of women did so in each year. Thus low pay has been, as it is now, a problem for the majority of women.

The State
The state's lack of neutrality in respect to social policies affecting women is well documented (Land, 1978, 1983a; David, 1983, 1986). There is considerable evidence to support the idea that state policy has consistently been framed with the intention of sustaining the traditional family form of breadwinning husband and dependent wife and children. However, policy outcomes have not necessarily been consistent with these aims. Furthermore, policies in areas not directly concerned with the family—for example, in health or education—have often been contradictory in terms of their effects on women's position.

Social security law has from the first merged the identities of husbands and wives. In practice this means that successive schemes have been administered through the spouse with the greatest attachment to and the most secure position in the labour market—the husband. The first National Insurance Act of 1911 essentially excluded married women, who could only join the scheme if they were insured workers in their own right. The Fabian Women's Group (1911) pointed out that such a scheme of contributory insurance was bound to exacerbate problems concerning women's economic position, dividing those living as their husband's dependant from what was before World War II the small minority of married women who worked full-time. The

Women's Industrial Council (1911) regretted the fact that National Insurance intensified the tendency 'to consider the work of a wife and mother in her home of no money value'.

These early critics were correct in their perception that any social security scheme administered on a contributory basis through participation in the workforce would always be of limited use to women because of their marginal position in the labour market. Assuming in his turn that married women's proper place was not in the labour market, Beveridge perpetuated the idea of women's double dependency on husbands—both for day-to-day maintenance and for state benefits—and summarised his views thus: 'on marriage a woman gains a legal right of maintenance by her husband as a first line of defence against risks which fall directly on the solitary woman' (Beveridge, 1942, p. 49). The assumption that married women should be financially dependent on their husbands has meant that state policy has been used further to restrict their access to benefits, thereby reinforcing the role of men as breadwinners and marginalising women as earners. Thus in 1931 in the depths of the Depression, the Anomalies Act assumed that any married woman who had left the labour force for whatever reason had effectively retired and was therefore ineligible for benefit. This legislation finds a parallel in recent changes in the regulations for unemployment insurance which, as Claire Callender describes in Chapter 7, now insist that married women claiming benefit must be able to demonstrate that they have made child-care provision and are thus effectively available for work.

While women's primary responsibility for home and family has been emphasised, state policy has shown meagre financial recognition of the time costs and forgone earnings involved. Maternity benefit in Britain is one of the lowest in Europe and child benefits fall far below those of many countries (Bradshaw and Piachaud, 1980). Thus unpaid work in the home is inevitably associated with women's poverty.

In some areas women have positively gained from direct

access to services such as the National Health Service. Nella
Last, recording for Mass Observation during World War II,
felt that the NHS would prove the greatest boon to married
women (Broad and Fleming, 1983). The contributors to
the Women's Co-operative Guild's collection of letters on
maternity a generation before would surely have agreed.
Indeed, women have used the NHS more than men because
they become mothers. Yet, while this may be interpreted
as women gaining more than men from a state service, it is
also not inconsistent with state policy to encourage women's
maternal role.

State policy continues to treat the household as a unit for
benefit purposes, aggregating the needs and resources of
its members and paying scant regard to the contribution
made by married women in particular to the family economy. In many areas of state provision there is now a formal
equality of opportunity but outcomes remain highly unequal. In general, state policy has accommodated rather
than attacked the structural causes of women's inferior economic position.

MEASURES OF INEQUALITY AND POVERTY

Here we draw together the quantitative evidence that is
available on the effects which the changes described above
have had on women's economic status relative to men, and
we examine how the nature of poverty among women has
altered. As we have said, comparisons of the extent of
poverty among women present many problems—different
concepts of poverty, changing poverty levels, the paucity of
data on the poverty of households and the virtual absence
of data on women's share of resources within households.
On many matters of importance there is simply no comparable quantitative data going back any length of time.

Changes in women's participation in the labour market
may be summarised as follows:

	1890s	1980s
Women as proportion of economically active population[1]	31%	39%
Women's earnings as proportion of total earnings[2]	19%	26%

Turning to social security benefits, in the past women were treated almost entirely as dependants so that benefits were paid to husbands for their spouses or to widows on the basis of their husband's contribution record. We may therefore distinguish between, first, that part of benefits which was paid *for* women, even if much of it was paid to their husbands, which in 1983 amounted to 51 per cent of social security;[3] and second, that part of benefits paid *to* women, including benefits paid for children and other family members, which in 1983 amounted to 44 per cent of social security.[4] Data on rates of poor relief and the marital status of recipients do not allow comparable estimates to be made for the past, but it is possible to compare numbers of recipients (though not the amounts received):

	1908	1983
Proportion of poor law/supplementary benefit recipients who were women[5]	61%	60%

Combining earnings and social security benefits and payments of rents and dividends, we can estimate the share of income directly paid to women—*direct* income. We distinguish this from *total* income calculated on the dubious assumption that household income is shared equally between household members. It would appear that, whereas women's share of *total* income has changed little, women's share of *direct* income has increased—although women still receive directly only a quarter of all income. (The figures for the 1890s are only approximate.)

	1890s	1980s
Women's share of direct income[6]	15%	25%
Women's share of total income[7]	45%	44%

Finally we examine the changing composition of poverty among women. We do this by re-analysing the results of the earliest systematic study of poverty carried out by Rowntree (or, more accurately, largely by his predominantly female staff) in York in 1899, and comparing these with recent government statistics on low incomes. The data for the 1980s are for Great Britain, but York was (and is) sufficiently representative for the comparison to be of interest. We

Table 2.5: Comparison of Causes of Poverty, 1899 and 1983

| | Among persons | | Among women | |
	1899	1983	1899	1983
Old age, sickness and disability	12%	39%	22%	58%
One-parent family	9%(a)	11%	18%	10%
Unemployment	5%(b)	27%	6%(b)	19%
Large family (see notes)	22%(c)	16%(d)	14%(c)	6%(d)
Low wages	52%	6%	40%	6%
All causes	100%	100%(e)	100%	100%(e)

(a) Widows plus deserted and separated women aged under 60.
(b) Chief wage earner out of work and irregularity of work.
(c) Five children or more.
(d) Three children or more.
(e) Omitting other causes, which amount to some 5 per cent of the total.

Sources: Rowntree, B. S. *Poverty a Study of Town Life*, Chapter V (Longmans 1902); *Low Income Families – 1983*, (DHSS, 1986 (Mimeo)); *Social Security Statistics, 1985* (DHSS, HMSO, 1986); and author's calculations.

Notes: For 1899, based on those in 'Primary Poverty', Rowntree's classification has been largely followed save for separating widows under and over age 60. Chief wage earners have been assumed to be male, spouses to be female, and other adults to be divided equally between women and men.

For 1983, based on those in receipt of Supplementary Benefit or Housing Benefit Supplement or with Relative Net Resources below Supplementary Benefit level. The DHSS division by economic status has been largely followed. It is assumed large families are distributed equally among the other types of families under pensionable age. Estimates of numbers of women have been based on proportions of women in each category among SB recipients in December 1983.

make no attempt to compare the poverty levels used; rather, we have for 1899 used Rowntree's 'primary' poverty level and for 1983 treated as poor those on or below the supplementary benefit level. The proportion of the population below the two levels in each year were 9.9 per cent in 1899 and 16.6 per cent in 1983. The results are shown in Table 2.5.

The causes of poverty among women have shown major changes. Most notably there has been a growth in the extent to which poverty is associated with old age, sickness and disability. There has also been a growth in poverty associated with unemployment. On the other hand, the proportion of women's poverty associated with low wages (predominantly of husbands) has declined. Predictably, large families are a smaller component, even using a lower definition of 'large' in 1983 than in 1899; but more surprisingly, women in one-parent families now represent a lower proportion of poor women than in 1899, primarily because of the decline in widowed women below pension age.

CONCLUSIONS

On the issues we have discussed we are severely constrained by limitations of data; for example, changes in marital status are a poor indicator of changes in patterns of living, cohabiting and sharing. Many important developments have not been considered, such as changes in training, promotion and occupational welfare in employment, patterns of inheritance, or treatment by the tax system. Our discussion has been generalised and has concealed many important changes. We do not distinguish the circumstances of ethnic minorities even though unemployment rates among women of West Indian and Asian origin are roughly twice those of white women (Brown, 1984); black women in Britain experience poverty much more than white women as Juliet Cook and Shantu Watt show in Chapter 3.

The evidence we have examined shows clearly that the

idea ʻhat poverty has only recently become 'feminised' is wrong. Women constitute a roughly similar proportion of the poor today as in 1900 and this reflects the position of women in society more generally. Paid employment is for the vast majority the main way of avoiding poverty; the nature of women's work, both paid and unpaid, and the undervaluing of both, lead in our social and economic system to women's relatively greater income insecurity throughout the life-cycle. While there are of course exceptions, it remains true that the great majority of women are trapped in a vicious circle of domestic responsibilities and low-paid, low-status employment.

While female poverty has been a constant fact, its composition has changed substantially. In the early part of the century, married women were the largest group of women in poverty because of the low wages paid to husbands and because of large families. Widows and elderly women were the next largest group. Today female poverty is concentrated among lone women, especially among the elderly. The balance of dependency has also shifted. Married women now have fewer children and higher material standards than their great-grandmothers, which means that potentially they have more leisure (subject to housework and child-care expanding to fill the time and little changing in the domestic division of labour between the sexes). Nor are married women as financially dependent on the generosity of husbands. Their share of direct income has risen, largely due to their increased labour market participation, and they have individual direct access to many social services such as the NHS—although not to social security. Lone mothers are more likely to be wholly dependent on the state than were their foremothers. The early twentieth-century state could not decide whether to treat lone mothers as mothers or workers; more recently the social security system has been prepared to support motherhood—however exiguously. In the case of the elderly, before 1948 the legal obligation to maintain covered three rather than two generations, so families were legally obliged to support elderly relatives (Crowther, 1982). Now state support has increased, but with the growing number of elderly dependants the work of caring, which falls largely on women, has probably increased rather than decreased.

The persistence of female poverty can only be explained in terms of women's position in society. Women's work is rewarded less than men's and this affects their well-being throughout their lives. That work now includes a large proportion of so-called 'economic activity' which is rewarded with earnings, but it still includes a wholly disproportionate share of unpaid work in the home, raising children and caring for husbands and other dependants. The latter, unpaid, work has a direct effect on the former, paid, work, contributing to inequalities in pay.

There is, of course, no reason why women should accept the ethos of the market-place and wish to maximise income or aspire to male models of full employment; women are not 'economic men'. Yet with existing child benefits and child-care facilities and the existing division of labour in society, whatever the personal rewards of unpaid work such as rearing children, it undoubtedly increases female dependency on men within the family or on the state. Children have, since Eleanor Rathbone wrote, been recognised as a source of poverty in families; they are, as things stand, above all a source of female poverty.

Poverty has been a central issue in social policy over the last century, but female poverty has been of only tangential concern. Poverty in old age and child poverty have received far more attention, with little recognition of their links with women's position in society. To a limited extent, a shift towards more collective responsibility for the elderly and towards recognition of changing family structures has led to developments that have allowed some women more autonomy. But for the most part social policy has assumed, or presumed, that women would continue to carry the burden of caring and remain unequal in the economy. It has therefore ignored the structural causes of female poverty. It is not surprising that women remain the principal victims of poverty.

NOTES

1. Calculated from Censuses of England and Wales and of Scotland for 1891 and 1981.

2. 1890s based on Census return of occupied population in 1891 and average wages of manual workers in 1886; *British Labour Statistics, Historical Abstract 1886–1968*, Department of Employment and Productivity (London: HMSO, 1971), Table 35. 1980s based on number of employees and mean earnings in *Family Expenditure Survey, 1983*.

3. Based on *Family Expenditure Survey, 1983*, Department of Employment (London: HMSO, 1985), Sources of Income. For each type of household the social security income for women = total social security income x W/W+M+O.5C (where W is number of women, M is number of men and C is number of children).

4. Based on *FES, 1983* (see note 3) calculated on the basis of social security payments to female heads of household and to wives (with *pro rata* estimates for other household types).

5. 1908 figures from GB 1909, Vol. I, Pt.II, paragraph 17. 1980 figures calculated from *Social Security Statistics, 1985* (London: HMSO, 1986).

6. 1890s based on the proportion of earnings to women (19 per cent) and the fact that women's shares of salaries (which constituted 17 per cent of income from employment in 1891; Feinstein, 1972) and of rent were small.

7. 1890s calculated on the assumption that the great majority of women were living with their fathers or husbands and that income is shared equally between adults, with children getting a half-share, i.e. women's share = W/W+M+O.5C (as in note 3 above).
   1980 based on FES 1983 on same method as in note 3 above using gross weekly income.

3 Racism, Women and Poverty

Juliet Cook and Shantu Watt

Writing about women and black women[1] in particular has too often concentrated on women as 'victims'[2] and not as strong, responsible, self-directed people in whatever circumstances they find themselves. Black women are part of a herstory where exploitation, abuse, violence and poverty are commonplace. But without romanticising their struggles, they are also part of a herstory of fighting back, of organising and challenging structures of inequality and oppression, of caring and creativity as well. The position of black women in Britain today illustrates these themes vividly in that class, race and gender inequalities combine in complex ways to produce poverty and other inequalities for black women. Equally, it demonstrates the ways in which black women have resisted the effects of these processes on themselves both as individuals and as members of groups. A good example is the very effective Organisation of Women of African and Asian Descent (OWAAD) (1978–83) which organised black women on a national basis and encouraged the growth of a multiplicity of local groups which still exist today (Bryan *et al.*, 1985).

Poverty has been defined in many ways but most definitions include not only the relative lack of financial and other economic resources, but also related qualitative dimensions such as the lack of family and other social relationships, the lack of opportunities for fulfilment, and feelings of insecurity (Townsend, 1979, Ch. 1). We want to capture not only the quantitative aspects of poverty for black women

and their families, but also some of the qualitative aspects—
for example, stress from racism and living in poverty in the
modern inner city; the effects of divided families, together
with the resourcefulness of women in maintaining families
and communities in the face of such pressures. In modern
advanced capitalist societies such as Britain, there is a clear
relationship between class (however defined) and poverty.
For black women in such societies racism and sexism as well
play a vital role in creating inequality, including poverty.

In recent years, there have been considerable developments in understanding and explaining sexism as both an
historical and a contemporary phenomenon. However many
black women have quite rightly pointed out that much of
this theory is predicated on assumptions that apply only to
white women, and that it does not address the ways in which
racism is always an overriding force in the experience of
black women. Parmar has therefore insisted on the need to
understand 'racially constructed gender roles' (Parmar,
1982, p.237). Similarly Westwood has urged us to 'theorise
[the] difference and unity' that both divide and unite black
and white women (Westwood, 1984, p.231). Brittan and
Maynard (1984) point out that class, race and gender
oppression cannot simply be added together in some crude
arithmetical way in order to explain the position of black
women in British society. These fundamental economic and
social processes interact and interwine to form what Westwood calls 'complementary and contradictory relationships'
(Westwood, 1984, p. 231).

Black and white women in British society, therefore, do
share some common experiences but they are also divided
by racism. For example, although the women in Westwood's
study fought together for higher wages, the black women
experienced racism from their white co-workers at work.
The racism that divides families and communities outside
the work place also meant that the women did not on the
whole socialise outside working hours (Westwood, 1984).

Both racism and sexism complicate women's relationship
to class and poverty[3]. First, women are class members
because of their role in production as paid workers. They

are usually poor as paid workers because of the low level of women's wages. Secondly, women have a further relationship to class because marriage can bring them more resources through access to men's wages. For black women, however, racism means that these resources are less because black men are paid lower wages than white men. Thirdly, women can be seen as having an indirect relationship to class via their unpaid domestic labour which, it is argued, helps to service the economy by supporting male workers (Kaluzynska, 1980). Historically however, this relationship is also different for black women because a high proportion of their paid labour under capitalism has been domestic labour (Parmar, 1982). Finally, the disproportionate effect of high unemployment on black workers including women and the low level of state benefits combine to produce poverty for black women.

To take the analysis still further and to keep racism at the top of the agenda, there are two additional assumptions which must be challenged if a real understanding of black women and poverty is to develop: first, the notion that black women are the economic dependants of men; and secondly, that the black family is oppressive for black women. It is a mistake to assume that black women are or were the dependants of men either in Africa, India, Pakistan, Bangladesh or in Britain. Research shows that black women have always made significant contributions to the economic well-being of their families and communities in a variety of ways (Carby, 1982; Parmar, 1982; Morokvasic, 1983). Angela Davis, writing about black women in the United States, expresses this clearly:

Like their men, Black women have worked until they could work no more. Like their men, they have assumed the responsibilities of family providers. The unorthodox feminine qualities of assertiveness and self-reliance—for which Black women have frequently been praised but more often rebuked—are reflections of their labor and their struggles outside the home. (Davis, 1982, p.231)

In the British context, it is important to recognise the vital role of black women workers in the migrations of the post-World War II period, particularly women from the Caribbean. As Carby (1982) points out, the pressures against mothers taking paid work in the early post-war period seemed to have applied to white women but not to black women. The immigration figures of the 1970s show that more work permits were issued to women from the Caribbean than to men (WING, 1985). Asian women were less likely to immigrate on the basis of work permits but, of course, they have undertaken extensive paid work since their arrival. Many young Asian women as well show considerable commitment to the notion of a 'working life' (Cross *et al.*, 1983).

However, it is clear that British immigration law is predicated on the notion of women's economic dependence on men, with disastrous consequences for some black women. Recent immigration policy has been directed towards reducing the number of 'primary migrants', a term which applies to workers or potential workers who are assumed to be male (Sivanandan, 1978). Indeed, the Home Office defence to the European Commission of Human Rights in May 1982 against the accusation of sex discrimination in the 1980 Immigration Rules was that 'society still expects the man to go out to work and the women to stay at home' (WING, 1985, p.147).

The black family, in popular ideas and in some feminist literature, has been seen as highly oppressive to black women. The black family itself has been treated as pathological. The debate surrounding the Moynihan Report in the United States (Moynihan, 1965) is but one example, while in Britain worries abound about the terrible consequences of the arranged marriage system for young Asian women in particular (Khan, 1976; Ahmed, 1978; Jamdagni, 1980; Edmonds, 1981). Often the issue is seen in terms of 'cultural differences' or 'culture conflict' between the culture of the black group and that of the dominant white group. Clearly no one can deny the reality of cultural differences nor the fact that at times cultural values may be in conflict. Equally, as Carby points out, black families are sometimes oppressive for women. However, what such perspectives tend to overlook is the role of racism in affecting the position of black women within the family and the contradictory nature of the family for black people. Thus for Carby, the black family has served as a major 'site of political and cultural resistance to racism' (Carby, 1982, p.214). The family must also be a refuge from racism for black people too, a place where the experiences of racism (including racial attacks) can be shared and mutual support and resistance generated (Brittan and Maynard, 1984).

Family networks have also been very important in black communities in helping to organise financial resources which are often in short supply. In Britain, Asian families have pooled money in order to buy houses of their own. Such a strategy clearly draws on cultural resources within Asian families and communities, but it is also made necessary by the racism in the housing market in Britain (Rex and Moore, 1967; CRE, 1984). A similar system, known as the pardner system, exists in Afro-Caribbean communities and women have been prominent in its operation (Bryan *et al.*, 1985). It is noteworthy too that it is part of the philosophy and organisation of the Rastafarian movement that poverty (or wealth) should be shared between men and women members (Catholic Commission for Racial Justice, 1982).

British social policy, particularly immigration policy, has not however facilitated the economic strengths of black women nor the unity of black families. Indeed, British immigration law has been severely criticised by the European Commission on Human Rights for its racial bias and for dividing families (*The Guardian*, 4 December 1979). Social policy does not seem to have much effect either on the relative poverty experienced by many black people in Britain—it is a poverty that is persisting (Brown, 1984). In addition, the recent Commission for Racial Equality Report on the immigration service showed the long waiting-lists that exist for people hoping to join their families here, and the almost insurmountable documentation and information that is required to validate their claims to family membership. Any discussion must therefore address issues of class and gender but, most centrally, issues of racism: 'I think if

you're a Black woman, you've got to begin with racism. It's
not a choice, it's a necessity' (Bryan *et al.*, 1985, p.174).

BLACK WOMEN AND THE LABOUR MARKET— PAID WORK AND EMPLOYMENT

The poverty experienced by black women in Britain is partly
a result of their own position in the labour market and
partly the result of the position of black men in the labour
market, since women are sometimes financially dependent
on men through marriage or other kinship ties. The distinc-
tively unequal position of black workers has been fully documented over recent years (Brown, 1984; Braham *et al.*,
1981), a position that Phizacklea has characterised as 'the
ghettoisation of migrant labour' (1983, p.107). Phizacklea
goes on to suggest that black women form a specific 'reserve
army of labour' for employers since not only are they made
redundant more quickly during a recession, but they are
also re-employed faster when business picks up. Clearly,
black women are also affected by the well-documented
effects of sexism in the labour market (Mackie and Patullo,
1977; Hakim, 1979), but for black women sexism does not
necessarily have primacy over racism in explaining their
inequality and poverty. It is a complex picture that needs
careful and specific analysis.

There has been little change over time in the racism faced
by black workers in the labour market in Britain. Black
men are located in rather different sectors of work from
white men and are more likely to work in jobs with low
pay and poor conditions. Brown's study (which reports the
findings of the latest Policy Studies Institute research
conducted in 1982) shows that 82 per cent of West Indian
men and 73 per cent of Asian men are manual workers
compared to 58 per cent of white men. They are more likely
to have to do shiftwork than white men. As far as job levels
are concerned, black men are less likely than white men to
hold supervisory positions. The effects of these differences
on median weekly earnings are striking. The same 1982

survey showed that median earnings for white men were
£20 per week higher than for West Indian men and £18 per
week higher than for Asian men (Brown, 1984, pp.167–9).
The low wages of black men might be one of the reasons
why a relatively high proportion of black women take up
paid work on a full-time basis. Certainly, Stone's research
(1983) indicates that for both black and white women the
main motive for working is to provide an essential financial
contribution to family income. The relationship is, however,
a complicated one since many Pakistani Muslim families
have the lowest incomes and yet the women are less likely
to take up paid work. Stone's work also shows that women
in all racial groups valued paid work because it helped to
reduce social isolation and boredom. Particularly prominent
in the labour market are women of Afro-Caribbean origin,
in part probably due to the tradition of women being the
'breadwinner' and in part, initially at least, because of the
greater opportunities for paid work for the early migrants
(Foner, 1979; Bryan *et al.*, 1985). Thus Brown found that
74 per cent of West Indian women compared with 39 per
cent of Asian women and 46 per cent of white women were
in the labour force in 1982 (Brown, 1984, p.186).

The struggle to combine paid work with child-care is one
that faces all working mothers but it is important to note
that there is differential access by race to scarce child-care
services (Parmar, 1982). As early as 1975 the Community
Relations Commission produced a study which showed the
way racism operated in child-care services. Black women
were less able to find childminders to meet their needs (for
example, long hours to cover shiftwork, childminders near
their home) than white women, and some minders refused
to take black children (CRC, 1975). The lack of flexible
child-care facilities is something that has persisted, if not
worsened, in recent years, forcing many black women into
less desirable and less well-paid jobs such as homeworking,
nightwork and shiftwork (Bryan *et al.*, 1985).

Brown's study indicates that there are on the whole fewer
differences in jobs and pay between black and white women
than between black and white men, which may well indicate

the pervasiveness of sexism in the labour market at a general level. However there are still important differences. For example, there are very few black women in professional or managerial jobs, and there are far fewer black women with no qualifications who manage to get non-manual jobs. Black women are also prominent in certain sectors of work rather than others. Many Afro-Caribbean women, for example, work in the National Health Service and local authority bodies (nearly 50 per cent of West Indian women compared with 25 per cent of white women and 16 per cent of Asian women). Asian women, on the other hand, work mainly in the private sector in manufacturing, particularly the textile and clothing industries (Brown, 1984).

The experience of Afro-Caribbean women in the National Health Service is captured by Bryan *et al.*, in the following way:

> For many Black women who join the NHS with the intention of becoming nurses, this was to remain an elusive goal. Relegated to the hospitals' kitchens and laundries, or trudging the wards as tea-ladies, cleaners and orderlies, we were to have first hand experience of the damning assumptions which define our role here. The patients saw it as fitting that we should be doing Britain's dirty work and often treated us with contempt. (Bryan *et al.*, 1985, p.43)

Extreme exploitation faces the many black women who have to take jobs as homeworkers with very low wages, job insecurity and many costs borne by the employee (Hakim, 1980; see also the chapter by Susan Lonsdale in this volume). The exact number of black homeworkers is not known, but Anwar (1979) in his study in Rochdale found that most of the Pakistani women there were homeworkers. An Asian woman homeworker in Wilson's study expresses her experience as follows:

> This is our fate, sister, to work, to slave, in Pakistan too some of us has to do the hard, hard work on the fields. Here it is a different kind of work, we are more lonely and in some ways the work is harder, but for us women as you know, life itself is very hard. (Wilson, 1978, p.49)

Earnings overall do not seem to differ for black and white

women as much as they do for black and white men (Smith, 1981; Brown, 1984). In Brown's 1982 study, the median weekly wage for white women was £4 more than for Asian women and £3 less than for West Indian women. The latter figure probably reflects the fact that many West Indian women work in large, public sector workplaces with unions where wages tend to be higher. The reasons for these relatively close wage levels are a matter of dispute (see for example, Smith, 1977; Parmar, 1982).

The devastating effects of growing unemployment amongst black individuals and in communities has been well documented over recent years, although solutions are thin on the ground. A wide range of government and non-government reports have pointed out that black unemployment has been rising significantly faster than white unemployment[4]. The particularly serious position of black youths has been noted by people such as Lord Scarman in his report on the Brixton disturbances of 1981 (Scarman, 1981). Clearly, the loss of a job, however poorly paid, immediately results in even less money coming into the family, bringing about even greater financial hardship. Smith (1981, p.54) has shown that only a tiny proportion of people receive more in benefits than they previously earned—3 per cent of white men, 5 per cent of minority men, 4 per cent of white women and 2 per cent of minority women.

Race has been shown to have a significant bearing on people's chances of becoming unemployed, irrespective of other factors associated with a greater risk of unemployment such as age, skill level or area of residence (Smith, 1981, pp.3–5). Gender also plays an important part. The 1971 Census showed that unemployment for minority men was slightly higher than for white men (6.8 per cent compared with 5.4 per cent). However even at that time when the recession was only just beginning to bite, there were significant differences between the rate for minority women (9.1 per cent) and the rate for white women (4.9 per cent).

These differences have remained. By 1982, the overall male national unemployment rate was 13 per cent, compared with much higher rates for black men—25 per cent for West Indian men and 20 per cent for Asian men. Black women also faced significantly higher rates at this time—10 per cent for white women, compared with 16 per cent for West Indian women and 20 per cent for Asian women (Brown, 1984, p.189). Black workers of either gender are also more likely to be out of work for longer periods of time. Brown's 1984 study showed that half the black men compared with a third of the white men were unemployed for over a year. Black women were more than twice as likely to be unemployed long term than white women.

The effects of the recession, particularly on young black women, cannot be overemphasised. Brown's data showed that young women of Asian and West Indian origin had the highest unemployment rates of any age group (47 per cent and 50 per cent, respectively). The response of successive governments to high and rising youth unemployment generally since 1978 has been to offer work experience and work training on two main programmes, the Youth Opportunities Programme (1978–83) and the Youth Training Scheme (1983—present). Black youngsters have taken up places on the Youth Opportunities Programme and the Youth Training Scheme in large numbers in the hope that the schemes would help them improve their work skills and job opportunities. Unfortunately these hopes have not been fulfilled, because they have been placed to a disproportionate extent on those parts of the schemes which offer lower quality training and less chance of permanent work afterwards (Cross *et al.*, 1983; Fenton *et al.*, 1984). A recent study of Afro-Caribbean young women in the Midlands has shown that race and gender inequalities are being perpetuated on the Youth Training Scheme in spite of the Manpower Services Commission's growing formal commitment to equal opportunities (Austen, 1984).

However, black women of whatever age have not passively accepted the effects of poverty and unemployment on their lives. Many young black women are responding to the lack of traditional work by setting up co-operatives, undertaking community work or moving into jobs that they can do on a self-employed basis in non-traditional areas such as carpentry (Cross et al., 1983; Bryan et al., 1985). Black women generally are prominent as union members, especially Afro-Caribbean women (Brown, 1984). Indeed, they have fought for union recognition and better wages and conditions in a number of important national and local disputes. Asian women, for example, were at the centre of the Imperial Typewriters strike in Leicester in 1974 and in the Grunwick dispute in London in 1976 (Wilson, 1978; Phizacklea, 1983). They have also fought in less well-publicised disputes about places like the clothing 'sweatshops' in Coventry in 1977 (Hoel, 1982). Afro-Caribbean women have played a significant part in fighting for better pay and conditions in the NHS (as well as in the defence of the NHS itself) in the strikes of 1972 and 1982/83 (Bryan et al., 1985). Such action shows some of the ways in which black women have worked together to resist the effects of sexism and poverty on their lives and the lives of their families and communities.

BLACK WOMEN AND SOCIAL SECURITY BENEFITS

Most black people in Britain are fully entitled to claim supplementary benefit and other kinds of state benefit and they should therefore face no more or less difficulty in claiming than anyone else. In practice, this is not so and the policy of linking immigration status to benefit entitlement has had the effect of excluding some black people from benefit on grounds which are not always clear. For example, a small number of black people are not eligible for supplementary benefit if they are defined as 'persons from abroad' who are not supposed to have 'recourse to public funds', a term which has yet to be clearly defined.

A passport is the obvious evidence of immigration status and the DHSS 'S' manual instruction, subsequently modified by Circular S/64, gives staff the right to ask for passports where there are 'reasonable grounds for doubt'.

There is considerable evidence, however, that the 'checking of passports [by the DHSS] is not just common, but so common as no longer to be an issue which black claimants complain of' (Gordon and Newnham, 1985, p.24). None the less the insecurity, anxiety and anger that such checking raises in black people should not be underestimated. Furthermore, DHSS officials do not always accurately interpret stamps and other notes made in passports and people may again be deprived unnecessarily of benefit (ibid.).

There are other ways in which racist assumptions operate in the benefit system. For example, assumptions are sometimes made that the Asian community is always closely-knit and that people can always call upon relatives for financial help. DHSS staff may therefore assume that Asian people have less need of benefits. On the other hand, there may be a complete lack of understanding of the way family and community networks *do* work. Informal transactions of money, shared property within the Asian community or resources abroad, for example, are quite common and have been used to invalidate claims for benefit by the DHSS (ibid.).

There are a number of issues that affect women claimants in particular and make their position problematic. In general women, particularly married women, are defined as the dependants of men in both immigration and benefit systems. Thus, for example, unless their husband is settled in the UK, wives do not have an independent right to stay (WING, 1985, p.94). Sometimes black women have had their benefits withdrawn because their husband's status is questioned for reasons of which they may or may not be aware. If the issue is one of illegal immigration, then their right to stay is also under threat. The campaign for Parveen Khan's case illustrates these issues. Ms Khan came to Britain in 1979 as the fiancée of Shaukat Khan whom she subsequently married. In 1980, Mr Khan's immigration status came under question and as a result so did the status of Ms Khan, although she had no knowledge of any irregularities. Eventually, in 1982, whilst their appeals were going through, her supplementary benefit and child benefit were withdrawn on the grounds that she was an illegal entrant. She remained under threat of deportation until June 1983, when the Home Office admitted that she was not an illegal entrant. Her social security benefits were not reinstated until the end of July 1983 (Gordon, 1984).

Married women face other difficulties in establishing their rights to benefits such as widows' pensions, retirement pensions and death grants because the validity of the marriage has to be established. If the marriage took place in the UK it is usually fairly easy to provide acceptable documentation. However, less acceptable may be documentation from abroad if the marriage took place overseas. Even more problematic for British officialdom is the issue of polygamous marriages. The DHSS has introduced two forms designed to overcome some of these problems, but the kind of 'proof' required is still often difficult to provide—for example, the names of witnesses if the marriage took place some time ago. Once again, women stand to lose benefits or to suffer long delays in establishing their rightful claims.

It is perhaps not surprising in view of the obstacles placed in front of black claimants that there is clear evidence of low take-up of benefits, particularly discretionary ones. The issue of unclaimed benefits is one that affects many poor people in Britain and the scale of underclaiming is immense. However, a number of surveys have shown that underclaiming by black people is higher than for white people (Gordon and Newnham, 1985, pp.57–9). Lack of information and the complexities of the system have been found to be the main barriers to claimants but in addition the racism of benefit and other agencies and their staff is keenly felt by black women:

There is no single area of our lives which better exposes our experience of institutionalised racism than our relationship with the various welfare services. Here we deal regularly with people who are vested with the power to control, disrupt and intervene in our lives on behalf of the state. Any black woman who has ever spent a day at the DHSS office trying to claim benefit or who has had a child taken into care quickly learns that once contact with the welfare agencies is made, her life is no longer her own. (Bryan *et al*., 1985, pp.110–11)

Finally it has to be said that there are costs to claiming from the state for black people, including black women, people whose labour as Bryan *et al*., (1985, p.111) point out: 'has propped up this country not only over the past four decades but for centuries. Far from draining its resources, we have been the producers of its wealth.' The many campaigns and appeals on individual cases are testament to the determination of black women to fight for their rights to state benefits should they need them. Appeals, when they are allowed, are held before tribunals and legal aid is not available for representation, despite the fact that all the evidence shows that representation is vital for a successful outcome (Evans, 1983). In addition the effects of the rising costs of acquiring British citizenship on black people cannot be ignored. Help with fees is not normally available through the social security system and the 1985 cost for discretionary registration or naturalisation is £160.

BLACK WOMEN AND THEIR FAMILIES

Current social policy in Britain including, in particular, immigration policy, makes it difficult for many black women effectively to fulfill their responsibilities to their families. Groups such as the Women Against Immigration and Nationality Group (WING) have been important in challenging these policies for black women. The sexism and racism embodied in official policies creates financial and emotional stress and the separation of family members from each other. Like most migrants, black people in Britain frequently have financial responsibilities to relatives in their country of origin. However, these obligations may persist not out of choice but as a result of the long delays in immigration procedures or, in some cases, the permanent separation of families. Brown's 1982 study gives some indication of the extent of such financial obligations. He found that 40 per cent of West Indian households and 10 per cent of Asian households send money mainly to relatives in their country of origin—the amounts averaged £17 a month for West Indian households and £26 a month for Asian households. Such payments indicate 'the strength of family bonds among minority ethnic groups, especially when it is remembered that their incomes are lower than those of whites' (Brown, 1984, p.302; see also Prescod-Roberts and Steele, 1980).

The relatively large number of women heads of lone-parent families in the Afro-Caribbean community has already been noted. The financial and social penalties faced by such families in the white community have been extensively highlighted by the Finer Report and other research (Finer, 1974; Letts, 1983). Black lone mothers, particularly single mothers, also have to face the pressure of racism and the insidious pathologising of black parents (Bryan *et al.*, 1985). It has been known for some years that a disproportionate number of Afro-Caribbean children are taken into care (Murray, 1983). It is highly likely that many of these children come from lone-parent families since it is known that, in the general population, a large number of children in care come from such families (NCOPF, 1978)[5]. It is hardly surprising that as a result many Afro-Caribbean women have learnt through bitter experience to suspect the 'help' offered by professionals such as social workers (Murray, 1984; Bryan *et al.*, 1985).[6]

Afro-Caribbean mothers may also face separation from their children against their will because of the way in which the immigration rules work and the costs of challenging decisions. In the early years of migration, many Afro-Caribbean women had to leave their children in the Caribbean while they settled and found work in Britain (Prescod-Roberts and Steele, 1980). Over the years it has become more difficult for children to join their parents, particularly a lone parent. The 'sole responsibility rule' introduced in 1968 has primarily affected Afro-Caribbean lone mothers. The rule means that they have to prove that they have sole financial and other responsibility for the child before s/he is allowed into Britain. Since other relatives in the Caribbean may well have given some help such proof may be difficult and costly to provide. As a result, some Afro-Caribbean mothers have been parted from their children who then have to be supported overseas without the help of child benefit or tax relief.

Changes in the immigration rules since 1969 have made it harder for women, particularly those of Asian origin, to be joined by their children (WING, 1985). One of the most famous campaigns by an Asian woman to be reunited with her children was that of Anwar Ditta. After five years and the help of the Granada television programme *World in Action*, who arranged for blood samples from her children in Pakistan to be sent to Britain for tests, Ms Ditta was finally reunited with them. The costs, financial and emotional, of such struggles and such separations cannot be overemphasised.

Many Asian couples have also been very hard hit by such separations. Whilst wives and intending wives have faced many difficulties, those hardest hit by the rules have been women in the UK wishing to be joined by foreign husbands (WING, 1985). The rules have in fact been successively tightened for women on the grounds that a wife should live where her husband lives, that Asian people should adapt to 'the customs of Europe' and that alleged abuses of the arranged marriage system to secure settlement must be stopped. By 1983 the rules allowed all women of British citizenship, regardless of ancestry, to bring in foreign husbands and fiancés. However women who were only settled here, or who were working or studying here subject to some immigration restrictions, were not so allowed.

Thus non-British black women have become more heavily penalised under the rules. As a result, three women took a case to the European Court of Human Rights on the grounds that the rules discriminated on grounds of sex. In May 1985 they won their case (*The Guardian*, 29 May 1985). However, the British government's solution has been to tighten the rules for men. From August 1985 husbands and fiancés will be able to join women with permanent residence but the restrictive criteria previously applied to them will now also apply to wives and fiancés (Runnymede Trust, 1985).

CONCLUSION

The title of this chapter is in effect charged with political significance. Without doubt the black community is doubly disadvantaged. Black people are concentrated disproportionately in the decaying inner areas of Britain's major cities and are therefore more vulnerable to the stresses of these areas. Individual households experience poverty, poor housing, unemployment and poor local facilities but with the added dimension of racial discrimination. Black women also have the unenviable task of having to contend with sexism in an already hostile environment.

Urban deprivation has been closely linked with race in all available research data but successive governments have sought to deal with the 'problem' of race by focusing on black immigration. In so doing, governments (and other official agencies) reveal that the central issue is how black people, their needs and concerns, are viewed in British society and are reflected in positions of power and authority. Black women in Britain have to face, and are still facing, the dual oppressions of racism and sexism which impinge negatively on their opportunities and consign them to low-paid and lower-status jobs. The major struggle for black women is not just to challenge the oppressive nature of the society in which they live but to create and provide their own positive images of the strengths, support and skills within the traditions of the herstory of black people. It is within the context of supportive and self-help groups that black women have been able to examine and address their own experiences of racism and sexism and develop their own political theory.

NOTES

1. Defining terms such as 'black', 'sexism' and 'racism' is a controversial activity. For the purpose of this discussion, we have formulated the following working definitions:

   Racism is a process of systematic oppression directed towards people who are defined as inferior, usually in pseudo-biological terms such as skin colour.

   Sexism is a process of systematic oppression directed towards women who are defined as inferior to men.

   Black is a political term used to refer to groups who have chosen to share their experience of racism (mainly) in British society, shifting that experience from a negative to a positive one. In the modern British context, it refers primarily to people of Asian and Afro-Caribbean origin. In some cases, research which uses different terms (e.g. 'West Indian', 'minority') will be cited.

   The discussion will also focus on family poverty rather than the very important wider aspects of poor housing, inner city poverty, the chronic under-resourcing of black self-help and community groups etc. We shall therefore be looking at black women with some sort of sole or shared financial responsibilities for family members (however defined), whether they are in paid work, unemployed, full-time housewives or heads of lone-parent families.

2. This point was strongly made at the recent Leicester International Women's Day conference on 8 March 1986.

3. The following framework draws on and extends helpful ideas from Westwood (1984, p.232), who in turn draws on work by Gardiner (1977, pp.155–63).

4. See, for example, Smith, 1981; Scarman 1981; Brown, 1984. Accurate data on unemployment by race and gender are problematic. Government sources have not consistently kept figures by race, and female unemployment is usually underestimated because it is not always worthwhile for women to register as unemployed. However, the data that exist from local and national surveys indicate similar trends.

5. We have been unable to trace any figures to support this point but we are grateful to Ben Brown (Assistant Director (Child Care), Dr Barnardo's, London) for helpful advice and sources.

6. Racism in social work is an issue that the profession has begun to address over recent years; see, for example, Husband, 1978; Cheetham, 1981; Ahmed, 1983; and Edmonds and Powell, 1985.

Part 2
Women, Paid Work and Poverty

4 Training for Low Pay

Carol Buswell

Youth training schemes (YTS) have been introduced during a period of unprecedented youth unemployment where the official rhetoric maintains that young people need to be trained in the 'skills' necessary for such jobs as may be available. Until 1986 the training consisted of 13 weeks 'off the job' in a college or training centre and the rest of the year on employers' premises. The young people are paid an 'allowance', but not by the employer. The scheme has now been extended to two years; the first year has the same requirements as the initial one-year scheme but in the second year only seven weeks is 'off the job' training. Employers have for many years been receiving free or cheap youth labour, as the YTS was preceded by the Youth Opportunities Programme. In addition the Young Worker Scheme reimburses employers for part of a young person's wage if this is below a certain threshold. Employers therefore have no need to pay proper wages to young people and since the inception of YTS have had no need to pay any wages at all, which helps to explain the lack of proper jobs for young people under 18 years. The choice, then, for most young people leaving school is between unemployment or a training scheme. In the first year of YTS more chose the former than was anticipated so young people now have to suffer reduced social security benefits for six weeks if they refuse a YTS place or leave a scheme during the year. These factors mean that, in effect, YTS is virtually compulsory for those young people who do not wish to be unemployed.

The introduction of youth training schemes in Britain has involved not only an extension of vocational training and education but also has antecedents in nineteenth-century education which for girls was shaped by an ideology of domesticity which embodied notions of femininity. This ideology, as will be illustrated, still underpins both current vocational initiatives and the present restructuring of the labour market. Case study material will illustrate how girls' experiences during their training year condition their expectations not only about future wages but also about the nature of the jobs they might expect to obtain. Service sector employment is currently being restructured to provide predominantly part-time work for older women and low-paid full-time work for young people. This will have far-reaching consequences beyond the individual and it is in this context that youth 'training' for girls is occurring.

BACKGROUND

In the nineteenth century the emphasis in education on 'useful' knowledge was, for working-class girls, not a vehicle for social mobility but a means of maintaining the status quo (Purvis, 1981). By the end of that century grants were being made available for the teaching of domestic subjects in elementary schools and it was argued that girls might be more attracted to 'going into service' if domestic duties were respected (Dyhouse, 1977). Vocational education for girls, with its emphasis on domestic skills was important both for unpaid family duties and for the waged sector of the labour market which working-class girls entered. In the twentieth century all recipients of vocational education became redefined as 'less able', but the extension of different kinds of waged work took gender-specific paths and the nature of 'women's employment' then contributed to notions of femininity (Marks, 1976).

Working-class education for both girls and boys has, historically, been vocational education; but for girls the vocationalisation was imbued with a domestic ideology which attempted to teach them to be good wives and mothers if they were middle-class, and to fit them for domestic occupations and be 'good women' if they were working-class (Purvis, 1983). The domestic ideology, in this sense, served both their home and labour market positions, although not without tensions. The ideology also served that stage of capital accumulation characterised by the separation of home and work; by male occupations which required a great deal of domestic servicing; and by a cheap pool of local labour. It is crucial in attempting to understand current developments in education and training not only to consider the social positions for which different classes and genders are destined but also to remember that class divisions exist *within* gendered groups. This is a truism when applied to men; but the 'myth of female classlessness' (Arnot, 1983) both gives primacy to a domestic ideology which homogenises women and also does not facilitate consideration of the very different nature of working-class girls' education and training.

FEMININITY

For younger women, clerical and shop jobs currently account for 43 per cent of their occupations nationally (OPCS, 1984a). The fact that just over one-third of YTS places offered are on clerical and service sector courses is therefore congruent with the actual labour market. Girls are encouraged to enter these areas of the labour market by the fact that the occupations are often presented with a 'glamorous' image. Griffin (1985), in fact, found that the distinction between office and factory work was the crux of the difference between a 'good' job and a 'bad' one for the girls in her study. Not only are the conditions of office working thought to be better; but it is also a site where an idealised form of femininity is represented. Griffin concludes that it is also a setting where girls think they might meet the 'right sort of man', and that it holds the illusion of upward mobility.

Office work can, of course, accommodate a wide range of girls and the skills of typing is only part of the requirement for the job. Griffin quotes a survey of male managers who looked for 'personality, good grooming, clear speech and a sense of humour'. As Curran (1985) notes, however, it is difficult in our society to disentangle notions of personality from those of gender; and where employers have an 'embarrassment of choice' with regard to workers the situation may facilitate the operation of personal preference and social stereotypes more than under conditions of low demand for jobs. Shop work can also be seen as an appropriate work setting if the shop concerned sells fashion goods or expensive items, where dealing with the commodities at a service level has higher status than manufacturing them. The public presentation of the secretarial image and 'boutique' assistant through the media and advertising is one that defines the elements of work in close connection with expectations about stereotyped female behaviour and appearance. These expectations will be not only a powerful determinant over which particular girls obtain such jobs as exist but also influential over the girls themselves.

In order to consider the place of girls on youth training schemes and their likely futures with regard to employment, it is necessary to take account of social processes that occur prior to this. It is well known that option choices in secondary schools serve largely to divide pupils by gender during the last couple of years of compulsory schooling; and that these choices are activated partly by assumptions concerning 'appropriate' studies for both boys and girls, partly by gender-typing of subjects themselves and partly by pupils' own self-identification and assumptions about their eventual place in the adult world. Many of the processes which occur during schooling to reinforce and maintain gender divisions are, however, both subtle and complex.

A two-year study of fifth and sixth formers conducted in a North of England mixed comprehensive school between 1980 and 1982 revealed the cultural reproduction of dependency relations which were shaped and legitimised by notions of femininity (Buswell, 1984). Gender stratification

structures, with males as the dominant group, are characterised by the dependency of women on men—in the private
sphere in terms of the social relations of domestic organisation and in the public sphere in terms of the social relations
of production. The school in question was one in which
most of the sixth formers were taught by men, so that female
pupils were therefore involved in dependency relations of
both a structural and an interpersonal kind.

Processes of nurturing, acquiescence and invisibility were
documented. These illustrated the various ways in which
girls 'managed' their interpersonal relations with male
teachers but, in so doing, became enmeshed in reinforcing
and reproducing dependency relations based on a limited
range of 'female-appropriate' behaviour, which served to
underline expectations of femininity.

The process of nurturing was illustrated by a girl who was
regarded as a 'problem pupil' in the fifth year but who
returned to the sixth form in order to attempt some 'O'
levels after disappointing job-seeking attempts. The first
part of her sixth form career was characterised by a continu-
ation of her fifth form behaviour—now indulged in with
some ambivalence, as there were certain male teachers
whose good opinion she was keen to elicit. This keenness
did not, however, prevent her from shouting at a senior
(male) member of staff, storming out of a (male-taught)
lesson, being rude to her (male) tutor and maintaining that
he had been 'trained to break her spirit'. This girl, far
from being regarded as rude and impolite, was variously
described by male teachers as highly strung, lacking in
confidence, neurotic, spoilt and manic-depressive. The
labelling of her attributes in this way was important because
it 'constructed' a person who needed nurturing rather than
punishment. This girl subsequently became adept at manip-
ulating the male teachers with such behaviour as pouting,
pretending to have no confidence and constantly asking for
help and advice that she did not need or had no intention
of following. The teachers, prior to her leaving, maintained
that she had 'grown-up'. What she had in fact grown into
was a person able to manipulate interpersonal relations of

an unequal kind, always remaining dependent on the person or group she thought she was controlling. In the end she fitted a stereotyped picture of a particular kind of female behaviour.

In contrast, for some girls in this school acquiescence earned them the reputation of good pupils; but doing what the 'school' wanted could also alter their choices and fundamentally affect their future lives. The invisibility of some girls is perhaps the most striking and obvious process in mixed schools and has been well documented by Stanworth (1983). To be invisible does not necessarily earn girls a positive reputation in teachers' eyes, as the criterion of 'ability' often shifts, later in school life, from being 'good' and working hard to being forthcoming, opinionated and having 'character'. Thus, behaviour that might have been functional early in the school career for eliciting teachers' good opinions becomes inappropriate for that purpose at a later stage.

The girls studied were in various ways attempting to cope with contradictory social messages and 'get by' in the best way they could. Thus they sometimes used 'female-appropriate' behaviour to resist the demands of work and teachers, and sometimes resisted and compromised in other ways. It is not being argued that the girls' behaviour turned them into 'types', as behaviour is partly the *product* of social relations within an organisation, but the girls' responses would serve to locate them in traditional positions *vis-à-vis* men. The modes of behaviour that are considered acceptable are also the ones which, if adopted, legitimate unequal gender structures.

Briefly, what this study showed is that besides the actual subjects studied at school, many girls, like boys, leave with certain behavioural skills which are gender-specific. It is not so surprising, then, that when given a 'choice' of future training for particular occupations predictable patterns emerge. This is not to minimise the fact that some careers officers, teachers, employers and training officers undoubtedly do make sexist assumptions and channel girls along particular routes, but also to suggest that girls themselves are not always open to other suggestions. These girls though, in choosing traditional paths, have a grasp of the reality of the labour market and of their future position within it.

However, while traditional forms of femininity are often encouraged within schools and sought by employers in service sector jobs, some girls may resist these even to the detriment of their own job-seeking attempts. In a study of girls on retail and clerical youth training schemes in a North of England city in 1985/86, this resistance was most marked among retail students for whom, in addition to the expectation of traditional female dress that pertains in many offices, there is often the added dimension of more general 'appearance', whereby not only dress but every aspect of the person is expected to conform to a particular stereotype. The following comments by retail students not only illustrate this but are also significant in as much as they were unsolicited and emerged during general discussion regarding the search for work:

'I was going to [national chain of chemist shops] but I changed me mind cos you've got to go with your hair all done up and make-up plastered on your face. I wouldn't do that—it's just selling yourself to them.'

'I was going to write away for that job in [franchise cosmetic firm] but they wanted a photograph of you. I thought "No way am I going to do a job like that." '

'I had an interview for a scheme at [national shoe chain] but before me interview I changed me mind cos I didn't like the uniform! Me mam was going mad, she said "You can't pick your uniform"—but it was a dead flarey blue skirt, a blue waistcoat, a white blouse and a big white tie thing. It was smart, like, but I didn't want to wear it.'

While the definition of femininity that contains prescriptions regarding dress and manner is an element of service sector jobs that appeal to some girls, with current levels of unemployment it is possible for it to be made virtually compulsory to the detriment of girls who do not, and do not want to, subscribe to that definition. The definition may be endorsed by some women and girls but it is generated and maintained by men. This is particularly obvious in certain chain stores where individual managers—usually male—have the authority to decide what form of matching

dress 'their girls' will wear for the coming season.
Complaints by some girls about blouses that are hard to
wash and the requirement to wear 'heeled' shoes indicate
the discrepancy between the appearance they would choose
and the one that is chosen for them in a direct and compulsory way to endorse the form of femininity which appeals
to white, middle-aged, middle-class men.

THE CHANGING LABOUR MARKET

It is now well known that over one half of the total employed
population currently works in the service sector of the
economy; that clerical and administrative workers make up
45 per cent of the total British workforce; and that one
quarter of total employment is in distribution, banking and
finance, personal services and hotel and catering occupations (CSO, 1985a). Disproportionately, three-quarters
of all employed women work in the service sector (Werneke,
1985). The fact that well over one half of employed women
aged between 30 and 59 work fewer than 30 hours a week
is also important for the present discussion.

Within the service sector retailing employs more than
twice as many people as any single manufacturing industry
and accounts for 15 per cent of women's employment
(Lewis, 1985). Just over a half of these jobs in 1981 were
part-time and almost all the part-time jobs were held by
married women (OPCS, 1984a). A continuing increase in
the ratio of part-time to full-time employees is a feature of
this sector, facilitated partly by the fact that it is cheaper to
employ two part-time workers for 18 hours each than one
full-timer, as no National Insurance contributions are paid
for the former.

In terms of the domestic ideology which, in the past,
underpinned both working-class women's vocational
education and their labour market positions it is suggested
that the consequences of such an ideology have not only
been a constant thread but, more recently, have actually
been 'capitalised' on (in the literal sense of the term). The

regions which earlier this century offered mainly single industry employment for a male workforce, in which long hours and shift-work were the norm, depended upon the domestic servicing provided by women. The subsequent introduction of 'female' part-time, badly paid employment rests on the same premise (although differently articulated) since part-time work is seen to be more 'compatible' with modern domestic commitments. But the incomes of the new 'female' jobs are still seen as secondary in the household economy, the labour market is structured to be part-time and the assumption is that workers can enter and leave—as women are not considered to be full-time, life-time, workers. During the current recession the occupational growth that has occurred has been in banking, finance, business services and retailing. However this growth has been in the number of part-time, as opposed to full-time jobs. Approximately a quarter of the total employed work-force is now part-time, some five million workers (Robinson, 1985).

In fact, women's pattern of working tends to change from being full-time before childbirth to a mixture of part-time and full-time after the first child. Approximately two-thirds of women's first return to work is to a part-time job and, at this point, there is a great deal of downward mobility (Dex, 1984). The move to part-time employment after child-birth is coinciding with or being used to shift the female workforce not only out of full-time into part-time employ-ment but also from manufacturing to the service and distri-bution sectors. These sectors are therefore *relying* on women having to take time off work during a certain phase of their life-cycle and 'the shift from manufacturing to services is being built, to some extent, upon elements of women's experience—domestic responsibilities, break for childbirth and consequent loss of earlier jobs' (ibid., p.106).

Working-class girls live in families where this pattern of working is part of life. The fact that shops and offices tend to recruit young people full-time and adult women part-time is a factor that might make these jobs 'attractive' in the light of assumed futures, if their expectations are that their lives will eventually be similar to their mothers'. But this future attractiveness may well be culturally disguised initially by the fact that these occupations are presented with a glamorous image for young full-time workers. So the labour market offers badly-paid full-time jobs for young women, which adult women can also do part-time. The 'desirability' of these occupations is emphasised for young women primarily through the ideal of femininity and for those same women after childbirth as a 'convenient' job which is congruent with domestic ideology. Current ideologies of femininity and domesticity therefore, far from being historical hangovers, are actually *central* to the restructuring of the economy, labour force and work processes.

The occupations in the tertiary sector for which young women are being trained are badly paid for both adults and young people. The average gross pay for a full-time adult shop assistant is £76, which compares with the average wage for girls under 18 years of £55.70, boys under 18 years of £87.70 and with the average full-time pay of adult women of £107.30 and adult men of £161.60 (CSO, 1985a). In the North of England some 60 per cent of all employees now work in the service sector and it has been estimated that 42 per cent of the total workforce in this region earns less than the 'decency threshold' specified by the Council of Europe (£108 a week or £2.75 per hour in 1985). Nearly 70 per cent of these low-paid employees are women and within the clerical and retailing fields the figures are bleak—90 per cent of women in shops in 1984 earned less than the decency wage, as did 86 per cent of receptionists and 56 per cent of costing and accounting clerks (Smail, 1985).

The official aim of youth training—'to provide opportunities for young people to learn not only job related skills but also to learn about the world of work in general' (Youth Training, 1984)—might be considered to have been successfully met if young women learn something of these aspects of work while they are training.

LEARNING DEPENDENCY

Young people on youth training schemes in 1985 received an 'allowance' of £27.30 a week plus any travel expenses over £2.50 a week. The terminology is important because it justifies the negligible amount by assuming that the training being received is the prime goal. Young people, however, only participate in 'off-the-job' training for 13 weeks of the year, the remainder of the time being spent 'on the job'. In effect the youngsters work full-time, one of the consequences of which is to introduce them to the *experience* of having too little money to participate fully in the adult working life they are pursuing.

Of 40 girls on retail and clerical schemes who were observed and interviewed in the course of research carried out during 1985 and 1986, the average amount of 'board' paid to parents was approximately £9 a week. After having paid travelling expenses most girls were left with about £16. They were therefore still dependent on their families for most things other than pocket money and some clothes. This dependence has consequences for whole households when, as in this sample, more than a quarter of them lived in single-adult families. Additionally, almost half of the girls were in households with only one adult wage, almost a quarter had no adult or only one part-time wage, and only a quarter lived in families with two full-time or one full-time and one part-time wage. Put another way, three-quarters of the young women were dependent on adults who had one wage or less to support the family. Thus the adults supporting these youngsters were themselves in households that were not the most affluent. Furthermore, as the amount of board paid did not fully cover the children's support, these parents were a fundamental part of the operation of the training schemes. Many parents, conscious of their children's circumstances, nevertheless did more than the minimum:

'Mam lends us money for clothes—but half the time when I go to give her the money back she'll say it doesn't matter.'

'Mam gives us 50 pence a day back for me lunch and she lends me the money for me clothes.'

'I only pays me mam £5 board. I was going to give her ten but she says "It's only a scheme so I'll just have the five"—and she pays for me dinners as well!'

This dependency also, for a few girls, extended beyond the family:

'Me boyfriend pays for everything when we go out—he earns £60.'

'I get paid to go out by me boyfriend.'

One consequence of training, therefore, is to enmesh young people in a web of dependency and obligation to individuals and families which, for some girls, has the added dimension of an early dependency on a wage-earning male. This is not to suggest that the girls themselves regarded this with equanimity, as economic independence was also valued. One girl explained this in relation to her divorced mother:

'I would've stayed at school if I'd got paid—but I would've felt stupid at Christmas with people giving me presents. I mean, I *like* giving presents, so I went crazy this year and bought everybody nice presents although I had no money for three weeks. I'd never *ever* been able to afford anything nice for me mam so I bought her something nice—she never expected it. Me mam's a one-parent family and we haven't got a man in the house to support us, so me mam can't afford anything nice—so I needed the money really.'

Another girl explained her presence on a scheme in similar vein:

'I didn't go to college to do a secretarial course because of the money. If you went to college you'd have no money and I'd have to have lived off me mam and dad and I didn't want to do that—I wanted to be independent but, I mean, £27—it doesn't go anywhere.'

While the meagre amount of money paid to these young people is officially regarded as a training allowance they experience it as low *pay*. Although trainees are intended to be 'extras' to their employers they are nevertheless present and correct for a full working week:

'The other people in the office say the money we get on schemes isn't worth it—they say it's slave labour, when I have to stay behind late me mam says that as well.' (Clerical trainee)

'I know people say "money isn't everything"—but you work nine till half five and come out with £27 —it really annoys us. You work so hard you're collapsing at the end of each day. The part-time people only work 15 hours and get more than I do. I'm the only full-time person there except the supervisor.' (Retail trainee)

'You'd get £10 for a Saturday job and that's only one day. I get less than a pound an hour—I thinks that's dreadful.' '(Clerical trainee)

In a few instances the young people were not, in fact, extras and they were aware that they were being employed to do a proper job:

'Somebody has to do the job I'm doing. The reason I got the job is that the girl who used to do it has left to have a baby and they haven't bothered replacing her, well—they've replaced her with me! If I wanted to take a holiday or anything I'd feel more dubious about taking it—especially if it was a busy time—rather than if I was just an extra, then I wouldn't be bothered.' (Clerical trainee)

'There used to be a woman there before me doing the job I'm doing but they made her redundant because they couldn't afford her—so I type everything that goes out of the office.' (Clerical trainee)

The demoralisation associated with the lack of money is highlighted for many girls on placements in offices and shops where particular kinds of dress are required and the young-ters have to comply—at their own expense. It costs to be 'feminine':

'It's terrible—every place you go to you've got to buy a new uniform. It's so stupid when you're on a scheme. . . . Fair enough if you're gettin' their wage—but otherwise there's no way. Then you have to wear tights all the time—and in a shop you're running around like a lunatic and always laddering your tights. Even if you buy cheap ones it still runs expensive.' (Retail trainee)

'I was always gettin' wrong for wearing skirts that she thought were too short—but, I mean, we couldn't afford to go out and buy a whole new wardrobe. I've got more trousers than skirts and she wouldn't let me wear them.' (Clerical trainee)

The girls' marginality also often seemed to be reinforced in offices where it is usual for employees to wear different clothes each day. The girls sometimes commented on their embarrassment at having to wear 'the same old thing'.

Some girls increased their incomes by doing other jobs as well. The traditional pocket-money source of babysitting was fairly common; one clerical trainee kept the Saturday shop job she had done whilst at school; and another clerical girl worked as a waitress after work two nights a week until 10 p.m. and for up to ten hours on a Saturday—in total a 57–hour week. Discussions about money peppered many of their conversations throughout the day, as this exchange between retail trainees illustrates:

Marie: I can't have lunch today—I've only got 12 pence to last until we get paid tomorrow.
Kirsty: I can't afford to go out at all now with Christmas presents and that.
Tricia: I only go to the disco on Tuesdays now, when it only costs a pound. I think we should get £37 over Christmas time.
Marie: Around £40 would be all right!

Experiencing relative poverty at the age of 16 or 17 for a year or two might not be considered to be too damaging in itself. A more important consequence, though, is that *expectations* are based on this experience, because future earnings are seen in relation to the base line of the £27 which they regard as their 'pay'. Most of these young people have applied for, and seen advertised, jobs in offices and shops where a wage, for their age, of about £40 is now usual—and in relation to £27 seems quite good:

'The people where I work get £40 and over, you know, I wouldn't mind that.' (Clerical trainee)

'My friend got an office job and gets over £50—so she's very well off. If you're permanent where I work you get between £40 and £60—that's good compared to what we get now.' (Clerical trainee)

'They say they don't get very good pay where I am—I think it's about £60. That would do me!' (Retail trainee)

Besides having lower expectations about what a 'proper wage' should be, there are even more serious consequences for these girls' views on what a 'job' should be. One retail girl was offered, during her training year, a part-time job in the shop where she was placed, and left the scheme to take it:

'He's offered me a 20–hour contract for £29 with the promise of overtime. That's pretty good because a lot of people who've been there quite a while have only got 15 hours.'

This girl, perhaps contrary to first impressions, is acting rationally in the light of the labour market conditions that prevail in much of retailing and certainly in the firm she worked for, where the main city centre shop employed only the manager and supervisor on a full-time basis and all the other employees were on part-time contracts ranging from 10 to 15 hours. These part-timers were not all older women, as there was at least one 18 year old who had not been able to obtain a full-time job. A 20–hour part-time contract was, therefore, as this girl pointed out, a better deal. This particular girl also said she might be in line for a 'trainee supervisorship' and she took that into account. The corporation for which she worked prides itself on the fact that 'Saturday girls' and part-timers can become supervisors and managers and, indeed, this is sometimes the case. What is not so obvious is the fact that 'supervisor' is merely the term used for the full-time employee who has charge of all the part-time employees, but who probably earns only the basic full-time wage. These supervisors, usually women, have responsibility but often no real prospects—as managers are more often men—yet the spurious 'status' is presented as a future prospect. This girl has got the measure of this labour

market and, incidentally, the labour process: 'If your face
fits you're OK. It's all down to personality and if he [the
manager] likes you.' In a year's time, therefore, she might
have acquired a full-time job as a trainee supervisor and
then 'it's all up to you'.

Clearly not all part-time workers are going to become
full-time in this sector of the labour market. Nevertheless,
part-time work is being accepted by some young people as
a possible route to a full-time job. Besides being an accurate
assessment of these particular sectors of the labour market,
some young people in small firms identify the wages paid
by their employers as a 'cost' that is high relative to *their*
understanding of wages. For example, the clerical girl
quoted previously who was doing all the typing since her
middle-aged predecessor had been made redundant said:

'When I was sorting out the filing cabinet I came across the old wage
sheets and she earned £100 a week. I'm not surprised they couldn't afford
her!'

In addition to the experience of poverty and the
conditioning of future expectations is the development of a
fatalistic attitude among some young people. With regard
to the £27 'allowance', comments like 'It's better than
nothing and more than the dole' and 'What you haven't
got you're not missing' were fairly common. It has to be
remembered that many young people experience a few
months of unemployment before starting training schemes
and their present income position is, at least early on in the
scheme, seen in relation to that:

'When I was on the dole I only got £17.30. I was bored and just doin'
housework for me mam all day.'

THE FUTURE

The service sector of the labour market, for which most
girls are being trained, has increased rapidly but technical

developments and restructuring are likely to make this sector problematic in the near future. With regard to office employment it is now estimated that word processors can do the work of 2½–5 traditional typists—and the estimated loss of 40 per cent of clerical jobs actually means between 400,000 and 700,000 people (Littler and Salaman, 1984). Resistance in this sector has been muted, not because of the passive nature of women workers, but because the occupation is characterised by high turnover and the widespread use of temporary and part-time workers. The introduction of equipment such as word processors is also likely to result in a change of office hours, with more shiftwork. Indeed some large British companies have already introduced a 'twilight shift' for clerical workers to enable women to work part-time while still fulfilling their domestic duties, a pattern that has hitherto been confined to factory work using local labour. Technical change in tertiary employment is therefore being introduced with reference to the ideology of domesticity which characterised women's work in the past. Littler and Salaman (1984, p.99) maintain that in the twentieth century 'office service replaced domestic service for working-class (and some middle-class) girls'.

The banking and finance sector is another area where the impact of new technology has fallen primarily on low-level, mostly female, staff. Child *et al.* (1985) report that senior bank officials freely admit that they have been introducing new technology within an unpublished dual employment policy, in which the stereotype of the female worker as a non-career-seeking, short-term employee has justified a lower tier of routine jobs.

With regard to retailing, a statement made in Australia in 1907 (quoted in O'Donnell, 1984, p.128) seems equally pertinent today: 'The futility of shop work as a life work for a woman is self evident. At its best it can only be a stop-gap between girlhood and matrimony for the majority. As a means of livelihood it is hopeless . . .' Changes in this sector of employment are proceeding rapidly as the average size of outlets increases, as diversification needs more sophisticated control and with larger shares of the market going to multiples. These circumstances are extremely favourable for the adoption of new technology (Marti and Zeilinger, 1985).

In order to respond to increasing competitiveness, attempts to decrease labour costs in retailing have therefore resulted in a pool of cheap labour—married women and young people—and it is these workers who are likely to be affected by the current phase of investment growth and microelectronic equipment. In these developments the multiples lead the way; their market power can be illustrated by the fact that in 1980 multiples had a 45 per cent share of the retailing market in Britain. In 1982 Sainsburys and Tesco accounted for 30 per cent of the *total* grocery market. However the introduction of new technology in retailing has hardly started for, despite the fact that 'electronic point of sales systems' have been on the market for over a decade, only 6 per cent of cashpoints in retail outlets had these systems installed by 1984. But investment is speeding up— it is estimated that in the next five years retailers will invest more than £200 million in these systems (Lewis, 1985).

Labour markets which recruit cheap full-time youth labour and part-time female labour are actually structured around the assumed dependency of these groups within a family context. It is assumed that both of these groups belong to households where the main expenses are borne by a higher earner. Changes in the labour market, therefore, are not simply about employment but about the connections between employment, home, class and gender. The occupations for which girls are currently being trained not only offer, in practice, low pay whilst they are young and full-time but are also being restructured to operate with part-time adult women. In this context it is worth noting that in 1984 one half of the part-time women workers in the North of England, for example, were paid less than £2 an hour (Smail, 1985)—this is the girls' future.

The training, as has been illustrated, also gives them first-hand experience of dependency, low pay and 'realistic'—in the light of the actual labour market —expectations. The future looks bleak in regions such as the North of England where the collapse of traditional male occupations and the possible consequent increase of men into such service sector full-time jobs as may exist will push women further to the margins (Buswell, 1985). Even if these girls eventually, as adults, form a traditional family unit—with one full-time service sector wage, one part-time wage and a couple of young people on training allowances or very low pay—they will experience not only individual, but also household, poverty.

5 Patterns of Paid Work

Susan Lonsdale

One of the most significant causes of poverty in Britain today is low pay, and the large majority of low-paid workers are women. The meaning and experience of work is quite different for women than it is for men. As a consequence, women's patterns of paid work are singularly different. Women are concentrated in lower-status and lower-paid jobs. They undertake a great deal of unpaid, and sometimes paid, work in the home. They often rely on part-time work which is inferior in rewards and conditions of service and is geared more towards the requirements of management than their own need for flexible hours. In general, women's participation in paid employment is of a kind that accommodates both domestic and employment commitments. The differences from men's patterns of work are largely due to the existence of a division of labour which separates men and women into gender-specific areas of work. The structure of this division of labour is underpinned by an ideology regarding the roles which women are expected to perform in society. Both structure and ideology profoundly affect women's access to income. This chapter will look at the role the sexual division of labour plays in characterising women's work as significant inside the home but deficient outside of it. It will show how women's patterns of paid work affect their earnings and conditions of employment. It will suggest that certain patterns of work which appear to give women relative autonomy are, in reality, enslaving them. Finally, it will evaluate recent policy measures designed to improve the situation of women in the labour market.

THE GREAT DIVIDE

Women's employment patterns are largely determined by beliefs about their role in society and by a structure of employment which subordinates them and uses their labour less to their own advantage than to the advantage of their employers. The sexual division of labour refers to the different tasks undertaken by men and women in society (Lonsdale, 1985a, pp.64–71). This and the ideology of sex role differentiation that goes with it affect employment in many ways. The paid jobs that women do outside the home tend to be very similar to the unpaid jobs they do inside the home such as cleaning, sewing, washing and cooking. However skills that are associated with the home (and learned within the home rather than in the industrial setting) are undervalued. Home-learned skills are defined as not being 'real' skills (as housework is not 'real' work) and, therefore, do not command a good wage (as housework does not command a wage). It is not surprising to find that wages in industries such as catering, clothing, laundry and cleaning are very low, nor that women are concentrated in such jobs. These industries therefore effectively set women's rates of pay. In addition to underestimating their skills, the dominance given to women's domestic life affects how they are regarded in the workplace. Suggesting that paid work is secondary to women's role in the home has the effect, as Oakley says, of 'characterising women as deficient labourers' (Oakley, 1982, p.135). From this it is an easy step to pay them a lesser wage for being lesser workers.

Some writers have suggested that the separation of home from work is a fairly recent phenomenon. It is argued that domestic work became devalued when the family lost its identity as a productive unit with industrialisation (Maynard, 1985). In this process, the work of the family was privatised until it no longer came to be seen as integral

to the production of commodities. The process of industrialisation itself also required a workforce that was more
flexible. Today, as then, a sexual division of labour serves
this purpose well, by providing the back-up services required
for primary, male workers and additional female workers
who can be drawn in and expelled from the labour force
when necessary.

SEPARATE BUT UNEQUAL

The sexual division of labour not only divides work into
unpaid and paid labour. It also influences what kinds of jobs
men and women do when both are in paid work. The degree
to which men and women are segregated into different occupations is crucial to an understanding of women's position
in the labour force and the wages they receive. Occupational
segregation is measured by the proportion of women who
work only with other women doing the same kind of work.
Studies have shown that there is a marked separation
between the kinds of paid work which men and women do
and that this has hardly changed this century (Hakim, 1978,
1981; Martin and Roberts, 1984). The jobs women do are
not only different from those that men do, but also tend to
be in lower-level, lower-paid occupations. Regardless of
occupation, women are also much more likely to work only
with other women if they work part-time (Martin and
Roberts, 1984). They are, therefore, segregated both hori-
zontally and vertically from male workers.

The sex structure of jobs has remained fairly constant
since 1970, with about a quarter of all jobs being typically
female and three-quarters being typically male. This has
had a significant effect on women's earnings and on the
impact of equal pay legislation, which will be dealt with
below. According to the 1980 Women and Employment
Survey, over three-quarters of all working women are to be
found in service industries and over half in clerical, catering,
cleaning and hairdressing. Three occupations were found to
have no women and ten out of all 18 occupations had one

per cent or less women in them (Martin and Roberts, 1984). The significance of job segregation is threefold. It has allowed a different wage structure to develop for men and women, keeping women's wages low. Secondly, it has removed women's jobs from the reaches of equal pay policy and legislation for a long time. Thirdly, it has resulted in men and women making quite different judgements regarding their relative status and abilities in the occupational and income hierarchy (Hakim, 1981). For instance in 1985 a woman would have had to be earning £189.50 a week to be in the top 10 per cent of female earners, whereas a man would have had to be earning £296.30 to be in the top 10 per cent of male earners (Department of Employment, 1985a, Part D). This would provide a more satisfactory explanation of why women are consistently found to be satisfied with less pay than men, than the more common suggestion that women only work for 'pin money' and therefore do not expect or need more pay.

It could be argued that occupational segregation is developing new dimensions which have not traditionally been thought of as part of occupational segregation. Two recently expanding types of work are now almost exclusively female; homework and part-time work. Homeworking refers to people working at home (rather than from home) for a wage, usually at piecework rates and for one employer only. Most surveys have shown that virtually all this kind of homeworking is done by women (Bisset and Huws, 1984; Hakim, 1984). Part-time work is also now a major feature of women's employment. In recent years, the number of part-time jobs has increased dramatically, mirroring the increase in married women's participation in paid work. In the 1984 Labour Force Survey, 55 percent of married women in employment worked part-time as against 4 per cent of men (OPCS, 1985a). Before considering the effect of this on women's jobs and pay, we need to look at women's earnings generally in relation to those of men.

SLIM PICKINGS

Their actual and perceived domestic responsibilities have limited the availability of most women to work the same hours as men. Whether women are economically active[1] or not, and whether they work full- or part-time, is largely determined by their age and marital status. Married women of childbearing age are least likely to be economically active or working full time. Most surveys now show that over 60 per cent of married women of working age are economically active, as against over 90 per cent of men and well over 70 per cent of non-married women (OPCS, 1982, 1984b, 1985a; Martin and Roberts, 1984; CSO 1986). Over the last 40 years, the proportion of married women in the labour force has increased substantially, but this increase has been very much in the area of part-time work. Between 1951 and 1981 part-time female employment increased fivefold from around 750,000 to nearly 4 million, while full-time female employment declined slightly over the same period (Robinson and Wallace, 1984a).

Women's earnings are significantly lower than men's and have always been so. In 1985 the average gross weekly wage of a female manual worker was 62 per cent of her male counterpart's weekly wage. Part of this difference is due to the greater amount of overtime work done by male workers. However even after taking this into account, female weekly earnings excluding overtime and female hourly earnings were still only 69 per cent of male earnings (Department of Employment, 1985a). It is interesting to note that this was ten years after the Equal Pay Act had come into force; and that there has been virtually no change in the male/female earnings gap since 1913 when it was 53 per cent, which demonstrates its remarkable resilience to change (Routh, 1980).

As well as earning less on average, women are heavily concentrated at the lower end of the earnings league. According to the *New Earnings Survey*, 27 per cent of female manual workers and 10 per cent of female non-manual workers earned a gross wage of less than £80 per

week in 1985, compared with 2.4 per cent and 1.6 per cent
of male manual and non-manual workers. Using the state-
determined family income supplement eligibility level of
£110 for 1985, we find 68 per cent of female manual and
38 per cent of female non-manual workers earning below
this amount, compared to 16 per cent and 8 per cent of
their male counterparts (Department of Employment,
1985a, Part A, Table 1). These figures are actually likely to
underestimate the difference between men and women's
earnings in so far as the NES does not cover those people
earning less than the National Insurance lower earnings
level, namely many part-time female workers and homeworkers.

These differences become most glaring at the level of
specific jobs. For instance, a female salesperson or shop
assistant earns an average gross weekly wage of £86.50,
while the man working alongside her would command
£121.00. Likewise, the average gross weekly wage of a
female cleaner would be £93.10 while that of a male cleaner
would be £129.50 (Department of Employment, 1985a, Part
A, Tables 8 and 9). While these figures give a clear picture
of the inequalities between men and women's earnings, they
do not give a picture of the real amounts of money which
women are left with at the end of working week. Once
deductions for taxation, National Insurance contributions
and travelling expenses associated with being employed are
taken into account, a woman on £80 a week would take
home a wage closer to £60 a week.

A clear pattern of earnings can be seen in Figure 5.1
where women overwhelmingly earn the lowest sums of
money. There is a clear hierarchy of employees, with white-
collar males at the top of the earnings league followed by
women working full-time and, much lower down, women
working part-time. The inequalities between men's and
women's earnings create a greater incentive in a two-earner
household for the woman rather than the man to leave
employment to bring up children. Even without an ideology
which would contribute to pushing her out of the labour
market, economic sense would dictate that the lowest earner

should be the one to go. The impact of this on her future employment career and earnings forgone, however, will be critical (Joshi, 1984; see also her chapter in this volume). Certain industries are notable as low-paying employers. These industries share a common feature in that they are covered by Wages Councils which each year set minimum rates of pay for the industry, known as statutory minimum remuneration (SMR). They also stand out as employing high proportions of women—estimated to be 75 per cent of all workers in the Wages Council sector—and a high proportion of workers registered as disabled, estimated to be 9 per cent (MacLennan, 1980). However the SMRs tend to be considerably lower than average earnings, ranging from about 30 per cent to 60 per cent, though employers can and sometimes do pay above them. They also sometimes illegally underpay their workforce.

There is evidence that women's earnings are less likely to exceed the minimum rates than men's earnings. MacLennan found that the actual earnings of female workers in Wages Councils exceeded the average SMR by only around 25 per cent, while male workers tended to exceed the SMR by nearly 100 per cent (ibid). The Department of Employment Wages Inspectorate does not collect data on underpayment of men and women separately. However there is evidence from studies of particular industries which also suggests that women are more likely to be underpaid. The Commission on Industrial Relations found that in retail distribution 2.4 per cent of men working full-time, 9.5 per cent of women working full-time and 36 per cent of part-time workers (largely women) were paid below the SMR (CIR, 1974). Generally, women are more vulnerable to underpayment because their wages are closer to the minimum set rates.

In 1985 10 per cent of male manual workers in Wages Council industries earned less than £80 a week but as many as 43 per cent of female manual workers did (Department of Employment, 1985a, Part A, Tables 19 and 20). Since 1970 there has been little improvement in the earnings of all Wages Council workers relative to the rest of the work-force. This means that the earnings of large numbers of

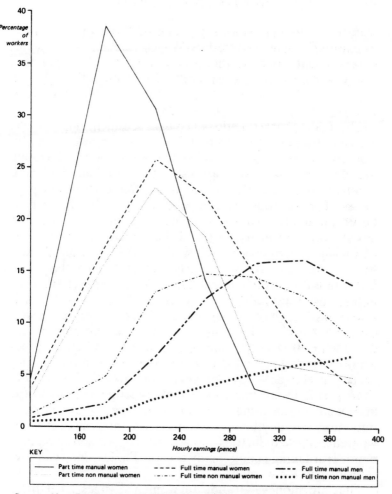

KEY

—— Part time manual women	– – – Full time manual women	— – – Full time manual men
Part time non manual women	–·–·– Full time non manual women	••••• Full time non manual men

Source: New Earnings Survey 1985 Part B Table 41 and Part F Table 173.

Notes:
(i) As might be expected, the distribution for all men and for non manual women working full-time starts to incline (steeply in the case of men) beyond 400 pence an hour.
(ii) Since the NES only includes earnings above the lower earnings level for National Insurance contributions, the inequality illustrated in this graph is actually likely to be even greater.

Figure 5.1: Distribution of the lower range of gross hourly earnings by different types of workers according to hours of work, sex and occupation, 1985

women are falling even further behind those of most men. In catering women covered by Wages Councils saw a small improvement, although their wages were still 15–20 per cent below women's earnings generally. In clothing, the earnings of women fell a further 12 per cent in some areas between 1970 and 1982 (Low Pay Unit, 1983).

The main characteristics of Wages Council employment are that it tends to be in small firms; it tends to be done by women and part-timers; and it has a high level of labour turnover. All of these features make it difficult for trade unions to organise. They also explain the low rates of pay. Many of these firms are competing with each other for an uncertain market. They rely on low wage bills and a flexible labour force. In many instances these factors lead to cases of illegal underpayment below the SMR and, as already shown, women are particularly vulnerable to this. The Department of Employment uses a Wages Inspectorate to police those establishments covered by Wages Council orders, with each of its inspectors being responsible for well over 3000 firms. The Low Pay Unit has monitored and documented the poor policing and small numbers of prosecutions undertaken; for example the prosecution of only seven out of over 9000 employers who broke the law in 1982 (ibid.). It is interesting to speculate whether the lacklustre approach to ensuring that firms do pay the statutory minimum has anything to do with the preponderance of women in these industries and attitudes to women's employment. Not taking action tacitly accepts the legitimacy of low rates of pay for women.

The 'pin money' attitude to women's wages (that their wages are less important to the household and a secondary reason for undertaking paid work) is open to serious doubt. Although it is doubtful whether this view has ever been realistic, it is particularly false at present. Most women work out of economic necessity, either to increase the low wage of a partner or as sole breadwinner. First, an increasing proportion of families are dependent on two wages. A government working paper has shown that the number of families in poverty would treble if it were not for the wife's earnings (Hamill, 1978). Lower income families are more likely to combine their resources (Pahl, 1985b), which suggests that both incomes are necessary to the household. The presence of children in a family leads to additional costs and one recent study of 2000 mothers found that 69 per cent felt the level of child benefit was too low (Walsh and Lister, 1985). Therefore the absence of a second earner in a family can have substantial financial consequences.

Secondly, the view that families consist of a breadwinning father and housewife mother is no longer appropriate. One in eight households is now headed by a single parent, and 91 per cent of these are women. As Jane Millar's chapter in this volume shows, the financial circumstances of lone mothers are usually very strained, with fewer opportunities for employment and a restricted earning capacity. Should these mothers be in paid employment, their earnings will clearly be vital to them. At least one study however has found that inadequate earnings were a common experience of lone mothers in paid employment (Letts, 1983). In 1979 nearly 250,000 lone mothers depended on earnings as their main source of income (House of Commons, *Hansard*, Written Answer, 27 July 1979).

Thirdly, in some 400,000 families women are the sole earners because their partners are unemployed. The earnings of such women can hardly be thought of as 'pin money'. Therefore although culturally there is a division of labour between men and women which determines existing patterns of paid work and wages, it does not reflect the real material needs which make women work.

FOOTING THE BILL OF FLEXIBILITY

Women with children face many constraints when taking on paid work. This section will look at different working patterns which, for women, represent responses to the problems of combining paid work with family responsibilities: part-time working, double or multiple job-holding, working unsocial hours and homeworking. These patterns of paid work are often perceived to be convenient for women, giving them greater flexibility and fitting in with primary domestic commitments. It will be argued that, in reality, they are neither. They often disrupt family life and are primarily suited to the requirements of employers. Far from accommodating family life, they often take little account of it, while at the same time reinforcing the ideology behind the sexual division of labour. The needs of women with children do not neatly fit together with the needs of industry. What usually takes place is a desperate balancing act by women between the need for money and a deep sense of responsibility towards the care of husbands and children.

In the face of declining profitability, companies can resort to a number of strategies to reduce costs, one of which is reorganising employment. One way of doing this is to replace full-time jobs with cheaper, part-time jobs which are more amenable to fluctuating orders and the use of capital-intensive processes. Another is to put work out to people who are prepared to work at home, thereby saving considerably on overheads and wages. For management, a flexible workforce has great advantages. Part-time workers are malleable in terms of hours of work; homeworkers may be even more convenient in terms of overheads, wages and hours of work. The ultimate expedient is to shift out whole areas of production to subcontractors, and there is growing evidence that this process has led to a new structuring of the labour market. It is argued by some that the labour market is divided in such a way that there now exists a core or primary sector of stable and well-paid jobs alongside a peripheral or secondary sector which is characterised by low wages, poor working conditions and job instability (Wilkinson, 1981; Gordon *et al.*, 1982; and Carol Buswell's chapter in this volume). The supply of labour to fill these peripheral jobs comes from marginal workers like immigrants, women, older workers and black workers. Highly disposable workers such as women are particularly suited to the secondary sector because of the instability of the work involved.

Part-Time Work

The growth of part-time work represents a long-term change in the composition of the labour force, but this has been almost entirely restricted to female employment. The expansion in part-time employment is unlikely to be a consequence of constraints in the supply of labour, since it has coincided with an increase in rates of unemployment. Neither is it likely to be a response to demands by women for employment that is more appropriate to their needs. Most part-time jobs have as their starting point the firm's desire to save money or to maximise productivity without incurring extra costs. A research project based on case studies of 21 organisations, both private companies and public services, found considerable evidence of this. Employers' demands for part-time rather than full-time labour were found to be 'essential to the adoption of more cost-effective employment policies dictated by pressures to improve efficiency in highly competitive conditions' (Robinson and Wallace, 1984a). Most importantly, it was found that part-time jobs existed in their own right and were not regarded as fractions of full-time jobs. The reasons for the move to part-time employment were different for manufacturing and service sectors. In the former, employers preferred part-time labour because it meant they could make maximum use of capital equipment and keep production continuous without overtime or shift premium costs. In service organisations it allowed firms to meet irregularities in trading patterns by taking on additional labour for peak periods. A good example of this in both private companies and public services is in catering (Robinson and Wallace, 1984b).

While the consequences of part-time employment for firms may be increased efficiency, greater productivity, more competitiveness and, therefore, greater profitability, the consequences for the women involved are somewhat different. One such consequence is a reduction in employment rights; the other is the lowering of pay. A working week of at least 16 hours (or eight hours for someone with five years' continuous employment) is necessary to qualify for cover under the Employment Protection Act 1975. These are the thresholds required for protection against unfair dismissal, entitlement to maternity benefits, the right to reinstatement after maternity, redundancy payments, and so on. The thresholds effectively create two classes of part-time workers: the protected and the unprotected. There are different ways of defining part-time work. The standard definition tends to be working up to 30 hours a week. In 1985 9 per cent of part-time employees worked less than eight hours a week; 25 per cent worked from 8–16 hours; and 65 per cent worked 16–30 hours (Department of Employment, 1985a, Part F, Table 183). However, Robinson and Wallace's study (which has the advantage of not excluding women below the National Insurance threshold and, therefore, not underestimating the numbers of very low-paid or short-hours workers) found that 37 per cent and 25 per cent of part-time local authority manual employees worked for up to eight hours and 8–16 hours respectively, suggesting that in certain areas the proportion of unprotected part-time workers is considerably higher (Robinson and Wallace, 1984b).

Part-time work can also reduce a woman's earnings. The hourly earnings of both manual and non-manual women in part-time jobs are less than those of men and women in full-time jobs (as shown in Figure 5.1). Furthermore the hourly earnings of women in part-time employment are actually declining relative to the hourly earnings of men and women employed full-time in the same industries and occupations. In 1975, for instance, a woman employed part-time in catering would have had hourly earnings of 96 per cent of those of her full-time female counterpart and 78 per cent of the hourly wages of her full-time male counterpart. By 1981 these had fallen to 88 per cent and 72 per cent, respectively (ibid.) In addition, by reducing the part-time working week, employers can keep wages below the threshold at which they become liable for National Insurance contributions (£38.00 in 1986), thus keeping down their wage bill. The consequences for the employee will not be immediately apparent, but will subsequently affect her rights to claim a range of social security benefits. The incentive to do this was given added impetus by recent changes to our sick pay system. By keeping wages below the National Insurance liability level, employers can now also save themselves the costs of paying employees statutory sick pay (Lonsdale, 1985b). Taking on two part-time jobs may be a response to this kind of financial pressure, as well as to the inability to find one full-time one.

Part-time work often reduces not only current earnings but also deferred earnings such as pensions and earnings replacements such as sick pay. An employee's remuneration package is made up of both wages and occupational benefits such as occupational sick pay and pension schemes. Part-time workers, mainly women, form one of the larger groups excluded from pension schemes. In 1979 only 0.3 million of the 4.45 million part-time workers were in pension schemes. Only 35 per cent of female employees were members of pension schemes in 1979 compared with 63 per cent of male employees (Brown and Small, 1985, p.162; see also Dulcie Groves' chapter in this volume). It is likely that the same patterns exist with regard to occupational sick pay schemes. Certainly female manual workers have less coverage (Lonsdale, 1980) and there is also lower coverage generally in those industries where women are concentrated (Brown and Small, 1985). In general, a principle seems to operate whereby the more tenuous the link between employers and employees in terms of hours of work and therefore hours of contact, the fewer obligations an employer has towards them. It is a principle embodied in employment protection legislation and is manifest in occupational benefits and pay.

Working Unsocial Hours
Part-time work is sometimes synonymous with systems of shift working. Shift working includes a number of different working patterns such as double day shifts, part-time shifts, split shifts, alternating day and night shifts, the three-shift system and night shifts. Like part-time work it has been increasing in recent years and for the same reasons of increasing efficiency and productivity. Much shiftwork takes

place in unsocial hours such as evenings or early mornings and allows intensive use of some machinery. Single adult male immigrant workers were often considered preferable to indigenous workers because of their willingness to work long unsocial hours, as they had no family commitments in Britain and a restricted choice of jobs. Their place is now often taken by women, especially black women. There is evidence that the proportion of women working shifts is rising faster than that of men (EOC, 1979). Working shifts is another way in which women can accommodate the pressures of child-care. Although women's hours of work are restricted by legislation, the Secretary of State for Employment may grant exemptions lifting these restrictions if s/he feels it is in the public interest to maintain or increase efficiency. The Equal Opportunities Commission has estimated that about 25 per cent of part-time workers are working under such exemption orders (EOC, 1979). There are conflicting views about the effects of shiftwork on health but much of the evidence seems to indicate that it is harmful.

Homeworking
Another form of work which, like part-time employment, is perceived to offer women greater freedom and flexibility is homeworking. This is probably due to its incorrect association with people who are self-employed or freelancing from their homes. But as Allen and Wolkowitz (1986) point out, the plastic bag packer cannot be lumped together with the redundant executive simply because both work at and from home. It is more useful to define homeworking as work done at home, for a wage, usually at piecework rates and for a single employer. In this way the starting point to understanding homeworking is to see it as part of the productive process rather than simply defining it by its location. This was the approach taken in the Homeworkers Protection Bill 1979, which was designed to give homeworkers basic employment rights in the belief that they are no different from other employees working on company premises. However, homeworkers are different in some other respects. They are subject to different working

conditions, rates of pay, control over their work and legislative coverage from other employees.

The scale of homeworking in Britain is not vast. A reasonable estimate of homeworkers as defined above is 300,000 (Bisset and Huws, 1984). Virtually all these homeworkers are women and many are from ethnic minorities. Most homework cannot be said to be undertaken out of free choice but rather from a strong sense of duty towards childcare. Factors influencing the decision to do homework have been found to be mainly child-care responsibilities but also ill-health, financial difficulties, language problems and the need to complement husbands' irregular work patterns such as shiftwork (Hakim, 1980). Most homeworkers probably go into the work because of the autonomy and flexibility they believe it will give them to combine paid work and family commitments. The reality of homework is that it leaves little scope for women to work to suit themselves. Many studies now show that homeworkers work to tight deadlines with little control over the amount and type of work they do, nor over when they do it (Leicestershire CPAG, 1983; Bisset and Huws, 1984; Allen and Wolkowitz, 1986). A common issue for homeworkers, for instance, is the irregularity of the work they do, ranging from meeting very short deadlines to going without work for lengthy periods. Women in this work situation are adjusting to the requirements of those who supply them with work rather than working to suit their own needs.

The significance of homework lies in its extremely poor rates of pay and the hidden costs and hazards for the women who do it and their families. A study of 50 homeworkers in Leicestershire in 1982 (Leicestershire CPAG, 1983) found that 70 per cent earned less than £1.00 an hour and 24 per cent less than 50 pence an hour. At the time the legal minimum hourly rate for work covered by Wages Council agreements was £1.40. Two years later, another study of 52 homeworkers found that 76 per cent were paid less than £1.00 an hour and 32 per cent less than 50 pence an hour (Bisset and Huws, 1984). Both these findings suggest that the real wages of homeworkers have deteriorated since an

earlier study by the Department of Employment in which
earnings were slightly higher (Cragg and Dawson, 1981).
However, in all cases rates of pay were well below most
standards of what constitutes low pay. Between 25,000 and
30,000 homeworkers are covered by Wages Councils and
should receive some protection from this. However, illegal
underpayment persists because homeworkers lack sufficient
knowledge and information about their rights, or fear that
they will lose what little income they have (Crine, 1981).
Payment in manufacturing homework is almost always on a
piecework basis and this method of payment seems to be
gaining ground among clerical workers too. This introduces
considerable pressure into the task. At times whole families
must help so that earnings can be guaranteed and deadlines
met to ensure future work. It is also unusual for homeworkers to receive other occupational benefits such as sick
pay or retainers when no work is available.

In addition to low rates of pay, homeworkers face
additional expenses which other workers do not. Working
at home uses heating, lighting and electricity (when industrial or other machines are used) and has the inconvenience
of noise and loss of space. These costs are rarely reimbursed
but when taken into account in calculating real wages,
reduce even further the low rates of pay. A disabled homeworker known to the author took telephone calls for a
finance company which did not reimburse her for her calls
relaying the information back to them—in another town.
The telephone calls came at all hours of the day and night
and were extremely disruptive. This was only one of a
number of jobs she was doing. The effect of these telephone
calls on the pace of other piecework was probably
substantial.

Inconvenience and disruption can become health hazards.
Although homeworkers are included in the provisions of
the Health and Safety Act 1974, no procedures have been
established for dealing with their particular circumstances.
Homeworkers can face a wide variety of different health
hazards. Machinery has dangers ranging from actual injuries
to badly mounted machines causing vibration and the need

for women to stretch uncomfortably to reach the equipment. Chemicals and materials causing fumes and dust respectively require additional ventilation which few homes can provide and, even if they can, homeworkers may be tempted not to ventilate properly to save fuel bills. Fire is always a hazard which can arise from storing large quantities of materials or using domestic wiring for industrial machines. It is important to establish that while the impoverishment of homeworking lies primarily in its very low rates of pay, it also imposes on family life and causes a very real threat to the health of many women and children.

THE ELUSIVE GOAL OF EQUALITY

The evidence that is available suggests conclusively that average earnings for women are well below those of men in virtually all industries and occupations and have been so for some time. Despite increases in their participation in paid work, women's average earnings have only reached two-thirds of men's earnings. Women also receive fewer fringe benefits than men. Most of this is due to the sexual division of labour which pushes men and women into different patterns of paid work. However the social processes which generate this supply of labour also respond to the demands of economic and industrial forces for certain types of labour at certain times. The most important factors determining the differential in men's and women's earnings are: the *type* of jobs they do and the segregation of women into low-paid occupations; the *hours* they work and the concentration of women into part-time, lower-paid jobs; and the *location* of their work, with women working for very low wages and in poor working conditions in the home.

It is these factors which have made women's equality at work such an intractable goal. The segregation of different groups of workers into separate labour markets, in separate industries, with different occupations, different workplaces and working different hours has meant that men and women are rarely in sight of one another let alone in competition with each other. At least part of the wages differential also has to be understood by reference to men and women's different relationship to working time and the different commitments each has outside of paid work. However job segregation and its roots in the sexual division of labour is crucial to an understanding of the failure of social policy measures designed to improve the situation of women in the labour market. It is increasingly clear that, as instruments of social policy, the Equal Pay Act (EPA) and the Sex Discrimination Act (SDA) have been unable to overcome job segregation and the forces that make it so attractive in the pursuit of profitability.

Under the EPA a woman must be paid the same as a man if she is doing broadly similar work; work which has been rated as equivalent by a job evaluation study, or work which is of equal value in terms of effort, skill and decision making. The latter criterion was only introduced in 1984, nine years after the Act came into force. Its exclusion allowed many inequalities to remain unchallenged because job segregation made many comparisons impossible. Under the SDA a woman can take her case to an industrial tribunal if she is being discriminated against contractually, whether this discrimination is by intent or effect. When both pieces of legislation first came into force in 1975 1742 tribunal applications were made under the EPA and 243 under the SDA. Over the next 7–8 years these fell dramatically particularly in the case of the EPA where only 35 applications were made in 1983 (Department of Employment, 1986a). There was evidence that a number of applicants faced a variety of pressures which caused them to withdraw or settle for less compensation than they felt was fair. Tribunal applications are withdrawn either because a settlement has been obtained or because of disillusionment. In a study of 82 women who withdrew applications, it was found that three-quarters were subjected to pressures which made them settle for less than they had hoped for, or for nothing at all. In a climate when factories are being closed or workers put on short time, few women will make claims of sex discrimination or for equal pay (Gregory, 1982). In any event, the extra labour costs arising out of making wages non-discriminatory may reinforce the existing processes of labour rationalisation referred to throughout this chapter. The Equal Opportunities Commission does not have a duty to assist tribunal applicants and at present does not have sufficient resources to do so.

However in 1984 there were signs of an upward trend in applications under the EPA and the SDA for the first time which seems to be continuing, at least for the EPA. The proportion of cases withdrawn by women has remained relatively constant between 1982 and 1985 suggesting that there are still grounds for caution (Department of Employment, 1986a). By and large the legislation rests on the assumption that the problem is one of equal opportunities. It accepts practices in industry which do nothing to break down, but instead reinforce, the division of labour between men and women both in work and at home.

The gains which have been made through equal opportunity legislation are likely to be undermined by current government policies of deregulating the labour market. These include the abolition of Wages Councils, the lowering of employment protection, the abolition of the Fair Wages Resolution which ensured that government contractors paid a fair wage, together with the privatisation of many female jobs in the public sector. All three are likely to affect women disproportionately (Coyle, 1985). Without equality at work, women will continue to be denied the chance of getting out of poverty through paid employment. But the goal of equality at work cannot be achieved through equal opportunities policies alone. It requires a fundamental restructuring of our private and public worlds.

NOTES

1. The term 'economically active' will be used in its traditional sense of referring to those in or seeking paid employment, but it is unsatisfactory in that it implicitly treats domestic work as being outside the economy.

6 The Cost of Caring

Heather Joshi[1]

Unpaid work caring for other people competes for the time and energy a person might otherwise devote to earning their own cash in paid work. Caring responsibilities are seldom undertaken at the expense of employment by men except occasionally in the absence of any available female. In contrast there are few women who do not, at some stage of their lives, take on a caring responsibility sufficiently demanding to have some impact on their capacity to earn cash. This chapter examines the earnings that women forgo as a result of their role as carer of first and last resort. The notion of forgone earnings is an example of what is known as an 'opportunity cost'. This concept compares a course of action with the best possible alternative that it pre-empts; opportunity costs are the value of what has to be given up to achieve a particular goal. Although some carers sacrifice a lot more than their potential money earnings, the cash they forgo is a crucial component of the opportunity cost of their unpaid work and of women's mutually reinforcing disadvantages in the labour market.

The recipients of care are generally, though not necessarily, members of the woman's own family and the degree of care they receive varies enormously, from the round-the-clock attendance required by a newborn infant or a severely disabled invalid to the laundering of socks and shirts for otherwise not very helpless adult males. The degree to which caring work interferes with a woman's capacity to earn depends not only on the helplessness of those she cares for, but also on the extent to which their care is shared by other people, paid and unpaid; and on expenditures on commodities such as domestic machinery, pre-cooked food or children's summer camp which can make multiple roles easier to perform well. Some very heroic simplifying assumptions therefore have to be made in any attempt to generalise about the opportunity cost of caring.

The idea of comparing the cash that women actually receive with what they might have earned without their caring role is not to deny that such activity normally has its material and emotional compensations, and that its value to the giver and receiver is sometimes beyond price. Neither is it suggested that 'labours of love' could be remunerated by wages in exact compensation. However they do need recognition, appreciation and above all support, rather than being taken for granted (Finch and Groves, 1983). The following description of how women's lives are affected financially by the current gender division of labour is intended to strengthen women's hands in the negotiations, private and public, which affect the allocation of work and income. An example of the application of the idea of opportunity costs to an issue of policy has been the success (in June 1986) of the campaign to extend eligibility for Invalid Care Allowance to married women. When this benefit was introduced to help compensate people for having to give up employment to care for the infirm the presumption was, as recently as 1975, that such costs were not incurred by married women.

An alternative approach to costing unpaid care is to value it at replacement; that is, what it would cost to pay somebody to do everything the unpaid carer does. This approach is particularly suited to the debate about policy on community care of the infirm and elderly (Henwood and Wicks, 1984) but it is not necessarily appropriate when considering the personal financial sacrifices which women make in the course of caring. In addition, estimating replacement costs raises some practical difficulties in observing the tasks performed and the time they take (or would take someone who didn't also live in the home), and in putting a price on the hours required. Piachaud (1985), for example, reported a survey of mothers' activities and concluded that the *extra* work involved in looking after a pre-school child amounted to 'round about 50 hours a week', before allowing for the time when the mother was 'on call' though not actually doing a specific tending task. Similarly, Nissel and Bonnerjea (1982) estimated from a time budget study that the time taken to perform the tasks needed by a handicapped elderly person ranged from 24 to 35 hours per week. They tentatively suggested valuing these tasks at the market rate for domestic work (£1.80 per hour in 1980). Henwood and Wicks (1984) suggest the official rate for local authority home helps (£2.90 in 1982–83). Either rate may be well below the market value of some of the nursing skills involved and, as Nissel and Bonnerjea show, well below what the carer might have been able to earn in her own occupation. They offer an annual valuation of caring tasks as replaced by paid workers of £2500, and two estimates of opportunity costs: £4500 for the earnings forgone by wives not in employment who would like to take up a job again (valued at the current rate for their previous occupation); and, for the earnings forgone by women working less than full-time, £1900, a little less than the 'replacement' estimate. At the level of earnings prevailing in 1986, these annual opportunity costs would amount to £7750 and £3275 respectively.[2]

The equation of opportunity costs with forgone earnings is not the whole of the story because it makes no allowance for the free time which may be diverted into caring for others nor, on the other hand, for the social and psychological benefits of avoiding isolation in the home. However, it has the advantage that it is possible to identify and quantify the cash opportunity cost of caring, by observing what women do in the public domain of paid employment and comparing the amount of paid work that women with and without domestic responsibilities manage to do. This approach is followed here to examine how caring—for children, husbands or disabled relatives—affects first, women's labour market participation and their hours of paid work; and secondly, their pay both in the short term and the long term.

THE EFFECTS OF CARING ON PARTICIPATION AND HOURS OF PAID WORK

The evidence used to quantify the effects of motherhood (and other caring activities) on employment participation was collected in the nationwide Women and Employment Survey (WES) conducted in Britain in 1980 (Martin and Roberts, 1984). Table 6.1 presents a regression analysis summarising and quantifying the most important identifiable determinants of a woman's chances of having any paid job and also of having a full-time paid job. The difference between the two formulae identifies the circumstances where women are likely to work part-time.

Multiple regression techniques control simultaneously for a number of possible influences on participation. The factors identified fall into three main groups; family responsibilities, potential pay and other sources of income. Thus at any given stage of the family life-cycle and level of alternative resources, the women who are most likely to be in employment are those who would find it most financially rewarding.[3] Similarly, all else being equal, women with the greatest need for cash are more likely to be employed (particularly in part-time jobs) than women who have other resources to fall back on.

As these economic considerations tend to cancel each other out, it is possible to generalise about women without caring responsibilities for children or older dependants. They could normally expect to be in the labour force (employed or looking for work) most of the time. The average chance of their actually having a paid job is more than 80 per cent over most of the ages from 16 to 59, albeit on a part-time basis for many older married women.

Table 6.1: Regression Analysis of Participation in Paid Work and in Full-time Work, Women and Employment Survey, Great Britain, 1980

Dependent variable	Working		Full-time		Mean	S.D.
					0.651	0.477
					0.380	0.485
Independent variables	b	t	b	t		
Constant	0.805	18.56	0.754	32.34		
Family responsibilities						
Pregnant	−0.144	3.96	−0.099	2.89	0.032	0.175
Presence of child 0–15	−0.763	23.56	−0.663	21.71	0.495	0.500
Age of youngest if 0–4***	0.085	10.51	0.018	2.37	1.915	2.252
Age of youngest if 5–10**	0.041	6.77	0.036	6.33	1.285	2.256
Age of youngest if 11–15*	0.022	2.33	0.066	7.28	0.320	0.971
Number of other children 0–4	−0.071	2.50	−0.039	1.46	0.061	0.254
Any other child 11–15	0.041	1.87	0.069	3.33	0.137	0.344
Number of children 16+	−0.005	0.90	−0.016	2.86	0.834	1.365
Any other dependant	−0.088	4.87	−0.062	3.63	0.139	0.346
Potential Earnings						
Imputed pay, top occupation	0.273	9.25	0.390	14.19	0.357	0.220
Local unemployment rate	−0.012	4.55	−0.003	1.27	6.594	2.788
Alternative Resources						
Currently married	0.217	3.53	0.277	6.69	0.735	0.441
Non-labour income, married	−2.3E-03	11.57	−1.4E-03	7.66	66.264	52.807
Non-labour income, not married	−4.9E-03	7.57	−6.0E-03	10.23	4.150	12.486
Mortgage	0.059	4.25	0.042	3.21	0.426	0.495
Husband not working	−0.272	10.05	−0.128	5.06	0.065	0.247
Age (years) if married	1.9E-04	0.14	−0.012	13.88	28.041	19.302
Age (years) if not married	2.5E-03	1.64			8.403	15.721
Square age since 40, married	−8.0E-04	5.53			36.735	83.543
Square age since 40, not married	−6.2E-04	3.01	−9.3E-04	7.43	11.779	53.306
North of Mersey-Tees	0.066	3.88	0.043	2.70	0.280	0.449
Adjusted R squared	0.316		0.409			

Sample of 4244 women aged 16–59, neither students nor permanently sick, no missing values on included variables.

Notes:

The b coefficients express the change in the participation rate associated with a unit change in any one of the independent variables when all others remain unchanged. For the categorical variables in the table a unit change reflects the change from a situation where the description does not apply to one where it does, and the mean value of the variable reported in the penultimate column gives the incidence of that state in the sample. For example 42.6 per cent of the sample had a mortgage and 49.5 per cent a child under 16.

The t statistics indicate the strength of each variable's explanatory power and the degree of certainty that can be attached to estimates of b. t values smaller than 2 indicate a margin of uncertainty at least as great as the size of the estimated b. Detailed definitions of variables are given in Joshi (1984). New transformations for the present analysis are as follows:

* s mark spline variables: all set to 0 when no child under 15.
These variables, though measured in units of years, are based on data reported in months.
***Set to youngest child's age, if that is 0–4; or 5 where it is 5–15.
** Set to age of youngest: minus 5 where youngest aged 5–10; 5 when youngest aged 11–15, or 0 when youngest aged 0–4.
* Set to age of youngest: minus 10 when youngest 11–15 or 0 when youngest aged 0–10.
Potential pay is the value of log pay imputed by formula used in Joshi (1986a) but with employment experience set to zero.
Non-labour income excludes respondent's net earnings and any benefit income received by virtue of her unemployment or retirement, includes net earnings of husband, if married.
E Notation indicates the number of places the decimal point should be advanced.

Effects of Motherhood

Responsibility for child-rearing is the major correlate of female labour force participation. It matters not so much how many children a woman has to care for, but how young is her youngest charge. The mother of an infant is very unlikely to have paid work, however many other children she has. The model fitted in Table 6.1 implies that if her other characteristics give her a 76 per cent chance of employment before child-bearing, it is certain that she would not work immediately after the birth. As the child gets older the chances of her having a job rise by nine percentage points per year until the child's fifth birthday, by which time the women in this example would have a work participation rate of 43 per cent. The chances of a mother being employed continue to rise, somewhat less steeply, as the youngest child passes through the ages of compulsory schooling. Mothers of teenagers are approximately as likely as women with no children to be employed—possibly slightly more so if they have more than one child in the age group. Mothers with more than one pre-school child have a somewhat smaller chance of being employed than those with just one, but this difference is minor compared to the contrast between families without any young children and those with at least one. The dampening effect of children on the chances of full-time employment is stronger than the effect on having some sort of job at all; women with children under 15 are more likely to work part-time than full-time. After a child reaches school-leaving age there are some minor effects, which continue to raise the chances of part-time rather than full-time employment. These are probably attributable to the long-term loss of labour market leverage (discussed further below) consequent upon the interruption in employment that most mothers have sustained.

The estimated effects of various patterns of childbearing on subsequent employment histories can be summarised in an implied average difference in lifetime workforce membership between hypothetical groups of women with and without children (but, on all other counts, identical and average).

Table 6.2: Impact on Average Lifetime Workforce Membership of Different Numbers of Children

Number of births	Ages at births	Fewer years of full-time employment	Extra years part-time	Net effect on time in paid work (years)
1	25	− 7.16	+2.83	−4.32
2	25,28	− 9.05	+2.80	−6.25
3	25,27,29	−10.44	+3.10	−7.34
3	25,28,31	−11.04	+2.80	−8.24
4	25,27,29,31	−11.77	+2.98	−8.79

As shown in Table 6.2, the time lost from full-time employment varies with the number of children but not proportionately, ranging from seven years for one child to twelve years for four, and is also sensitive to the spacing of births. There is an extra propensity to work part-time which is almost invariant with the number of children (roughly three more years than would be the case without children). The net effect on the average employment record of having one child rather than none is equivalent to 4.3 years of workforce membership. The net effect of a family of four, provided the births are closely spaced, is only double.[4]

Effects of Marriage

After dependent children, the next most common candidate requiring a woman's time to be diverted (or freed) from paid work is the husband. Married women are no less likely to have a job than those living with no partner, but their jobs are more likely to be part-time. To some extent this must be because of the greater need for cash by those (especially lone mothers) who cannot share in income earned by a partner, but as I have argued elsewhere (Joshi, 1986a), the lower propensity of married women to take full-time jobs even when they have no young children must also partly arise from the extra demands on their time of looking after husband, home and social network.

Ironically there is stronger evidence of this aspect of a wife's role in the low work participation of wives whose husbands are not currently earning. The timing of a husband's retirement often dictates that of his wife. Among a number of explanations for this phenomenon are: the desire to enjoy leisure activities together; the need for special care if the husband is in poor health or to cook his midday meal even if he is well; and the threat to the husband's status as chief breadwinner. Some similar considerations may also help account for the low rate of employment, other things being equal, of the wives of unemployed men, although there are also considerations connected with a benefit 'trap' and the likelihood that individuals at high risk of unemployment might have married one another. In any case, women in zero earner couples are at high risk of poverty.

Marriage, even to a healthy husband, impedes employment participation to some extent (and can also affect a woman's pay and prospects if it restricts her freedom to move, stay or travel), but such sacrifices of earnings may in fact be 'good value for money'. It is very difficult to say how far they might be outweighed by the benefits of the pooling and transfer of resources that normally take place between spouses. Some wives do very well out of the 'domestic bargain', but all too many do not (see Hilary Graham's chapter in this volume).

Care for the Physically Dependent

Responsibility for handicapped, sick or disabled people potentially presents the most exacting and thankless claims on a woman's unpaid time. 'Community care' of the aged is typically undertaken by daughters or daughters-in-law, which in some ways complements the story of motherhood sketched above. The most difficult caring situations are relatively uncommon among women under 60. Only 14 per cent of the women in the Women and Employment Survey reported that they had responsibility for someone needing care. Of these a quarter were actually providing constant attention. Among those cared for were handicapped children and invalid husbands; some of the others, mainly elderly people, were living in separate households. The existence of these varied caring responsibilities on average lowered the employment rate, all else being equal, by nine percentage points, which is about the same order of magnitude as the effect of the average dependent child. Caring responsibilities for the disabled are often, like maternal responsibilities, combined with some employment. Detailed studies of their situation stress the emotional as well as the financial benefits of the carer having another role outside the home (Parker, 1985a). When the handicapped person is a child, the WES-based model predicts about the same reduction of employment rates as found by Baldwin and Glendinning (1983) in a study comparing families with disabled children with a control group. As the physical dependency of a disabled child is prolonged, mothers with handicapped children are less likely to manage the part-time employment that typifies mothers of healthy schoolchildren.

EFFECTS OF FAMILY RESPONSIBILITIES ON THE RATE OF A WOMEN'S PAY

If current and past caring responsibilities affect the rate of remuneration while a woman is in work, this too should enter the calculation of the opportunity cost of caring.

Current Effects
Through a variety of mechanisms, current domestic ties can lower the rate of pay a woman receives relative to what she might get if she were a free agent. Some women take jobs for which they are over-qualified in order to fit in with the demands of their dual role. Among mothers in the Women and Employment Survey who had made a return to work after their first birth, 37 per cent had returned to a lower level of occupation than their previous job (Martin and Roberts, 1984). In other cases the woman's need for her job to have convenient hours and location permits employers to pay her less than they would have to pay to get the work done by someone else. Low pay for those with family responsibilities is doubtless also reinforced by their lack of time and opportunity to organise collectively. The poverty wages received by homeworkers are an extreme example of this process, but it also occurs in other circumstances. Freeman (1982) argues that the employed mothers she studied were primarily concerned to preserve employer tolerance of flexibility in their working arrangements rather than raise their rate of pay. Craig *et al.* (1985) cite among other examples employers near outer-city housing estates taking advantage of the local women's inability to travel further afield to maintain low levels of pay. These mechanisms are particularly prevalent in part-time jobs, where employees are virtually all women (Robinson and Wallace, 1984b).

Postponed Effects—Care Now, Pay Later
The effects of caring responsibilities in the past also have an impact on a woman's current rate of pay, even after she becomes more of a free agent in the labour market, for the

market rewards accumulated employment experience just as it penalises workers with interrupted employment records. Employees with uninterrupted careers gain experience which may enhance their value to the employer, if only because they have had a chance to learn by making mistakes or to acquire, formally or informally, training on the job. Continuous service in large organisations also affords opportunities for earning increments and promotion within and between occupational grades. These pay-augmenting effects of employment experience are particularly strong in early adulthood (when people are most likely to be starting families) and in the knowledge-using non-manual occupations where the majority of women are now employed.[5]

Quantifying the Effects
In an analysis of employees in the Medical Research Council's National Survey of Health and Development of a cohort born in 1946, Joshi and Newell (1987b) compared the hourly pay of mothers who had returned to work by the ages of 26 and 32 respectively with that of their female contemporaries who had no children. The average mother employed at age 26 received 29 per cent less per hour than her childless colleagues. The regression analysis, controlling for other relevant differences, suggests that a differential of at least 14 per cent was attributable to maternal responsibilities. This 14 per cent is a product of a loss of 8 per cent on the rate of pay from lost employment experience (2.3 years on average); 4 per cent from the mother's higher chance of being in a part-time job; and 2.5 per cent from downward mobility[6] into manual and sales jobs. Among mothers employed at age 32 the corresponding estimates of effects of motherhood on pay are: 4.5 per cent less due to an average loss of employment experience since age 26 of 1.8 years; 5 per cent less due to the higher incidence of part-time employment and again about 2.5 per cent attributable to downward mobility—a total differential of 12 per cent attributable to motherhood out of an average shortfall of 26 per cent below the pay of childless women. The relative importance of lost employment experience among mothers

returning to paid work at later stages could be expected to increase, because they would tend to have had longer gaps in their records. However there are other indications that once a woman has returned after a given length of break, the penalty she sustains for having had an interruption in the past diminishes over time; as the break recedes into the past, some 'catching up' is possible.

Main's exhaustive analysis of the pay of a cross-section of women workers of all ages who reported their pay in the 1980 Women and Employment Survey found that broken employment histories dominate occupational and industrial mobility as factors which explain statistically the variations in women's pay (Main, 1986).

A somewhat simpler analysis of the same data is presented in Table 6.3. Differentials in pay per hour are statistically explained by a set of variables which record the woman's education, employment experience and whether or not her current job is part-time.

The coefficient of -0.101 in the penultimate row of Table 6.3 estimates a 10 per cent on the reduction in pay per hour of otherwise identical employees having part-time rather than full-time work. This is very close to Main's estimate of the same phenomenon and also very similar to the 9 per cent estimated by Joshi and Newell (1987a) in two snapshots of young female workers in the 1970s. Our interpretation of this consistent finding is that it reflects the low grading of most part-time jobs, which in turn reflects the influence of domestic constraints.

The model used to analyse the WES pay data does not explicitly allow for domestic commitments having a direct negative effect on the pay of any full-time workers, though such effects probably apply with at least the same force to those whose lack of alternative income impels them to work full-time (such as many of the lone mothers not reliant on supplementary benefit). There were insufficient cases in this general sample to provide this type of statistical evidence for a phenomenon which is well documented in case studies, such as those reported by Craig *et al.* (1985).

Table 6.3: Regression Analysis of Pay Differentials, Women and Employment Survey, *Great Britain, 1980*

	b	t	mean	S.D.
Dependent variable				
Natural logarithm of hourly pay			0.518	0.389
Explanatory variables				
Years of post-compulsory education	0.068	15.3	1.332	1.967
Highest qualification attained:				
A level or above	0.179	7.4	0.183	0.387
O level or equivalent	0.050	2.9	0.203	0.402
CSE, etc.	0.036	2.0	0.156	0.363
(Age (years) − 40)² ÷ 100	−0.041	6.5	1.54	1.51
Years worked full-time	0.017	5.8	11.043	8.770
Years worked part-time	0.013	4.5	4.275	5.854
(Years worked)² ÷ 100	−0.031	4.4	3.061	3.856
Proportion of time since leaving education in employment	0.226	7.2	0.743	0.217
Years in current job	0.006	3.8	4.381	4.831
Current job part-time	−0.101	6.7	4.39	0.496
Constant	0.147	3.9		

Adjusted R squared 0.369	Degrees of freedom	11
Residual sum of squares 276.16		2893

Note: The b coefficients express the expected change in the log of hourly pay associated with a unit change in each explanatory variable. They are the logarithms of the proportional differentials in pay which are associated with each variable when the other variables are held constant. The t statistics indicate the strength of each variable's explanatory power and the degree of certainty that can be attached to the estimates of b.

Though women workers on average would appear to gain financially from clocking up and maintaining an employment record, these returns diminish as the total amount of accumulated experience rises. They are also affected by whether the experience gained is with the same employer and by whether or not it is full-time. A curve describing the formula rises gradually less and less steeply over a hypothetical life-cycle even for someone with continuous employment, and then turns down at high hypothetical values of experience. It seems unrealistic to assume that the profile of hourly pay for an individual living through a hypothetical

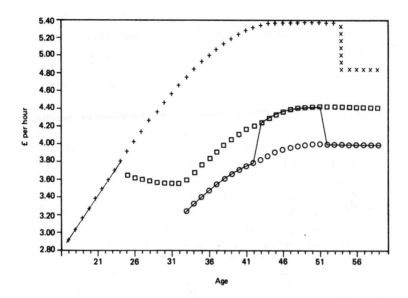

Note: Continuous line illustrates example discussed in text.

KEY TO HYPOTHETICAL SCENARIOS

	Full-time job		Part-time job
□	Children, born 25 and 28	○	Children
+	No child (assumed to switch to part-time employment at age 54).	x	No child

Figure 6.1: Pay per hour over the life-cycle: illustration of 8 year break in employment

life-cycle would actually turn down if she worked continuously. This pattern probably reflects the fact that the data are actually comparing a cross-section of women of successively earlier generations who have other unmeasured differences in attitudes and aptitudes. Accordingly, the curves plotted in Figure 6.1 on the basis of the formula in Table

6.3 describe the upward sloping segment of the fitted curve, but have been arbitrarily fixed to level off once they reach the late career peak. The scale on the vertical axis of Figure 6.1 has been arbitrarily chosen to fit the case of someone who at the age of 24 would be paid an annual salary of £6000—in 1986 the sort of level available to fairly junior secretaries. Inflation is assumed away, the value of money in 1986 is assumed to apply over the whole of the hypothetical lifetime. Using these assumptions, Figure 6.1 shows what would happen to the pay of such a woman if her continuous full-time employment were interrupted. The continous line illustrates a full-time career with a single employer, inter-rupted at age 25 for the birth of a first child and followed by a complete gap of eight years. This could happen if, say, a second child were born when the woman was 28 and she stayed away from employment until this second child was five (and she was 33). In our example she returns initially to part-time work for 10 years and resumes full-time employ-ment when she is 43 and her younger child 15. She reverts to part-time employment after another nine years, as other life-cycle factors reduce her chance of working full-time. In the scenario where she never has children she is assumed to switch out of full-time into part-time employment at the age of 54, and to sustain the drop in pay per hour illustrated in the top line of Figure 6.1. These hypothetical scenarios are fairly arbitrary, but they have been informed by the participation analysis discussed above.[7]

The lower lines in Figure 6.1 tell us what the woman's rate of pay per hour would be, given her employment record to date, if she started a full-time job and also, once she had made her return to employment as a mother, what it would be at the part-time rate. The rates that she would actually receive are joined by a continuous line. While she is out of employment her hypothetical rate of pay in full-time work falls because of lost seniority within her original firm and because of the estimated effect of time spent out of employ-ment during her adult life. Thus when she eventually returns to work after an eight-year gap, her pay per hour is 55p per hour lower than what she last earned—35p because she is now working part-time rather than full-time, and 20p through loss of seniority and reduction of the proportion of her working life spent in employment. On the other hand if she had stayed in her original job her pay would have gone up by 96p over those eight years (even in the absence of inflation). The total gap of 151p between actual pay and what might have been is equivalent to 32 per cent of what she would have earned had she maintained continuous service with the same employer. The difference between the mother's actual rate of pay and what she might have earned does however eventually decrease—on these assumptions, in the long term, the differential levels out after age 50 to 17 per cent of what it might have been.[8]

EFFECTS ON TOTAL INCOME

Figure 6.2 reports the story of Figure 6.1 in terms of total income, year by year. Annual hours of work are assumed to be 1650 when employed full-time and exactly half that whenever the job is part-time. If the woman has no children, her total earnings over the ages of 17 to 59 are £293,000. On the assumption that childbearing entails an eight-year break followed by 12 extra years of part-time employment (compared with those of her childless counterpart), the grand total falls to £158,000. The £135,000 forgone (more than twentyfold her annual salary when she dropped out) can be accounted for as follows:

Earnings forgone while out of employment	£54,000
Earnings forgone while working shorter hours	£49,000
Earnings forgone because of lower rates of pay	£32,000

These headings account for 40 per cent, 36 per cent and 25 per cent respectively of the total forgone. The 25 per cent effect on lower rates of pay consists of £4700 attributable to current domestic constraints and £27,600 from loss of previous work experience. The total effect is more than double the immediate and most apparent absence of earnings while the woman is not working at all.

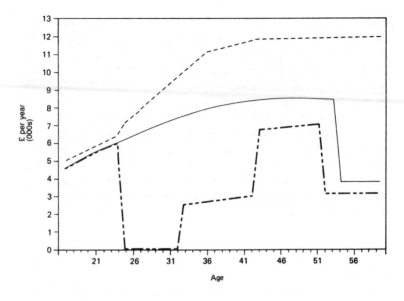

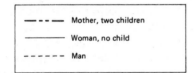

Figure 6.2: Annual Earnings over the life-cycle: illustrative comparison of men and women

The size and composition of the forgone earnings depend on the assumptions adopted. Earlier childbearing for example has a relatively minor effect on the eventual difference in hourly rates, but it exposes women to their effects for longer. A history with a shorter break would suffer less from years of absence and show a smaller drop in pay on return to work, but would also involve exposure to reduced rates of pay for longer. The costs would however be smaller if the woman's employment would anyway be less than continuous (or even if she occasionally changed employer).

Women whose caring responsibilities take them away from employment at later stages of the life-cycle clearly incur the opportunity costs of the constraints on their employment while they are caring. Nissel and Bonnerjea (1982) estimated opportunity costs of £7750 per year (uprated to 1986 levels), if full-time employment is given up entirely to care. Similarly, in our example, a childless woman would forgo £8500 and a mother up to £7000 per year if she gave up full-time employment at the later stage of the employment cycle. If and when carers manage to return to employment unconstrained by these responsibilities, the formula adopted here suggests that subsequent pay might be reduced through loss of seniority, though other effects of losing work experience are probably more severe at younger ages.

These lost earnings do not constitute the whole of the cash opportunity costs of childbearing because pension entitlements would also be affected. The home responsibility credits of the currently (1986) proposed version of the state pension scheme would protect a mother from losing out on account of her years without any employment. Nevertheless the earnings-related component of the pension would still reflect the lower pay and hours while in employment after childbearing in this case reducing earnings to 34 per cent below what they might have been. Occupational pensions would also be affected by lost years of service as they do not provide home responsibilities protection. The precise extent to which the cash penalties of motherhood are carried into retirement depends on the particular pension scheme involved, and whether a woman qualifies for any pension rights at all while working part-time. Nevertheless, the proportional loss of occupational pension rights could easily be at least as high as the 46 per cent loss of lifetime earnings.

THE COST OF BEING FEMALE

Forgoing earnings as a result of parenthood is a price of this pleasure and privilege which is paid by women but not by men. Yet it is not the only penalty in the labour market of being female. Despite improvements attributable to equal opportunities legislation (see Zabalza and Tzannatos, 1985; and the chapter by Susan Lonsdale in this volume), women with no actual caring responsibilities and uninterrupted employment records still tend to be paid less well than the equivalent man. Our analysis of employees born in 1946 attempted to quantify this 'price of being female'. Although it varies between people of different social backgrounds, the gap between men's and women's pay tends to open up during their late twenties. The top line in Figure 6.2, based loosely on estimates from 1977 data (Joshi and Newell, 1987a and b) puts the advantage of being male at 17 per cent of female pay at age 26, 32 per cent at age 32 and fixes it, somewhat arbitrarily, at 40 per cent by age 36. The man's curve is boosted by 8 per cent at age 25 on the basis of the enhancement of pay associated with men (but not with women) getting married. We would suggest that the caring work of a wife may also help to raise the amount that men are paid.

The extra income that the person in Figure 6.2 would have earned between the ages of 17 and 59 had they been male rather than female is represented by the area between the two top lines. It amounts, on these assumptions, to about the same as the earnings a woman typically gives up by becoming a mother. If this general disadvantage, to which all women are exposed, is itself an indirect outcome of the social expectations about the female caring role, the costs of caring are compounded—in this case, roughly doubled. Whatever its fundamental source, unequal treatment in the labour market helps to perpetuate gender inequalities in the home, for the opportunity costs of men taking on caring would generally be higher than letting them devolve upon women (see Ungerson, 1983).

The price a man pays for parenthood is generally being

Part 3
Women, Welfare And Poverty

7 Redundancy, Unemployment and Poverty[1]

Claire Callender

The purpose of this chapter is to demonstrate the inadequacy of redundancy payments provisions and social security benefits in alleviating the impact of unemployment and poverty upon women. By exploring some of the financial consequences and other implications of job loss for a group of redundant women, the appropriateness of existing policy provision will be assessed.

Unemployment is not equally distributed among all groups in society but is concentrated amongst some of the poorest and least powerful in the labour force and in society as a whole. One such vulnerable group is women. However, little is known about either the scope or nature of women's unemployment.

Many women workers exhibit labour market characteristics traditionally associated with vulnerability to unemployment. They frequently work within structures of insecurity—their jobs are unskilled, poorly paid and often part-time; they have few fringe benefits; and they may work unsocial hours in poor working conditions, lacking the security of trade unions or protective legislation (See Susan Lonsdale's chapter in this volume). However, there is considerable debate on the extent to which women or certain categories of women workers are particularly susceptible to unemployment in comparison with men (Callender, 1985b). Official statistics suggest that women's unemployment has risen at a much faster rate than men's, although the absolute and percentage numbers for men remain higher. Figures based upon those claiming social security benefits show that between 1979 and 1986 male unemployment rose by 146 per cent while female unemployment increased by 276 per cent (*Employment Gazette*, Table 2.1, various volumes).

These statistics and other measures of unemployment, all of which are socially constructed and based on certain assumptions, need to be treated with caution. They underestimate the levels of unemployment and are incomplete and biased (Unemployment Unit, 1986). However, they particularly misrepresent the numbers of women who do not have paid work and want employment or who are underemployed (Callender, 1985b). Moreover the variation in the definitions of unemployment used in these statistics creates differing estimates. For example, the 1984 Labour Force Survey, which enumerates women who would like a job and are available for work, puts the figure of female unemployment between 1 and 1.25 million higher than the Department of Employment monthly claimant count.

Non-working women do not comply with our male-dominated conceptual framework for defining who is unemployed. If a man is healthy, of working age and not working, then he is unemployed. However, women in a similar position are not necessarily ascribed that status. Hence women may not 'fit' the classifications and categories used in statistics (Roberts, 1981). They may also be excluded because they are not entitled to benefits, do not register for work, or do not define themselves as unemployed. In other words, women's invisibility in the official statistics reflects both social security arrangements and differences between men and women's experiences of unemployment—all issues which will be explored in more detail in the following pages.

Unemployed women are often defined out of the labour market by structures and ideologies which regulate that market. These forces not only exclude women from unemployment statistics but also from 'legitimate' experiences of unemployment. Their experiences are marginalised so that their unemployment is not considered a problem or worthy of comprehensive social policy responses. One such experience which is peripheralised and rendered invisible is the poverty associated with unemployment (Townsend, 1979). We shall examine some of the structures and social policies which shape women's experience of unemployment and poverty before exploring some of those experiences.

ACCESS TO REDUNDANCY PAYMENTS

Many myths about redundancy payments have evolved (Levie *et al.*, 1984), primarily from the media's treatment of ex-gratia payments which are privately and separately negotiated in collective agreements. However ex-gratia payments are, like other occupational fringe benefits, unequally distributed (Sinfield, 1978). Because of women's location in the labour market they do not have equal access to them and consequently are more dependent than men on the less generous statutory minimum payments. It is to these statutory payments that we now turn.

The economic rationale behind the redundancy payment legislation which originated in 1965 was to facilitate labour mobility so that industry could adapt itself to changing economic and technological requirements. The payments were part of a package of benefits which were to act as a carrot to persuade workers to accept being made unemployed. Today the redundancy legislation is used to reduce the labour force because of economic decline. However the ultimate aim of the legislation—to shed labour and alter workers' consciousness so that they accept being sacked—remains the same.

The Wages Act 1986 radically altered the financing of redundancy payments by abolishing the government's subsidy of employers' redundancy costs.[2] These changes, which herald another shift in the purpose of the legislation, put a high premium on dismissing the cheapest workers and bring into question the role of redundancy payments and their relationship with the social security system.

The Employment Protection (Consolidation) Act 1978 (amended in 1984, 1985 and 1986) secures the rights of redundant workers to financial remuneration (Department of Employment, 1984b). Eligibility for payments is restricted to workers under retirement age who have a minimum of two years' full-time service since the age of 18. Payments are calculated on the basis of the worker's age, length of continuous service, and pay. These three criteria are discussed in turn below.

Redundancy payments are calculated on a sliding-scale according to age, so the cheapest workers to dismiss are the youngest workers and/or those with the shortest service. Certain groups of workers are likely to be excluded at both ends of the age spectrum (Callender, 1985a). In practice workers under the age of 20 do not receive payments and this especially affects women because girls tend to leave school and enter paid employment earlier than boys (Deem, 1978). Women are also penalised because service after retirement age is ignored in the calculation of payments. Yet women are less likely than men to leave paid employment at the statutory retirement age (Parker, 1980). In addition, women receive proportionately smaller payments on their 60th birthday because the number of years included in reckonable service is less for women. Finally, because of differential retirement ages, payments based on age, and the ceiling of 20 years' maximum that can count towards payments, women can *never* receive the maximum compensation.

The value of redundancy payments increases with a worker's length of service and any break deprives workers of their rights to payments. An employee must work a minimum of 16 hours for two years continuously with the same employer to be eligible for payment. This clearly affects women adversely because it overlooks their discontinuous patterns of employment (Martin and Roberts, 1984) which arise out of their domestic responsibilities. Moreover, part-time workers, the majority of whom are women, are doubly disadvantaged. If they work between 8 and 16 hours a week they need five years' continuous employment before they qualify for payment, while those who work less than eight hours a week have no entitlement to redundancy payments.[3]

The final component in calculating compensation is weekly pay levels. This also disadvantages women because, despite equal pay legislation, men and women's pay remains unequal. Moreover these disparities in earnings increase with age over the lifetime, varying according to occupation (see Heather Joshi's chapter above). Consequently, proportionately fewer women receive payments based on their peak earnings.

The cumulative impact of these three determinants of redundancy payments is that women are discriminated against both directly and indirectly by the legislation. The 1980 Women and Employment Survey showed that 36 per cent of employed women were not covered by the employment protection legislation and were therefore not eligible for redundancy payments, primarily because they had insufficient lengths of service (Martin and Roberts, 1984, p. 35). In fact, those who benefit most from this gender-blind legislation are non-manual male workers. This is verified by Anderson (1981), who showed that a higher proportion of redundant women were not entitled to any payments compared with men. Furthermore, eligibility for statutory payments declined down the occupational ladder and those eligible for payment earned more than those ineligible—findings particularly significant for women. Women's disadvantaged position is confirmed by unpublished figures from the Department of Employment[4] which show that in 1985 only about a third of all payments went to women. The median payment for men in 1985 was £1595 while for women it was only £617. The distribution of the payments likewise shows considerable differences between the sexes. Over half (57 per cent) of women's payments were under £750 and three-quarters under £1250. By contrast, just over a quarter of the men received under £750 and 43 per cent under £1250. Only 4 per cent of all women received payments between £3251 and £4750 (maximum payment for 1985) while the respective figure for men was 26 per cent.

The above figures highlight the low level of statutory minimum redundancy payments. Furthermore, it is women who are more reliant than men on these less generous payments. However, women receive lower redundancy payments than men and a larger proportion of them are ineligible for payments altogether. This makes it cheaper for employers to dismiss women, which in turn contributes to making them more vulnerable to redundancy. The legislation therefore perpetuates women's disadvantaged position in the labour market and reinforces their economic dependency out of employment, as will be shown shortly. Nevertheless, redundancy payments play a special role for married women workers because they may be the *sole* source of financial compensation for job loss. This is due to the nature of social security provision to which we now turn.

ACCESS TO SOCIAL SECURITY PAYMENTS

Men and women's claims to state maintenance have been subject to different constraints. As discussed in Chapter 1, assumptions about the economic relationship between men and women in the family and the sexual divisions of labour in the home and workplace underpin social security provision. These assumptions are very apparent in relation to unemployment benefit.

Until the Social Security Pensions Act 1975 married women were either ineligible for full unemployment benefit or, by opting for reduced National Insurance contributions, were excluded altogether. Since the implementation of this legislation in 1978 only married women and widows already paying reduced contributions could continue to do so, provided they did not leave the labour market for more than two years. Married women, like single women and men, therefore became eligible for unemployment benefit (if they had paid full National Insurance contributions). However, in 1984 34 per cent of married women were still paying reduced National Insurance contributions compared with 64 per cent in 1978 (DHSS, 1986, unpublished statistics).

There are other reasons why women are unable to build up sufficient National Insurance contributions and are thereby denied access to unemployment benefit. Recent changes in contribution conditions mean that the higher paid now qualify for benefits faster than the lower paid and this especially affects women who make up the majority of low-paid workers. The Social Security Act 1986, which abolishes the reduced rate of unemployment and other National Insurance benefits where contributions are not fully satisfied, also especially affects the low-paid and those with discontinuous employment patterns. In particular, it denies unemployment benefit to women who had previously been eligible to at least some benefit in their own right. In 1985, 21,838 women received reduced rates of benefits, of which an estimated 78 per cent would be unlikely to have any independent entitlement to any other benefit, thus rendering them economically dependent upon their partners (DHSS, 1986, unpublished statistics).[5]

Part-time workers who earn below the National Insurance earnings threshold pay no contributions and receive no contributory benefits. In 1984 three fifths of part-time workers—some 2.75 million women—were earning below the National Insurance threshold (Department of Employment, 1984c). Even where part-time workers earn above the limit they still may not qualify for unemployment benefit unless they can demonstrate the existence of part-time work in their area and a 'reasonable chance' of obtaining such employment. Furthermore, under a recent stricter 'availability for work' test, women with children may find themselves disqualified from unemployment benefit if they cannot satisfy the DHSS that they could make adequate child-care arrangements if they found a job. These women are therefore not only subject to more stringent requirements than comparable male claimants but the presence of young children is also used as a means of excluding women from benefits. The even more recently 'strengthened' test of availability for work penalises women for their domestic commitments yet further. Under the test, introduced in phases during the second half of 1986, newly-unemployed claimants are required to provide evidence that they are actively seeking work; take *any* full-time job immediately; work beyond the normal travelling distance; and make immediate arrangements for family care (*The Guardian*, 28 October 1986). This test will potentially affect their eligibility for supplementary as well as unemployment benefit.[6]

Unemployed people may, depending on their circumstances, be eligible for means-tested supplementary benefit in addition to unemployment benefit. Once their entitlement to unemployment benefit expires (after 12 months) they are totally dependent on supplementary benefit. Until November 1983 married women could not claim supplementary benefit. The introduction of 'equal treatment' following the EEC Directive 79/7 means that married or cohabiting women can now claim supplementary benefit even if their partner is employed (although in practice the couple's income is aggregated which often wipes out the wife's entitlement altogether). In certain restricted circumstances a married or cohabiting woman can also claim supplementary benefit as the 'nominated breadwinner' when she or her partner are unemployed (Cohen and Lakhani, 1986). However, whilst the new conditions apply to both men and women they favour the man becoming the nominated claimant.[7] And although these changes accommodate role-reversal they are unlikely to have a significant impact on the vast majority of families which depend on both partners earning.

Significantly, there has been no systematic monitoring of the equal treatment regulations but DHSS figures for October 1984 indicate approximately 7000 successful claims in the first ten months after their introduction compared with an original expectation of around 17,000 (Kidd, 1985, p. 22). Kidd suggests this low take-up can be attributed to inconsistencies within the regulations and the low priority accorded the measure by the government and DHSS.

One result of all these factors is the low percentage of

women claiming unemployment and supplementary benefits. Moreover, as suggested in the introduction to this chapter these figures under-represent the number of unemployed women, rendering their unemployment invisible.

Table 7.1: Benefit Position of Unemployed Claimants in Great Britain, May 1985

Benefits received	Women[1]	Men[2]	Total	Women as a % each recipient group
Unemployment benefit only	33.4	18.5	23.0	44.0%
Unemployment benefit and supplementary benefit	3.1	8.8	7.1	13.4%
Supplementary benefit only	42.4	61.6	55.8	23.1%
Not in receipt of benefit (Creditation)	21.0	11.1	14.1	45.4%
Total	100	100	100	

Notes: 1. As a percentage of all women claimants.
2. As a percentage of all male claimants.

Source: Department of Health and Social Security, 1986 (unpublished).

In these social security provisions we see a set of values and institutional arrangements which conditions the position and experience of those out of work, and which is both premised upon and reinforces a male-dominated social construction of unemployment. It is to these experiences of unemployment and social security that we now turn.

WOMEN'S EXPERIENCES OF SOCIAL SECURITY AND UNEMPLOYMENT

There is debate on the extent to which women's varying experiences of social security and unemployment are different to those of men. Coyle (1984) stresses the differences, while Dex (1985) emphasises the similarities, although she acknowledges the lack of research in this area. Several factors point to the differences: women's position in the labour market; their domestic roles and the dominant familial ideology; their lack of control over resources; their problematic identification with the 'unemployed status'; and their treatment by the DHSS, Job Centres and the Manpower Services Commission.

Ironically, these qualitative differences between men and women have actually been used to explain away and neglect women's unemployment; their unemployment is not perceived as a problem because it is not the same as men's. The 'real' problems, which are associated in politics, policy and academe with persistent high unemployment, are those of men. The following empirical evidence suggests that despite the existence of some dissimilarities, women's unemployment is a significant issue, although the nature of women's problems and concerns do differ. However, significant similarities exist too. These similarities belie the assumptions (based on the declared differences) that women's unemployment does not matter. The point is that the differences and similarities are not necessarily mutually exclusive; rather, they both raise gender-specific issues.

Some of these issues will now be illustrated by the experiences of a group of married women following the partial closure of a clothing factory in South Wales. The clothing factory, which was opened in 1939, is part of a multinational company and until recently the major employer of female labour in the area. The factory is located in a sub-region where both male and female unemployment rates are well above the national average. The redundancies took place in stages from 1979 to 1981 reducing the workforce from more than 1500 to 500. However, certain types of women were 'selected out' by the redundancy process; they tended to be disadvantaged in human capital terms, which made them vulnerable to poverty (Callender, 1986b).

All the women in the study were or had been married and were aged between 20 and 59. They had been made redundant involuntarily and had worked full-time in the factory in low-paid, unskilled manual jobs on the shopfloor.

When the women were made redundant in 1981 their weekly take-home pay averaged £55 and for half of the women it was the only wage in the household. The majority of the interviews took place between 9 and 12 months after the women's redundancy.

The women's financial situation on becoming unemployed depended on their eligibility for redundancy payments and unemployment benefit. Redundancy payments, ranging from £50 to £598, were received by most of the women. The majority of payments were too small to replace the income lost from earnings and were therefore used to supplement other income, to buy goods for the home or saved for emergencies. The women recognised the inadequacy of their compensation:

'If Brian [husband] was working . . . maybe I could have put the money away for a rainy day, but in our place . . . you more or less need it. What is £300? It's nothing, is it? Nothing compared with when you've got a wage of £60 a week, is it?'

Claiming Unemployment Benefit and Registering for Work
Once unemployed, redundancy payments were the only monies received by half the women interviewed, because they were ineligible for unemployment benefit. Older women were least likely to be eligible because they had started working at the factory when the married women's option (i.e. to pay reduced NI contributions) was in full operation and the majority had not considered it financially worthwhile to pay full contributions. They had entered into complex calculations, weighing up the potential loss of both short- and long-term benefits against the extra cash in their pay packets and had decided to maximise their already low pay at the time they most needed it. Other women had thought their employment would only be temporary and so believed they would not be in the labour market long enough to build up sufficient contributions. Yet others had correctly calculated that they were too old or their employment patterns too discontinuous to be eligible for pensions. However not all women were aware of the consequences of

having paid reduced contributions but none of them had anticipated being made redundant.

All the women who had paid full National Insurance contributions had sufficient contributions to be eligible for unemployment benefit. Most of these women had negative experiences of claiming benefit. Like men in similar situations, the women stressed the feelings of stigma, shame and humiliation in claiming benefit. Encountering unsympathetic staff in a physically depressing environment ('It's a depressing place, cold, the clocks don't work') many women found the experience alienating and impersonal: 'I just sign my name, feel like a convict, lining up and all that.' Another woman observed: 'You are nothing. You go in a line like everybody else, you feel the same as everybody else. . . . You are just one of a million.' It was an experience which could not be divorced from the notion of scrounging. Indeed a recurrent theme among these women was that they felt they had no right to benefit, that they were getting something for nothing, in marked contrast to a wage. As one woman said:

'It's the thought of having to go there. . . . You feel you're going begging—oh, give me a job, give me a job sort of thing. You feel you're begging for something that isn't there. You feel you're begging for money. . . . Probably it's money that's coming to me because I have paid insurance. But it's not the same as having a wage, it's not the same as having a pay-packet. You sign this piece of paper, you feel as if you're scrounging, you're getting something for nothing.'

The 'street-level bureaucracy' (Lipsky, 1981) which the women faced added to their sense of powerlessness, alienation and distrust of officialdom. Only a small minority had claimed unemployment benefit before and so they found the complex procedures bewildering and confusing. As one woman said, 'It all made me feel uncomfortable. What questions are they going to ask now, and have I got the right answers. Oh I don't like signing on the dole.'

Women's receipt of unemployment benefit automatically meant they had registered for work.[8] However, several women who received no benefits also registered, although the majority in this position did not because they desired to be self-sufficient and free from official agencies. They preferred to avoid contact with what they considered an alienating agent of the state's authority. This feeling was compounded by confusion over the respective roles and functions of the Department of Employment, the Department of Health and Social Security, the Manpower Services Commission, the 'dole', unemployment benefit offices, employment offices and Job Centres. Not surprisingly, there was a widespread uncertainty about what registration entailed, about whether they were eligible to register, and about whether it was relevant to their needs, as Cragg and Dawson (1984) also discovered.

Some women did not perceive themselves as unemployed and so felt it was not legitimate to register. This rejection of the 'unemployed' label is probably associated with the blurring of the boundaries for women between employment and economic inactivity and between unemployment and economic activity which renders their classification in the labour market problematic (Callender, 1985b). Other women did not want to adopt the 'unemployed' label associated with registering for work or did not want confirmation of their unemployed status. Some women did not register because they were discouraged from looking for paid work because of the poor state of the economy. Finally, the attitudes of some women illustrated the 'queueing principle' (Martin and Wallace, 1984), namely that in times of high unemployment certain social groups are felt to have greater claims to paid employment. In other words, some women defined themselves out of the labour market because they felt that they were unlikely to get paid work or because they believed that they had no right to paid work. However it must be emphasised that all the women who chose not to register for work actually did want paid employment and took up any employment opportunities which arose (Callender, 1986a). Moreover as Cragg and Dawson (1984, p. 43) also found, there was no significant correlation between registration and success in finding employment.

The Financial Impact of Unemployment
Townsend's (1979) work has firmly established the links between unemployment and poverty. His notion of relative deprivation, with its focus on social wellbeing, activities, and the social construction of need highlights the importance of employment as a major source of participation within society. However his analysis is gender-blind and he fails to consider how experiences of unemployment and thus poverty are gender-specific. The following analysis attempts to rectify this omission, it incorporates Townsend's emphasis on the non-material aspects of poverty but, in addition, exposes the gender-specific dynamics of poverty.

A common assumption made about female unemployment is that it does not cause financial hardship in the same way it does for men. Such assumptions have been used as a partial justification for women's ineligibility for social security benefits. However, the loss of income of the women studied did have a considerable impact upon them and their families.

The extent of financial hardship varied among the women depending upon the size of their redundancy payment, whether they received unemployment and/or supplementary benefit, their earning status in the household, the employment status of their partner, whether there were other sources of income, and how the family managed their income. Inevitably the financial consequences were most immediate and dramatic for those women who were not in receipt of benefit or who were the sole wage earners. In fact about a third of the women were both the sole earners *and* were ineligible for unemployment benefit. However, without exception, all the women had to make some economies because their wages had been an essential part of the household economy and the benefits they received were too low to compensate for their lost earnings. Interestingly it was only with this loss that many husbands realised the importance of their spouse's wage to the family.

There were large variations in the systems (Pahl, 1983) used by the households both to manage and control their income (see both Hilary Graham and Gillian Parker in this volume). Nevertheless, in the majority of cases it was the woman who managed the money by taking responsibility for day-to-day budgeting arrangements, paying the bills and organising the family finances. Consequently they had the worry of juggling the finances and trying to make ends meet. However they did not always have control over the money nor make the key decisions over how it was spent and distributed.

In general, the women in the study had spent their wages on food, items for the children or had saved some money while their husband's wages were spent on larger bills. Usually the women kept some money 'for their own' to buy themselves make-up, tights or clothes, and to pay for the occasional trip or night out. Once unemployed, this small sum was the first economy all the women made. Even if they received unemployment benefit it was usually spent entirely on food. In other words, they cut first and most their personal consumption rather than collective consumption. With the loss of their pay-packet and 'their' money they lost a sense of independence and freedom—vital ingredients to women's social well-being. They lost their 'little treats' and 'extras' which were an important bonus of paid employment. By contrast the husbands, irrespective of their employment status, nearly always had some 'pocket money' (although the sum may have been reduced) which reflected their control over the family finances.

The economies made on collective consumption and their effects on the family ranged from cutbacks on savings, which had little immediate impact but rocked their sense of security, to cutbacks on essentials like food, which signalled hard-hitting poverty. Most women were more cautious and conscious about how they spent the household's money but about half were just 'living from week to week', struggling to meet their financial commitments with every penny of the weekly budget accounted for. They curtailed their social activities, they abandoned trying to save, they dispensed with their holiday plans, home improvements and repairs, their cars, telephones and televisions. As one woman who had a disabled unemployed husband commented:

'The telephone bill came, it was only £24. Well it was either that or stuff for the kids. You can't see the kids without so he [husband] let it be cut off. Of course to have it put back on would cost another £9 extra. With his leg and one thing and another it does make a difference having a phone . . . . Now it's like robbing Peter to pay Paul, you're not living, you're just existing. Now you've got to think twice before you can breath tidy.'

They cashed in insurance policies and used up their savings and redundancy money. They cut down on cigarettes, food, heating and lighting, and they stopped buying clothing and presents. Little or no monies were allocated to maintaining their worker status—they could not afford special trips to the Job Centre or to visit factories. All these economies were necessary not because the women's husbands were unwilling to share the money but usually because none was available.

It was the women who had to make the hard decisions and choices as to what expenditure to cut or what bill could be postponed for yet another week. They dreaded the unan-ticipated bill or unforeseen expenditure. It was primarily up to the women to devise strategies for saving money, especially within spheres of expenditure that they both managed and controlled. They shopped around for bargains and cheaper food; were more selective as to what food was bought; and cooked cheaper but filling meals which often took longer to prepare. As one woman remarked: 'I used to buy a lot of biscuits and things. Well, cake, we don't even know what it looks like now, a piece of cake. It's a luxury isn't it? Meat, you just can't run to it.' Shopping was a skilled but painful exercise, as one woman observed:

'Shopping in the supermarket, you're going around and looking and you know you can't have it, you have to leave it. That's the hardest thing. . . . You can't just go in and pick up everything you need, you've got to stop and you've got to think. And you'll have one thing one week and some-thing else another.'

Other strategies to 'save' money included joining clubs to purchase essentials which they could not afford to pay for in a lump sum, although being aware of the extra costs of the high interest on such purchases; having slot meters installed to control electricity consumption; and delaying lighting the fire until later in the day to conserve coal:

'In the morning some get up and light the fire straight away, I can't afford to. When the children go to school I leave Brian [unemployed husband] and Kim [unemployed daughter] to stop in bed. Well, perhaps I won't light the fire until half past eleven or something to try and make it go that bit further.'

It was the women who had to face their children's disappointment at their unmet wants and it was the women who constantly had to say no:

'You tell the kids they can't have this and they can't have that. And they want to know why . . . 'cos the other children have got them and why can't they have this and why can't they do this . . . it's hard, it's really hard on them. The children would come in, perhaps their friends are going to the pictures, and sometimes I'd cry because I know mine can't go. Whereas before, when I was working, I could give it to them. But not now and they don't understand.'

And often it was the women who sacrificed their own needs to satisfy those of the rest of the family. It was a draining and depressing experience, as one woman commented:

'You do get a lot of tension trying to make ends meet. . . . And the worst part of being unemployed is having to be always broke . . . thinking over where's the next money going to come from.'

The Social Effects of Unemployment
The material deprivation many women and their families experienced was only one aspect of their poverty. A major economy all the women faced was a reduction in their social lives. They could no longer afford to go to pubs, clubs or bingo, nor for the occasional day out or trip. These activities had to be either totally abandoned or curtailed. Fun was an expensive commodity that many of the women could no longer afford. With this reduction of social activities came a sense of social exclusion. Even prior to redundancy many

of the women did not have a particularly extensive social life because of the constraints of their working and domestic lives. They had had little time to socialise and some had lost contact with friends and neighbours as a direct result of being in full-time work. Most socialising had been concentrated within the private, domestic sphere with their female kin and children. Unemployment exacerbated and accentuated the already privatised nature of their lives. With the loss of their paid employment outside the home both their social contacts and horizons were radically curtailed. Their world became even more confined and focused on the home. They thus became excluded from the social networks of the employed which were vital for job-acquisition (Callender, 1986a). With this constrained lifestyle came boredom and loneliness. In this way unemployed married women probably find their circumstances significantly different from those of unemployed men, many of whom are likely to have their wives at home to provide company (Martin and Wallace, 1984).

Two of the things the women had valued most when they were in employment were the social interaction and companionship of their friendly workmates. It was this company they sorely missed once unemployed. For most of the women paid work had been a route out of the family and domestic and financial dependence. As one woman commented:

'I have missed working. I've missed the company as much as the money. Before, I loved being at home but I loved being in work too and I do miss it, the girls and all. I still haven't really settled to it because my nerves have gone all wonky being in the house. It's all right when the children are here but when everybody goes I am back on my own all day.'

With the loss of their jobs they not only lost a sense of financial security; they also lost a sense of personal security. Being in employment had given these women personal confidence, a sense of independence, autonomy and pride. As one woman said:

'I think you feel more of a person because you're independent. I loved that. You are more independent, you're contributing, not only helping and doing in the home but you're bringing in some money as well. You're not entirely dependent on your husband. And I think you have much more confidence, you're bound to, mixing with people. As I say you feel more of a person.'

Time and again the women stressed their loss of independence and with that loss came frustration, insecurity and a sense of worthlessness 'commensurate with that which men experience over the loss of their breadwinner status' (Coyle, 1984, p. 107).

It should be stressed that the women did not question their roles as housewives and mothers. Rather, it was the financing of that role that led to the feelings of dependency. Moreover housework was a highly privatised activity which was not as well regarded and was much less interesting than paid employment. Nor could these married women return easily to their previous domestic roles if in the course of their employment their children had grown up.

In short, the expectations and attitudes of these women had changed as a result of their experience of paid work. Going out to work had become the normal pattern of their lives, not a deviant one. The loss of paid work therefore did not mean a return to a 'normal' way of life, but a change to a new, more restricted and less rewarding one. As Martin (1983, p. 22) suggests: 'When full-time working women become unemployed they do not move from one role to another, they simply lose one —like men.' Nevertheless, the family did cushion the blow of job loss for some women and their domestic role did offer a way of making sense of their experience. Indeed, a few women embraced domesticity and the family and tried to become more involved in, for example, their extended family. One woman 'decided to have a baby so I wouldn't be so lonely in the house on my own and there was not much chance of me getting a job'. What is evident from the women studied is that they wanted and needed paid work for economic, social, psychological and personal reasons. These wider, non-material aspects of unemployment and poverty remain untouched by any legislative provision.

For a third of the women these hardships were temporarily alleviated when they obtained new paid employment. However, with one exception none of these new jobs was permanent; some were part-time, and all were low-paid. Yet again therefore these women continued to be excluded from both redundancy and social security provisions but this time in rather different ways. None of their jobs lasted long enough for them to be eligible for redundancy pay so they remained unprotected by employment protection legislation. Some jobs were too short lived for them to build up sufficient contributions to acquire eligibility for unemployment benefit. Several jobs were paid below the National Insurance contribution threshold, while other women did jobs like running catalogues which were not recognised as 'work'.

These women's experiences reflect the disenfranchisement and casualisation of women's work. They highlight the false assumptions which underpin much social security provision. Women's role in the labour market was not secondary to their domestic responsibilities. For many of the women, paid employment was part of being a 'good' mother and providing for their children—providing not extras but vital necessities. These women did not work for 'pin money'—their contribution to the family economy was paramount. Part-time employment was often the only paid employment they could find, while others had little choice but to work part-time if they were to fulfil their changing domestic commitments. Discontinuous employment was an integral part of these women's working lives.

CONCLUSION

Poverty exists not only as a consumption experience but it is also related to labour market experience. We have seen how the redundancy payments scheme disadvantages women in comparison with men. Its effects are to make women more vulnerable to job loss, to exclude or only inequitably compensate them, and to perpetuate poverty through insufficient payments. Once women are unemployed, social security benefits are also unlikely to provide an adequate (if any) replacement income for their lost wages. Both these payments and benefits are totally inappropriate for dealing with today's long-term structural unemployment and play no role in compensating for recurrent unemployment or the casualisation of work. Their shortcomings help swell the growing numbers of the 'new' unemployed and the 'new' poor; women whose unemployment and poverty remain hidden. Neither redundancy payments nor social security benefits are rooted in the reality of women's working lives. Rather, they are based on misplaced assumptions and upon male dominated notions of employment. They therefore fail to consider the position of women in the labour market. But that market by its very nature leads to gender inequalities and poverty too, as the unemployed women's replacement jobs illustrate.

These women's experiences of poverty demonstrate its different facets. Being unemployed has all the social, psychological and moral effects characteristic of men but with additional gender specific dynamics. The women in this study may not have identified with the 'unemployed' status but employment remained a central organising principle of their lives. They acutely felt its loss; the loss of their independence in both the public and private spheres, the constant financial pressures; and the frustrations of having 'to live every day at home in poverty'.

NOTES

1. My thanks to the editors for their helpful remarks on the first draft of this chapter.
2. Employers received a rebate of 35 per cent of their redundancy bill from the Redundancy Fund. In future employers with ten or more employees will be responsible for all their redundancy costs.
3. At the time of writing, a White Paper *Building Businesses . . . Not*

Barriers (1986) proposes to raise the hours of work threshold from 16 to 20 hours to qualify for redundancy payments after two years and from 8 to 12 hours to qualify after five years. The proposal disproportionately affects women, who constitute 87 per cent of those employees working fewer than 20 hours a week (Quoted in EOC, 1986b).

4. These figures are based upon a 5 per cent sample of people receiving redundancy payments direct from their employers.

5. This estimate is based on the assumption that these women would not be eligible for supplementary benefit. Twenty-two per cent of female recipients receive the reduced rate of unemployment benefit plus supplementary benefit. However, when this clause was announced Mr Tony Newton MP explained that:

> Over half the recipients receive no financial advantage from the benefit because they also draw supplementary benefit. The rest are likely to have a partner who is working or to have other resources of their own. (Quoted in EOC, 1986a)

This change was introduced in October 1986. Other changes in the Social Security Act 1986 are also likely to have an impact on women's eligibility for social security benefits.

6. Doubts about availability for work include assessing whether people are prevented from taking certain jobs because of domestic circumstances; whether they impose restrictions on their hours of work or wages; and whether they have skills or qualifications which preclude taking a certain type of job.

7. When the equal treatment clause was introduced the conditions under which claimants were eligible for benefit were tightened. Claimants now have to demonstrate some contact with the labour market over the previous six months or acceptable reasons for not having that contact. Therefore, women who have looked after children full-time for over six months cannot become the claimant.

8. At the time the fieldwork was conducted and until the Social Security and Housing Benefit Act 1982, it was compulsory for all those claiming unemployment benefit to register for work at a Job Centre. Registration is now voluntary at Job Centres. However, registration for work (and receipt of benefit) is still often used as a criterion for eligibility for MSC schemes such as the Community Programme.

8 Lone Mothers[1]

Jane Millar

Currently there are about one million lone parents in the UK caring for 1½ million children. Nine out of ten of these lone parents are women and well over half of these women and children are living in poverty. Lone mothers are perhaps the most 'visible' of all poor women. As discussed in Chapter 1, measures of poverty which are based on the family or the household as the unit of measurement cannot accurately reflect the true extent of poverty amongst women; women can be poor in 'well-off' families. Lone mothers, however, do show up more readily in the statistics (that is, when they are not partially hidden in the category of 'lone parent'). But the fact that we know more about the extent of poverty amongst lone mothers than among other women does not mean that the causes of poverty are different for lone mothers. On the contrary, it is precisely because lone mothers are women that they are poor. The situation of lone mothers—their position in the labour market and their treatment in the social security system—is the inevitable outcome of the situation of women in general. Both follow from the same assumptions about women's roles. Thus it is only by analysing the economic position of lone mothers in the context of the economic position of women in general that we can really understand the causes of their poverty. Conversely, by examining the situation of lone mothers, where the consequences of the economic inequalities between men and women are so clearly seen, we also cast light upon the nature of these inequalities.

THE EXTENT OF POVERTY AMONG LONE MOTHERS

Lone mothers have a much higher risk of poverty than any other family type, apart from elderly women. The most recent government statistics on the number of low-income families refer to 1983 (DHSS, 1986a) and show that of an estimated total of 950,000 lone-parent families, 570,000 were either in receipt of supplementary benefit or had incomes of less than 140 per cent of the ordinary scale rates of supplementary benefit. The DHSS does not provide a breakdown of these figures by the sex of the lone parents but almost all (91 per cent) lone-parent families are headed by a woman (Haskey, 1986) and a number of studies (e.g. Finer, 1974; Knight, 1981) have shown that lone mothers are much more likely to be poor than lone fathers (see also Chapter 1, Table 1.1). Thus the vast majority of these low income lone parents are lone mothers. As Table 8.1 shows, the number of lone-parent families in or on the margins of poverty has increased substantially in recent years; from

Table 8.1: Low-income Families Great Britain, 1979 and 1983: Lone Parents with Dependent Children

	1979		1983	
	Number	% of total lone parents	Number	% of total lone parents
In receipt of supplementary benefit	320,000	37.6	460,000	48.4
Incomes below level of supplementary benefit	40,000	4.7	30,000	3.2
Incomes between 100 and 140 per cent of supplementary benefit	70,000	8.2	80,000	8.4
Total in receipt of supplementary benefit or with incomes of below 140 per cent	430,000	50.6	570,000	60.0

Source: Department of Health and Social Security, *Low Income Families 1983* (1986).

430,000 (50 per cent of the total) in 1979 to 570,000 (60 per cent of the total) in 1983.

As Table 8.1 shows, much of the increase in poverty amongst lone parents in recent years is a result of increasing dependence on supplementary benefit. In 1984 there were 491,000 lone mothers (caring for 784,000 children under 16) in receipt of supplementary benefit. Many of these women were long-term claimants with about three-quarters (73 per cent) having been in receipt for at least one year, and a quarter (24 per cent) for at least five years.[2]

However, neither the fact that lone mothers have a very high risk of poverty nor the fact that they are very likely to be dependent on state income support are particularly new. According to Rowntree's figures, in York at the turn of the century the second most common cause of poverty after low wages was the 'death of the chief wage-earner', accounting for 28 per cent of all poor households and 16 per cent of all poor persons (Rowntree, 1902, p. 120). Most of these women were widows, although a small number (3 per cent) were 'deserted or separated' wives. Not all of these widows would have had dependent children of course, but a significant proportion must have had as there were 460 children under 14 in the 403 households in this group. Rowntree's later study in York (Rowntree, 1941) suggested that the introduction of widows' benefits had led to a substantial decrease in the extent of poverty amongst lone mothers. But of course these benefits did nothing for the increasing number of lone mothers who were not widows but who were unmarried or, more commonly, divorced or separated. Thus in the early 1950s—after the post-war welfare reforms— lone mothers were again heavily over-represented amongst the poor. In 1953/54 19 per cent of all poor families with dependent children were 'headed' by a lone mother compared with only 5 per cent of all families with dependent children (Abel-Smith and Townsend, 1965, p. 33). This over-representation of lone mothers among the poor has been found over and over again (e.g. Finer, 1974; Fiegehen *et al.*, 1977; Layard *et al.*, 1978; Townsend, 1979; Mack and Lansley, 1985).

Similarly, there is a strong tradition of dependence on state income support. Snell and Millar (1987) have calculated that about 30 per cent of all families receiving parish relief under the old Poor Law (prior to 1834) were lone mothers; and Pat Thane (1978) has pointed out that, throughout the period of the operation of the new Poor Law, women (often widows or deserted or separated mothers) made up the majority of adult recipients of relief. Today, of all the families with children living on supplementary benefit, 47 per cent are lone-parent families (DHSS, 1986b).

The general situation of lone mothers has thus probably not changed very much over the last 100 years, but it has come to be seen as a particular problem because the number of such families has increased so dramatically in recent years—from about 474,000 in 1961 to 570,000 in 1971, and up to 940,000 in 1984 (Haskey, 1986). About 13 per cent of all families with children are now headed by a lone parent. However, even this situation is not 'new' if looked at over the longer term. As Anderson (1983) has pointed out, marital breakdown rates in the nineteenth century were probably not very different from those found today, the difference being that divorce rather than death is now the main cause of lone parenthood. It has also been suggested that the current proportion of families headed by a lone parent may actually be quite low in comparison with that found in the past. Estimates based on parish records suggest that in the late eighteenth and early nineteenth centuries on average about 19 per cent of all families with children were lone-parent families (Snell and Millar, 1987). Nevertheless increasing divorce rates and increasing numbers of lone mothers (two-thirds of whom are women who are divorced or separated) have created something of a 'new' problem for the modern welfare state.

As well as having a very high risk of being in poverty, lone mothers are also very likely to stay poor. Most of the information we have on the extent of poverty is cross-sectional—it refers to only one point in time. However an analysis of the data collected in the Family Finances Survey

(FFS) and the Family Resources Survey (FRS) provides some information on the persistence of poverty over time. The FFS consisted of a sample of about 3000 families with children interviewed during the course of 1978 and 1979. All families in the sample had a net family income, after meeting housing costs, of not more than 140 per cent of ordinary rate supplementary benefit. Nearly two-fifths (37 per cent) of these poor families were headed by a lone mother. The same families were interviewed again 12 months later for the FRS. Although this is a fairly short period over which to look at changes in income, comparisons between the lone mothers and the two-parent families did reveal some interesting differences in the extent to which the families were able to 'escape' from poverty. As Table 8.2 shows, whereas 35 per cent of the two-parent families had crossed the poverty line (140 per cent of supplementary benefit) between the two interviews, this was the case for only 11 per cent of the lone mothers. Two-parent families therefore were three times as likely as lone mothers to escape from poverty. The analysis showed that the best way to do this was through full-time employment and especially (for two-parent families) through the employment of both adults. Indeed the only families in the sample with any significant chance of crossing the poverty line were two-earner couples. Among these two-earner couples (that is, families in which one or both parents had taken up employment between the two interviews) 73 per cent were no longer defined as poor at the second interview, compared with 39 per cent of the families where only the man was employed. Thus the earnings of both the husband *and* the wife were necessary if the risk of poverty was to be significantly reduced; the husband's earnings alone were not always sufficient (see Hamill, 1978; Layard *et al.*, 1978, both of whom show that without the earnings of the wife the numbers of poor two-parent families would be very much higher). Among 'new' two-parent families (or reconstituted families—that is, families which had been lone-mother families at the first interview but where the lone mother was living as part of a couple at the second interview) a similar pattern is apparent. At the second interview 48 per cent of these women were living in families with a family income above the poverty line, many of these being in two-earner

Table 8.2: Proportion of Families Crossing the Poverty Line of 140 per cent of Supplementary Benefit between the Family Finances (1978/79) and Family Resources (1979/80) Surveys by Family Type and Employment Status

Family type and employment status at FRS	% of families in category at FRS	% of each category crossing the poverty line
Two-parent families		
One earner	56	39
Two earners	17	73
No earner	27	3
All two-parent families	100	35
Base[1]	999 (1254)	
Lone Mothers		
Not employed at FFS, in part-time job at FRS	10	29
Not employed at FFS, in full-time job at FRS	4	63
Employed at both	13	24
Not employed	74	4
All lone mothers	100	11
Base	464 (508)	
Lone Mothers who Changed Marital Status[2]		
One earner	43	63
Two earners	24	79
No earner	33	4
All lone mothers who changed marital status	100	48
Base	87 (94)	

Notes: 1. The sample was weighted to increase the number of large families. Percentages and numbers refer to re-weighted sample, number in brackets to the number actually interviewed.
2. Presenting these figures in a slightly different way shows that of the original lone mothers at the FFS, 17 per cent were in the 'non-poor' families at the FRS. Of these women 56 per cent were still lone mothers while 44 per cent were not.

families. Eekelaar and MacLean (1986, p. 72) report similar results; of the divorced women in their sample only 21 per cent of those who were lone mothers had incomes above supplementary benefit levels, compared with 70 per cent of those living in re-constituted families.

It should be remembered that these results are based on the total *family* income and we should therefore be cautious in interpreting what they mean for the living standards of the families and the individuals within these families. We cannot necessarily conclude that the married mothers were automatically better-off than the lone mothers simply because their total family income had increased. Again there is the question of how fairly the resources are distributed within the family and the extent to which women actually have access to the increased family resources. In addition while paid employment for married women both increases family income and provides an independent source of income for the women, it also usually means that their workload is substantially increased—that they add the demands of paid employment to their domestic responsibilities. Nevertheless the contrast between the financial situation of the women who remained lone mothers and those who married or remarried is very striking. Women alone are very likely to be trapped in poverty and, just as there are substantial economic pressures on women to marry, so there are even more substantial economic pressures on women to remarry. As Christine Delphy puts it:

the potential market situation for women's labour . . . is such that marriage still offers them the best career, economically speaking. If the initial or potential situation is bad, it will simply be aggravated by the married state, which becomes even more necessary than ever. (Delphy, 1984, p. 97)

EMPLOYMENT

For lone mothers the most successful route out of income poverty—being part of a two-earner household—is obviously not available. Furthermore even if a lone mother is in full-time employment, this is no guarantee that she will not be poor. Full-time employment for women, on average, gives them earnings equivalent to only about two-thirds of the full-time earnings of men (based on the average earnings of manual workers). Thus while a two-earner couple will have the equivalent of 1⅓–1½ of full-time wages (assuming, as is usually the case when there are children, that the woman has a part-time job), lone mothers in full-time jobs will have only about two-thirds of an average male manual full-time wage. If the full-time earnings of men are often insufficient to prevent family poverty, then it is hardly surprising to find that neither are the full-time earnings of women. Thus among the FFS lone mothers, of the 10 per cent who took up part-time jobs during the subsequent year, 71 per cent still had incomes below the poverty line. Of the 4 per cent who took full-time jobs, 37 per cent remained below the poverty line. This means that for 62 per cent of the women who took employment this gave little or no improvement on their supplementary benefit incomes.

The FFS and the FRS covered only one year and we therefore cannot say whether the small minority of women who were able to increase that incomes by taking up employment were able to maintain their position. However there is much to suggest that their chances of doing so would not have been very good. As Susan Lonsdale has described in Chapter 5, the jobs available to women tend to be low-paid, low-status jobs in a highly sex-segregated labour market. The primary role of women is still seen as being in the domestic sphere rather than in the labour market. This has two major consequences. The first is that women's earnings are assumed to be the secondary, not the sole or major source of family support and therefore low wages for women are not seen as a particular problem. Secondly, it means that the state and employers make little or no recognition of the demands of domestic responsibilities —and particularly of the demands of caring for dependent children. Working mothers themselves must therefore take responsibility for coping with both employment and child-care. This is seen most clearly in the lack of collectively provided child-care provision, but it is also reflected in limited maternity rights and benefits and in the lack of parental leave arrangements. Both low earnings and the fact that domestic responsibilities are ignored in the labour market put special pressure on lone mothers; they cannot survive financially on part-time earnings alone and, without adequate child-care facilities, cannot take full-time jobs. In addition, when mothers return to paid work following child-bearing this is often associated with occupational downgrading (Martin and Roberts, 1984; Joshi, 1984; and Joshi in this volume). Some divorced and separated lone mothers will presumably have experienced this downgrading before becoming lone mothers and will therefore already be in a weak position in the labour market.

Lone mothers apparently do not fall into two separate and clear-cut groups of those in employment and those who are not employed. As with married women, those with pre-school children are less likely to be employed than those with only older children, but otherwise there are no clear differences in the characteristics of the employed and the non-employed (EAO, undated; Weale *et al.*, 1984). In addition a substantial proportion of non-employed lone mothers—half in the FFS sample, two-thirds in Evason's (1980) study of lone mothers in Northern Ireland—say that they would prefer to be in employment, if they could find suitable jobs and if child-care facilities were available. The unequal position of women in the labour market means that lone mothers find it difficult to maintain stable, full-time employment. Consequently the employment experience of lone mothers is likely to be one of short-term and often low-paid jobs which fail to provide the full-time, full-year employment that would be at least the first line of defence against poverty.

In recent years the employment situation of lone mothers seems to have deteriorated. As Table 8.3 shows, whereas from the mid-1970s to the early 1980s about half (47–48 per cent) of all lone mothers were employed, by 1982–84 this had fallen to 39 per cent. Particularly disturbing is the fact that most of this fall is accounted for by a fall in the proportion of lone mothers in full-time jobs, from 24 per cent in 1976–78 to 17 per cent in 1982–84. The proportion in part-time jobs hardly changed. Lone mothers are apparently finding it increasingly difficult either to find or to keep full-time jobs, and this is undoubtedly related to the generally poor employment situation (Tarpey, 1985).

Table 8.3: Proportion of Lone Mothers in Employment by Age of Youngest Child, Great Britain, 1976–84

	1976–78	1978–80	1980–82	1982–84
All Lone Mothers	%	%	%	%
Employed full time	24	22	22	17
Employed part time	23	25	25	22
All employed	47	47	47	39
Base (100%)	1276	1313	1318	1253
Youngest Child under Five Years				
Employed full time	15	14	11	6
Employed part time	13	12	13	11
All employed	28	26	24	17
Base (100%)	366	381	386	416
Youngest Child over Five Years				
Employed full time	27	26	27	23
Employed part time	28	30	30	27
All employed	55	56	57	50
Base (100%)	910	932	932	837

Source: OPCS Monitor (1985) *General Household Survey*, preliminary results for 1984, Table 14.

THE EXPERIENCE OF POVERTY

Although the causes of poverty may be much the same for married as for lone mothers, the ways in which they experience their poverty are likely to be different. A number of studies (Houghton, 1973; Evason, 1980; Pahl, 1985a) have found that some lone mothers, despite their low incomes and restricted life-styles, say that they 'feel' better-off as lone mothers than they did as married women because they at least have control over their limited resources. (See Hilary Graham's chapter in this volume for a fuller discussion of this.) However, the other side of this 'independence' is that very often they have exchanged dependency on a man for dependency on the state. In particular they are very likely to be dependent on the state for two very basic needs: housing and income.

Almost two-thirds (62 per cent) of lone mothers are local authority tenants, compared with only 26 per cent of two-parent families (OPCS, 1985c). Marital breakdown often means that families must move (Eekelaar and MacLean, 1986) and many lone-parent families—especially single mothers—are sharing accommodation. Almost a quarter (22 per cent) of lone mothers share housing with other adults compared with only 5 per cent of two-parent families (OPCS, 1985c). Although the access of lone mothers to council housing has become much easier since the Housing (Homeless Persons) Act 1977, the type of housing they are offered tends to be of poorer quality than that offered to 'ordinary' families. In part this is a consequence of their route into council housing, which is often as homeless persons (in 1979 one third of all homeless households were lone parents: Popay *et al.*, 1983); and people housed in this way tend to get the worst accommodation. Lone mothers are more likely than other families to be living in sub-standard or over-crowded accommodation with inadequate amenities—often in flats rather than houses—and in poor quality housing areas (Ferri, 1976; Burnell and Wadsworth, 1982). Many lone parents live in the inner-city areas, where housing conditions and amenities are often very poor. In 14 of the 33 London boroughs more than 20 per cent of all families with children are headed by a lone parent (NCOPF, 1982).

Supplementary benefit is the main source of state income support for non-employed lone mothers and most lone mothers will spend at least some time, and often lengthy periods, in receipt of supplementary benefit. In 1982 the two groups of lone mothers most likely to be recipients were single women (76 per cent) and separated women (77 per cent) rather than divorced women (37 per cent) or widows (8 per cent). This is partly related to the different character- istics of these groups; both divorced women and widows are less likely to have pre-school age children and hence are less likely to be constrained in finding employment. More important, however, is the fact that both widows and divorced women are more likely than single or separated women to have other sources of income. This means that they are not forced into either full-time employment or dependence on supplementary benefit, but can 'afford' to take part-time jobs. Widows with dependent children may be eligible for widowed mothers allowance which, although it is taxable, is not (unlike supplementary benefit) directly reduced if the widow has earnings. For divorced women maintenance—if received regularly—can also be used as a supplement to earnings. Maintenance payments are in general fairly low and by themselves often do not provide an adequate level of income. According to estimates from the *General Household Survey*, 49 per cent of currently divorced women with children receive some maintenance, but this is usually (32 per cent) for the children only and it has been estimated that only 6 per cent of lone mothers rely on maintenance as their main source of income (Popay *et al.*, 1983). Maintenance can be used to boost low earnings, although for women on supplementary benefit it provides no addition to their income because the amount of supplementary benefit is reduced accordingly.

The higher rates of dependency on supplementary benefit among single and separated women also suggest that lone motherhood is very likely to begin with a spell on benefit. This was certainly the case with the FFS sample; among the two-parent families who separated between the two interviews, as many as 78 per cent of the 'new' lone mothers were on supplementary benefit at the second interview. Many of the women who come onto benefit at this time will eventually go on to become long-term claimants. Others will move on and off benefit as they move in and out of jobs (and may therefore only ever qualify for the lower short-term rate). In the FFS sample 58 per cent of the non-widowed lone mothers had been in receipt of supplementary benefit continuously for the two years prior to the second interview while 31 per cent had had intermittent spells on benefit interspersed with periods in employment. Only 11 per cent were never on benefit at all during those two years. Similarly Berthoud (1984) found that 44 per cent of the lone mothers in his sample of supplementary benefit recipients had had at least one prior spell on benefit before their current period in receipt.

A number of studies have reported that lone mothers often find the experience of claiming supplementary benefit very negative. Claiming any means-tested benefit involves of necessity a detailed investigation of personal circumstances. In addition, for lone mothers claiming supplementary benefit there are rules regarding 'liable relatives' and 'cohabitation'. Under the regulations relating to liable relatives the husband is liable to maintain both the woman and children if the couple are separated but only the children if the couple are divorced. The fathers of 'illegitimate' children are also liable to maintain the children (but not the mother). Under the cohabitation rule a couple who are 'living together as husband and wife' are treated in exactly the same way as a married couple, that is, their resources are aggregated and only one of them (usually the man) can make a claim.[3] Thus if a lone mother is deemed to be cohabiting, her benefit can be stopped and she must either become dependent on the man's earnings (if he is employed) or he must make the claim for both of them. The administration of both these rules—particularly the cohabitation rule—is fraught and they have always been controversial. As well as assuming, or indeed forcing, women into financial dependency upon men, they also mean that lone mothers may be subject to detailed and intrusive questioning about their living arrangements; put under pressure to name and pursue the liable relative; and generally treated with suspicion of fraud (Marsden, 1973; Letts, 1983; Smith, 1985). The negative impact of these rules may be further compounded by the attitudes of those administering the scheme. Both Howe

(1985) and Cooper (1985) have described how the attitudes of officials can influence their treatment of claimants. Lone mothers, because they are seen to bear responsibility for their own situation, may also be seen as less 'deserving'.[4] In Marshall's (1972) study the women were asked what they disliked most about being on benefit. Dislike of going to the local office, of questioning by staff and of feelings of stigma and dependency were mentioned more often than criticisms of the level of benefit. Berthoud (1984) found that lone parents were particularly likely to see supplementary benefit as a charity rather than as a right.

For lone mothers, therefore, poverty and dependency on the state are dominant characteristics of their lives. As Townsend has pointed out, poverty is not only a matter of low income but also of the social exclusion that those on low incomes experience, being unable to participate in the 'activities, customs and diets commonly approved by society' (Townsend, 1979, p. 88). There is much evidence to show that lone mothers have a very restricted lifestyle. In the FFS sample the basic necessities of food, fuel and housing accounted on average for 65 per cent of their total expenditure, leaving little to spend on anything else. Going into debt and doing without seemed to be common features of their lives. Nine out of ten said they had difficulty in affording children's clothes and shoes and seven out of ten recorded no expenditure at all on entertainment. The isolation caused by low incomes is further compounded for lone mothers by their position as 'women alone' in a society where much social life is geared towards couples (Letts, 1983) and where the stigma attached to lone motherhood (especially for the unmarried mother) has not entirely disappeared. For non-employed lone mothers there is no opportunity for social contacts through employment, which many married mothers see as an important aspect of their jobs, providing a relief from the 'private' world of home and family (Cragg and Dawson, 1984). Lone mothers are also unlikely to have access to the consumer goods which might reduce their isolation; only 29 per cent have access to a car and 61 per cent to a telephone (Department of Employment, 1986b).

INCOME SUPPORT POLICY

The policy response to the growing numbers of lone-mother families and to the clear evidence, going back over many years, that they are very likely to be poor, has been to add to or modify the existing system of benefits rather than make any fundamental changes. Thus in the supplementary benefit scheme lone parents are not required to register for work and hence can receive the long-term rate after one year on benefit. They also have a more generous and tapered earnings disregard than other claimants. In the family income supplement (FIS) and housing benefit schemes the qualifying levels of income are set at the same rate for lone parents as for couples, and lone parents can qualify for FIS if they are employed for at least 24 (rather than 30) hours per week. There is also an addition to child benefit for lone parents in the form of one-parent benefit (paid per family rather than per child) and the tax allowance for lone parents is equivalent to that of a married man rather than a single person. The changes now proposed to reform social security (DHSS, 1985a) follow the same general pattern; the needs of lone parents will continue to be met through the mainly means-tested assistance available to all low-income families with children, with some differences in the rules of entitlement and the rates of benefit. The assumption behind this is that the needs of lone-parent families are not fundamentally different from the needs of all families with children, and therefore that both can be met through the same overall structure. What this focus on families tends to obscure, though, is the extent to which the needs of mothers—whether lone or married—are similar. Furthermore, neither lone mothers nor married mothers have their needs adequately met under the current system, precisely because of the focus on a particular definition of 'family' needs.

Family needs are addressed in current income support policies on the basis of an underlying model of the family which assumes a clear separation of the two main functions of the family with regard to children—the caring function being the province of the mother and the providing function the province of the father. The man is the 'breadwinner' and the woman is financially dependent upon him while she performs what Beveridge called 'the vital though unpaid' work of the housewife (Beveridge, 1942, p. 107). This has led to the different treatment of women and men in social security provision with the central core of these provisions being income replacement for the male breadwinner. Furthermore, this male breadwinner is assumed to be unambiguously in full-time work or out of work; the needs of part-time workers are virtually ignored. Effectively the social security system gives benefits to the 'providers' when they are unable to provide (through unemployment, sickness or old age) but not to the 'carers' (except in a limited way through child benefit and the invalid care allowance— the latter until very recently denied to married women).

Lone mothers, of course, must combine the roles of provider and carer within an income maintenance system which separates these two roles. The options under the current system are to treat lone mothers as *either* mothers *or* workers. In fact, they are treated primarily as mothers; hence their first duty is assumed to be child-care (not employment) and it is also assumed that they are, have been or will be financially dependent upon men. The particular rules which apply to lone mothers on supplementary benefit reflect these assumptions: they are not required to register for work;[5] only very tentative approaches to encourage employment (through the tapered earnings disregard) have been made; and their status changes when their children reach the age of 16, when they are required to register for work. The liable relative and cohabitation rules reflect the assumptions of past and present dependency on men. Paradoxically, although the current structure of benefits, together with the weak position of women in the labour market, tend to trap lone mothers in dependency on benefit, the family-based model also means that in some respects lone mothers are treated more generously than other families with children. For lone mothers the question of incentives to work and the extent to which benefit levels might erode work incentives (which is so important in keeping down benefit levels for the unemployed) is considered to be largely irrelevant. Thus lone mothers receive the higher long-term rate of supplementary benefit after one year while the unemployed never receive the higher rate. In the short term the family-based model and the view of lone mothers as 'mothers' acts partly to their advantage but nevertheless it also contributes to their long-term disadvantage.

It is the women who become lone mothers through marital breakdown (who are, as we have noted, the majority of lone mothers) who are particularly difficult to fit into this family-based model. First, there is the popular fear that adequate benefits for these women would lead to an increase in marital breakdown or in collusive separation. Secondly, there is the question of the interaction between the public and the private systems of income support. State support for lone mothers could be seen to be releasing husbands from their obligations and responsibilities, to be forcing the community in general to bear the costs of private choices. However, in some ways, this is more of a problem in principle than in practice. As noted above, maintenance is already only a minor source of income support for divorced women, and the Matrimonial and Family Proceedings Act 1984 has, in any case, severely undermined the principle of a life-long liability to maintain in favour of clean-break divorce. As yet it is too early to judge the impact of this change but it does illustrate the potential dangers to women of policies which ignore the consequences of dependency. Given that dependency within marriage still exists for women, this change in the legislation removes the notion of dependency when marriage ends but does so leaving women continuing to suffer the consequences of their dependency within marriage. As Carol Smart puts it, the Act 'reduces women's access to private sources of maintenance while

refusing to improve other sources of income support'
(Smart, 1984, p. 141).[6]

In the short term, the main policy priority must be to
seek ways to reduce the dependence of lone mothers on
supplementary benefit. The most obvious way to do this
would be through an extension of the widowed mothers'
allowance to all lone parents (as has been suggested by,
among others, the National Council for One-Parent
Families (1984) and the National Consumer Council,
(1984)). Marital breakdown is now an event which one in
three couples faces and providing a non-contributory
National Insurance benefit for the parent who has care of
the children would mean that the costs of this risk would
be shared more equitably instead of falling mainly on the
women as they do at present.

However in the long term it will be impossible to improve
the financial situation of lone mothers simply by treating
them as a separate and discrete group for whom a specific
benefit can be provided. Lone mothers are not such a
group—they are drawn mainly from the ranks of married
women—and their situation is a result of the failure to tackle
the problems that women face in combining the roles of
paid employee, mother and unpaid domestic worker. Thus
it is only by considering the needs of women in general that
any long-term solution to the poverty of lone mothers can
be found.

NOTES

1. The analysis of the Family Finances Survey data reported in this
   chapter was carried out with financial support provided by the ESRC
   (grant number G00232074). I am also grateful to Eileen Evason for
   her comments on this chapter.
2. *Social Security Statistics 1986*, Tables 34.82 and 34.89.
3. Unless the couple can meet the conditions under which the women
   can be the 'nominated' claimant. However to do so she must meet a
   number of conditions, including a recent work test, and these
   conditions probably limit the number of cases where the woman can

be the claimant. See Cohen and Lakhani (1986, pp. 21–3) for a description of the rules.

4. Geoffrey Beltram (1984, p. 97) also notes that lone mothers may face unsympathetic attitudes: 'others among the junior staff shared the common resentment of other low-paid people towards "undeserving" claimants (mainly young single unemployed and single parents).'

5. The fact that lone mothers are not required to register for work may also exclude them from the various 'job'-creation and training programmes for the unemployed, which does little to improve their long-term chances of getting off supplementary benefit and into employment.

6. On the same lines, in the Green Paper on the reform of social security a similar point was raised with regard to widows:

> The present benefits date from days when far fewer married women worked. Today two-thirds of all married women with children over school age, and a half of all widows between 40 and 60, go to work. The present pattern of benefits nonetheless provides support without regard to widows' other income, in many cases long after they have ceased to be responsible for bringing up children. (DHSS, 1985a, vol. 1, para. 10.9)

Although widows tend to be older and have older children and are therefore in a better position in the labour market than other lone mothers, some of the same problems would apply to them if they lost their right to benefit. As the National Consumer Council points out, the 'abolition of any compensation for those widows would flagrantly disregard the effect on most of their careers of raising a family' (NCC, 1984, p. 116).

9 The Poor Relation: Poverty among Older Women

Alan Walker

Elderly people dominate the poverty statistics and have done so ever since the systematic studies of Charles Booth (1894) at the end of the nineteenth century. But poverty is not evenly distributed among the elderly, and gender is one of the clearest lines along which the economic and social experience of old age is divided. Thus more than twice as many elderly women as elderly men live in poverty or on its margins. Among those in advanced old age (80 years and over) the ratio is around five to one. The dual purpose of this chapter is to describe and explain this major division in the distribution of resources in old age.

The main themes underlying this examination of poverty among older women may be summarised as follows. Poverty in old age is a function, first, of low economic and social status *prior* to retirement, which restricts access to a wide range of resources; and, secondly, of the imposition of depressed social status through retirement. Within these social processes which are responsible for the construction of poverty in old age (and, incidentally, the social construction of old age itself), the situation of older women is significantly different from that of older men. The economic and social status of women before retirement is, of course, related to the advantages secured by men in the social division of labour (see the chapters by Susan Lonsdale and Heather Joshi in this volume). This distorted access to resources in youth and middle age—institutionalised in segregative and discriminatory employment and other social policies as well as in the domestic division of labour—is reflected, in due course, in the relative disadvantage of women in old age. The process of retirement too has a differential impact on men and women, but the experience of women has remained obscured because old age is regarded, in Simone de Beauvoir's (1977, p.101) terms, as 'a man's problem'. Women have been neglected in studies of the transition to retirement even though the proportion of women participating in the labour force, and therefore undergoing retirement from paid employment in their own right, has been growing steadily—an example of the male-dominated construction of retirement both in practice and in policy analysis and research.

So, underlying this chapter is a theory of ageing based not on the analysis of biologically-based differences in senescence or individual adjustments to the ageing process but, instead, on the social creation of dependent status and on the structural relationships between the elderly and young adults and between different groups of elderly people, especially men and women. (For a more detailed account of this approach see Walker, 1980; 1981.) The main practical implication of this theoretical position is that social policy is the main focus of attention in explaining poverty in old age and in attempting to overcome it. Thus social policy must be critically evaluated not only for its failure to eradicate poverty among elderly women (and, to a lesser extent men), but also because it occupies a central role in producing and legitimating both the poverty of a substantial proportion of elderly people and the marked inequalities between elderly women and men. The starting point for this analysis is a description of the current financial status of elderly women.

POVERTY AND LOW INCOMES AMONG ELDERLY WOMEN

The principal financial problem faced by elderly people is poverty. This fact has been demonstrated in official and independent research studies spanning the last century. Moreover this pattern of poverty and financial insecurity among elderly women is common to all patriarchally-organised societies, both developed and underdeveloped (Storey Gibson, 1985). Poverty among elderly women in Britain has endured to the present day, despite the significant political commitment given to pensions in the 1970s, which culminated in the legislation in 1975 introducing the state earnings-related pension scheme (SERPS) and in the series of pledges to uprate pensions in line with earnings or prices whichever was the greater (Walker, 1985a), policies which did result in some improvement in the relative position of elderly people in the national income distribution (see below). Poverty is one important aspect of the substantial inequalities in income and other resources between the majority of those under and those over retirement age (Townsend, 1979). While just under one in five (18 per cent) of all persons in Great Britain are over retirement age, they comprise two in every five of those living on incomes on or below the supplementary benefit level, the official or social standard of poverty. The risk of experiencing poverty is three times greater for those over retirement age than it is for those below retirement age (DHSS, 1983).

Within the generally impoverished status of elderly people, elderly women and especially lone elderly women (i.e. those living alone, including single, widowed, separated and divorced women) are often particularly disadvantaged (see Table 9.1). In 1981 (the most recent information available from the government) nearly two in every five elderly women (38 per cent) were living on incomes on or below the poverty line as defined by supplementary benefit levels, compared with 28 per cent of elderly men. Over half of lone elderly women compared with just under two-fifths of single elderly men had incomes on or below the poverty line. In all, more than two-thirds of elderly women were living in or on the margins of poverty (i.e. with incomes of up to 140 per cent of the appropriate supplementary benefit rates).

The preponderance of women among the poor elderly is

Table 9.1: Numbers and Percentages of Elderly Men and Women Living in or on the Margins of Poverty, Britain, 1981

Family income in relation to supplementary benefit level	Women over 60 (000s)			Men over 65 (000s)		
	Lone	Married	Total	Lone	Married	Total
Below SB level	520	240	760	120	240	360
Receiving SB	1210	285	1495	170	285	455
Up to 140% SB	920	825	1745	230	825	1055
Total	2650	1350	4000	520	1350	1870
Percentage of all pensioners	79.6	51.4	67.2	67.4	64.4	65.2

Source: DHSS (1983); House of Commons (1984).

of course partly due to the larger number of women than men in the elderly population as a whole. This results primarily from the greater longevity of women compared with men; life expectancy at birth is 76 years for women and 70 years for men, while at 60 it is 21 years for women and 16 years for men. The main contributory factor here is the greater decline among older women than older men in mortality rates over the last 40 years or so, with cancer and circulatory diseases now being the main causes of the higher mortality rate among men (Ermisch, 1983). As a result of their greater longevity, elderly women are more than twice as likely as men to be widowed and, as a consequence of this and the lower propensity of the current generation (if not succeeding ones) to have married in the first place, they are three times as likely to be living alone. More women than men therefore survive into old age and advanced old age. But as Table 9.1 shows, the incidence of poverty among elderly women, especially lone women, is strikingly high compared with that of men.

Table 9.1 underestimates the poverty of elderly married women in two main respects. The calculation of the numbers of married women and men living on low incomes has been forced to assume an equal division of income *within* the income unit. However, as Pahl (1980) and others have shown (see particularly Hilary Graham's chapter in this volume), the distribution of income within the family is likely to give women unequal access to total household resources. Secondly, it is not possible to distinguish in the aggregate figures either those married women who are not entitled to pensions until their husbands reach the age of 65 or those aged 60–64 whose husbands do not appear in the statistics. As a result the procedure of dividing the numbers of married persons by two artificially deflates the numbers and proportion of married women in poverty.

As a much greater proportion of women than men survive into advanced old age they increasingly dominate the poverty profile of successively older age groups. For example, among single people in 1981 the ratio of women to men who were living on supplementary benefit increased from five to one for those aged 65–69, to six to one in the 70–79 age group, to eight to one for those aged 80 and over (House of Commons, 1984). Women who have never married are over-represented among the very elderly. However, as Table 9.2 shows, it is *not* simply that there are more women in the older age groups. Elderly lone women

Table 9.2: Percentage of Pensioners Supported by Supplementary Benefit in 1982 by Age, Sex and Marital Status

Age	Married couples	Lone men	Widows	Other lone women	All pensioners
60–64	—	—	23	27	25
65–69	9	20	33	28	15
70–74	14	21	42	31	23
75–79	17	28	43	27	28
80+	18	20	38	21	26
All 65+	13	22	35	27	23

Note: Single people (i.e. widowed, unmarried, separated and divorced) are included in this table if they are over pension age and married couples if the husband is 65+. Couples are classified by age of husband.

Source: DHSS (1984) *Population, Pension Costs and Pensioners' Incomes*, p. 17.

are more likely than lone men to have to rely on supplementary benefit and widows are much more likely than widowers to do so.

Further evidence of the disadvantaged position of elderly women in relation to men can be gained from information on the distribution of income. Elderly women in the bottom quintile of the income distribution have slightly lower incomes than men in the same quintile and elderly men in the top quintile have much higher incomes than women in the top quintile. Thus in 1982, the spread of disposable incomes for elderly lone women ranged from £32 per week to £77 per week compared with £34 to £91 per week for elderly lone men (DHSS, 1984, p.18). Table 9.3 shows the inequalities in average disposable income between elderly women and men.

Table 9.3: Average Disposable Income by Age, Sex and Marital Status, 1982; £ per week

| Age | Marital status | | |
	Married Couples £	Lone Men £	Lone Women £
60–64	—	—	57
65–69	96	67	49
70–74	86	54	49
75+	78	47	46
All ages	88	55	49

Note: See note to Table 9.2.

Source: DHSS (1984), p. 18.

Two important features of Table 9.3 should be noted. The inequality between lone men and lone women is greatest among those just over retirement age. Secondly, very elderly women are poorer than young ones.

The significant inequalities in income between elderly men and elderly women are mirrored in the distribution of other resources. For example, in his national survey of household resources and standards of living, Townsend found that a higher proportion of elderly lone women than lone men had less than £100 worth of assets and fewer than six consumer durables. The acute disadvantage experienced by widows was also noted by Townsend:

Not only were there more of them than of other groups living in poverty or on the margins of poverty; more had no assets or virtually no assets, and fewer possessed substantial amounts of assets. . . . According to a variety of indicators of economic situation, widowed women were least advantaged. (Townsend, 1979, p.796).

A similar pattern of inequality was discovered in a recent survey of all those aged 60 and over living in their own homes in the city of Aberdeen. Men had higher incomes and savings than women. Moreover even when household income was controlled for marital status, women were still disadvantaged. These objective inequalities were reflected in subjective appraisals; for example, men envisaged less difficulty in obtaining emergency cash than women (Taylor and Ford, 1983, p.190).

In addition to sex-based inequalities in income and household resources, elderly women, in general, are more disadvantaged than men according to a range of other indicators of deprivation. They are three times more likely than elderly men to be living alone and only half as likely to have a spouse. Elderly women report more illness and longstanding health problems and consult their GPs more frequently than men (OPCS, 1985c). They are also more likely than elderly men to suffer from psychological problems such as loneliness and anxiety and to have lower levels of morale or life satisfaction (Atchley, 1976; Abrams 1978).

The elderly person's experience of poverty is an enduring one and, because of their greater longevity, the poverty of elderly women is particularly longlasting. In 1981 the proportion of pensioners who had been in receipt of supplementary benefit for ten years or more was nearly seven times greater than that for younger people (40 per cent as against 5.7 per cent). A national survey of supplementary benefit claimants carried out in 1982 found a similarly large proportion of long-term claimants among pensioners (Berthoud, 1984, p.A5).

It is important to emphasise before concluding this section that, contrary to the implications of flat-rate social security benefits and pensions for the elderly, *needs* as well as resources are unevenly distributed in old age. For example, disability is a major indicator of the need for additional income and other resources among those both under and over retirement age (Townsend, 1981). People with disabilities are more likely than the non-disabled to experience poverty, have lower incomes and fewer assets. The combination of old age and disability substantially increases the risk of poverty; those over retirement age with minor or appreciable disabilities are twice as likely as those of middle age (40 to 60/65) to be living in households with incomes below or on the margins of poverty, while those elderly people with appreciable or severe disabilities are nearly twice as likely as younger adults to be poor (Townsend, 1979, p.712).

Elderly women suffer from disablement more often than elderly men. In the 65 and over age group there are twice as many severely and very severely disabled elderly women as men and more than five times as many in the 75 and over age group (Harris, 1971). The higher incidence of disability among elderly women is partly attributable to their greater longevity, but in addition some disabling conditions affect women more than men. For example, the number of women suffering from arthritis is more than three times that of men. The current generation of elderly women were more likely to have contracted poliomyelitis, are more likely to have strokes or develop multiple sclerosis. They also have a higher prevalence of high blood pressure and rheumatic complaints (Campling, 1981b, p.142). A significant proportion of women with these disabling conditions are also responsible for caring for a male spouse or other relative with a disability.

Primarily because of their greater experience of disability, the needs of elderly women are often greater than those of elderly men. In other words, it is not just that elderly women experience a higher incidence of poverty according to the supplementary benefit standard of poverty. The gap between their needs and resources is likely to be even wider than the social security based poverty line suggests.

EXPLANATIONS OF POVERTY AMONG ELDERLY WOMEN

Why are elderly women poor, and why is the incidence of poverty greater among this group than any other, including elderly men? It would be wrong to conclude that it is simply because women live longer than men. We have already seen that even within age cohorts women are more likely to experience poverty and low incomes. An adequate explanation of the greater incidence of poverty amongst women in old age must reflect on the social and economic status of women *before* as well as after retirement and, therefore, the systems of distribution which determine status and access to resources. Chief among these are employment and, linked to it, the occupational pension system and social security. Inequalities forged or reinforced in the labour market are carried into retirement via occupational and state (earnings-related) pension schemes. Thus the poverty of elderly women is a function both of life-long low access to resources (including the non-participation of some in the resource-generating potential of joint households via marriage); and of the restricted access to resources which is imposed by retirement and the assumptions about the level of state pensions which are allied to it. These factors imply that poverty in old age is not solely determined by gender; there are some acutely deprived groups of older men and some relatively affluent groups of elderly women. Nevertheless the severe disadvantage experienced by a large proportion of, in particular, very elderly women rests on the social production and distribution of resources in relation to the *combination* of social class, age and gender.

Some of the systematic disadvantages encountered by women in the labour market—especially working-class women, lone parents and those from ethnic minorities—are discussed elsewhere in this book and will only be mentioned here. Similarly the role of occupational and private pensions is covered fully in the chapter by Dulcie Groves and it is therefore necessary only to highlight here the main features which disadvantage women.

Occupational Pensions
It is primarily through access to the ownership of occupational pensions that inequalities forged or reinforced in the labour market are carried into retirement. Rights to occupational and private pensions are built up during the individual's employment. These schemes and the benefits they provide, in general, are organised hierarchically according to employment status and occupational class (James, 1984). Since women are much less likely than men to be employed full-time, to be in highly paid secure jobs or to hold managerial or professional posts (see Susan Lonsdale's chapter in this volume) they are less likely to be members of occupational pension schemes. Those working in the public sector and those in jobs with strong union organisation are more likely to have occupational pensions. The proportion of women belonging to occupational pension schemes is about half that of men (37 per cent compared with 65 per cent). This difference in participation is particularly marked among those employed in the private sector, with 24 per cent of women compared to 52 per cent of men belonging to occupational pension schemes (Government Actuary, 1986, p.6). Seven out of ten employees covered by occupational pension schemes are men. Essentially these schemes are designed by men with male 'family wage-earners' and male middle-class career patterns in mind; so not only do they exclude the majority of part-time workers, but they tend to assume that earnings peak in the final years of working life, which is much less often the case for women than for men. Part-time women workers are particularly disadvantaged here.

The implications of this unequal access to occupational pension schemes during paid employment are that elderly married couples and lone men, *regardless of age*, are much more likely than lone women to have occupational pensions; nearly two-thirds have such pensions compared with one-third of lone women (DHSS, 1984, p.18). Among the very elderly (75 and over) the proportions of married couples, lone men and lone women with income from occupational pensions are 59 per cent, 43 per cent and 28 per cent respectively.

There are two forms of inequality related to occupational pensions which also serve to disadvantage very elderly women, especially widows. In the first place, there is the differential distribution of occupational schemes between men and women. Secondly, there is an inequality between younger and older women in their ability to gain access to the newly emerging occupational pension opportunities. Thus two-fifths of lone women currently aged 60–64 receive income from occupational schemes compared with only a quarter of those aged 75 and over.

Retirement Policies
The growth of retirement and, more recently, early retirement has ensured that an increasing proportion of older people have been excluded from the labour force over the course of this century. This social process of exclusion has denied older women and men access to earnings and the other economic, social and psychological aspects of the workplace. Largely because of the reliance of many older married women on their husband's state pension contributions, the proportion staying in the labour market beyond the age of 60 has remained fairly high (around one quarter compared with 5 per cent of men working beyond 65). There is however a sharp decline to only 5 per cent remaining economically active by the age of 65 (OPCS, 1985c, p.101). The position of non-married women is rather different. Their rates of economic activity over recent years have followed the male pattern of rapid decline in the 60–64 age group (from one-third in 1973 to one-fifth in 1982) with a slight decline in the 55–59 age group (69 per cent to 64 per cent).

The operation of this social process of exclusion from the formal economy (called retirement) has been closely related to the organisation of production and the demand for labour. Accounts of the emergence first of retirement and then of early retirement suggest that older people have in fact been used as a reserve army of labour, to be tapped when labour is in short supply and to be shed when demand falls (Graebner, 1980; Phillipson, 1982; Walker, 1985b). The advent of large-scale unemployment in the 1930s was crucial to the institutionalisation of retirement, and its return in the early 1980s has resulted in the growth of early retirement.

Like the experience of employment, attitudes towards retirement and the experience of retirement itself are socially divided. Although a large proportion of women remain economically active until the age of 60 or even 65, retirement is still regarded as a predominantly male experience. Of course, with economic activity rates among women peaking at around two-thirds for married women in middle age and four-fifths for non-married women in their twenties and early thirties, there is a significant proportion who never experience 'retirement' from paid employment in their own right because they have withdrawn from the labour market long before formal retirement age. But since this proportion is relatively small, the main explanation for the neglect of women in the study of retirement is more likely to be a combination of two particular factors. First, women's labour market participation is regarded as marginal in comparison with that of men. Secondly, the vast majority of economically active women are engaged in at least two roles—formal and informal—and there is no retirement from the latter domestic role. The assumption appears to be therefore that women do not experience the same degree of loss as men when do they retire from paid work.

The experience of retirement is also divided on the basis of occupational class. There are those, mainly salaried, workers who are able to choose whether or not to leave work at the retirement age, leave prematurely, or perhaps work on. Then there are those, predominantly manual workers, who are effectively coerced into retirement and sometimes early retirement by poor working conditions, ill-health, redundancy and unemployment (Walker, 1985b). Thus for large numbers of older workers poverty is experienced *prior* to the official retirement age. In fact, sickness and unemployment account for one quarter of women (and two-thirds of men) who retire prematurely (Parker, 1980, p.10). So for some older workers the retirement age is effectively lowered by unemployment, sickness or injury. As with unemployment itself, semi-skilled and unskilled workers are over-represented among the early retired (Parker, 1980, p.16).

Because the arbitrary pension ages of 60 and 65 have been adopted as customary retirement ages, women are forced to retire five years earlier than men. In general, the earlier the retirement the sooner the imposition of poverty and, especially in the case of elderly women, the longer that poverty must be endured.

The recent ruling by the European Court of Justice in the case of Ms Marshall represented a major step towards the equalisation of retirement ages, if not pension ages. Ms Marshall was compulsorily retired by Southampton Area Health Authority at the age of 62, whereas men employed in a similar position were able to continue working until the age of 65. The Court found that the dismissal of a woman solely because she had attained or passed the qualifying age for a state pension constituted discrimination on the grounds of sex, contrary to EEC Equal Treatment Directive 76/207. However this ruling applies only to those employed in the public sector. Even if the proposals in the Consultative Document, aimed in response to the Court ruling, are adopted and the Sex Discrimination and Employment Protection Acts are amended to make unlawful the dismissal of women on grounds of age at a younger age than comparable men, the five-year differential in state *pension* age will remain. Moreover, the achievement of equal retirement ages, though significant, would do nothing to remove the tyranny of fixed age retirement for both women and men.

The main implications of age-barrier retirement are, first,

that it results in an average fall in income of about one half. As a result those who continue in employment after retirement age are less likely to experience poverty. The impact of retirement can be illustrated with reference to lone women aged 60–73. In 1977 53 per cent of those in paid employment had net weekly incomes under £30 compared with 85 per cent of the retired; the figures for women in two-person households were 5 per cent and 28 per cent respectively (Parker, 1980, p.31). Secondly, for those who do continue in employment, retirement age can produce a dramatic downward shift in occupational status (Walker, 1981, p.82). So, for example, between the age groups of 50–59 and 60–73 the proportion of women in junior and intermediate non-manual socio-economic groups falls from nearly half to nearly one third, while the proportion in the unskilled group rises from one in ten to nearly one in four. One study found that one half of elderly women who changed jobs at retirement age had done so because of forced retirement from previous employment. In addition 46 per cent of women (and men) who gave up work at retirement age would have liked to go on working (Hunt, 1978, p.61). These changes in employment and socio-economic status are reflected in earnings. In 1977, 37 per cent of full-time female workers aged 50–59 had weekly earnings of under £40 compared to 55 per cent of those aged 60–73. The comparable figures for men aged 55–64 and 65–73 were 8 per cent and 20 per cent (Parker, 1980, p.35).

Pension and Social Security Policies
The corollary of this social process of exclusion from he labour force, coupled with restricted access to alternative forms of post-retirement income, is that elderly people and women in particular are heavily dependent on the state for financial support. They are, in effect, trapped in poverty by virtue of their reliance on state benefits. We have seen that retirement has a differential impact on elderly people which depends primarily on their prior socio-economic status and the access which this grants to resources which might be carried into retirement. In addition, because of social press-

ures to limit the level of state pensions and other benefits for those outside the labour force, retirement imposes a lowered social status on the majority of elderly people in comparison with younger adults in the labour force (Walker, 1980).

The dependency relationship between elderly people, the state and the labour market was institutionalised by the 'retirement condition', introduced in 1948, whereby state pensions are conditional on retirement rather than age. This has encouraged an end to labour force participation and has established arbitrary ages as customary retirement ages. (Ironically, Beveridge had hoped that the retirement condition would encourage workers to defer retirement.)

The social security system is also one of the main mechanisms through which the income inequalities between older women and men are both generated and reinforced and by which the dependence of women on men is encouraged. Elderly married women are less likely than men to receive a National Insurance retirement pension in their own right and overwhelmingly less likely to receive a state earnings-related pension.

The basic pension is payable according to a contributions formula which stipulates that to gain a full pension sufficient contributions have to be paid in nine out of every ten years of a 'working life' (i.e. paid employment). Many women are unable to qualify for a full pension because of periods spent out of the labour force or in part-time work while caring for children or disabled relatives. Some limited home responsibilities protection was introduced in 1978 in order to help women in this position, but in order to qualify for a full pension they still require 20 years' worth of contributions or credits. While single women receive a single person's pension, married and divorced women can choose to claim a pension in their own right (if they have sufficient contributions) or as a dependent wife. However the dependent wife receives only 60 per cent of the single person's pension—a fact that reflects not only the dependent status of married women but also the failure of the social security system to adapt to the increase in economic activity (particularly in part-time jobs) among women since the Beveridge scheme was introduced.

The state earnings related pension scheme also tends to disadvantage women as much as the basic pension, and if the proposals made by the current government are enacted after the next election, their position will be further worsened. SERPS was introduced in 1975. It applies only to those reaching pensionable age since April 1978 and is not expected to reach full maturity until 1998. Because it is an earnings-related scheme, if women do qualify for SERPS the pension they receive will reflect their tendency to earn less than men. The vast majority of current pensioners, both women and men, do not receive SERPS.

Ironically, the introduction of SERPS did represent an attempt to improve the pension position of widows and other women. It allowed the surviving spouse to inherit the full SERP entitlement of a contributor, provided both were over retirement age. It also provided for home responsibility credits towards the basic pension. This relative 'generosity' to women has been one of the main sources of official criticism of the scheme (Bornatt *et al.*, 1985, p.31). The government's original proposal for SERPS in the Green Paper on the *Reform of Social Security* was to abolish the scheme (DHSS, 1985a). However the weight of influential opinion against this option, which included the Confederation of British Industry and the National Association of Pension Funds, and the public outcry which greeted the proposal, caused the government to modify its plans. Thus in the White Paper (DHSS, 1985b) four main proposals were made to reduce the cost of SERPS. Two of these will have a significant impact on women by reversing the main attempts of the 1975 scheme to begin very slowly to adjust state pensions to the economic experiences of women.

In the first place it is proposed that the calculation of earnings-related pension should be based on a lifetime's earnings (40 years) rather than the best 20 years. This had been considered to be 'over-generous' to those, especially women, who have shorter than average periods of employment or non-incremental earnings. Moreover, because

SERPS provides the basis for the guaranteed minimum pension within occupational schemes, if this measure is enacted the disadvantage experienced by women in the public sector will be mirrored in the private sector. Secondly, the proportion of SERPS that can be inherited by a spouse would be half rather than the full amount as at present (Walker, 1986, p.193). These and other proposed changes to SERPS have been deferred until 1988, so the limited steps made by women towards more equal treatment in the provision of state pensions rest on the outcome of the next election. The proposals made by the DHSS for the rest of the social security system, including supplementary benefit, have not been deferred and, indeed, are in the process of being implemented. On the basis of the government's own estimates these changes will make 1.9 million pensioners aged 60–79 and 350,000 of those aged 80 and over worse off, the vast majority of them being women (DHSS, 1985b).

This brief review of retirement and pension policies should be sufficient to indicate that the economic dependency—and therefore the poverty—of elderly people in general and elderly women in particular has been socially manufactured. Two sets of policies are in operation. On the one hand, age-restrictive social policies have been used by the state both to exclude older workers from the labour force and to legitimate that exclusion through the notion of 'retirement'. On the other hand, sex-discriminatory policies, particularly in the provision of pensions, have restricted the access of older women to even minimal income entitlements on a par with men. When coupled with the impact of life-long low social and economic status resulting from the influence of social class, the effect of these policies is to impose the very severest deprivation on very elderly working-class women. For example, in the recent study of elderly people in Aberdeen, younger (60–74) middle-class men and older (75+) working-class women were the two groups at the extreme ends of the income distribution. None of the middle-class men had incomes below £30 per week and over half had incomes in excess of £60. By comparison more than three in five of the older working-class women had an income of less than £30 per week and none had over £60 (Taylor and Ford, 1983, p.192).

CONCLUSIONS

Because the widespread poverty of elderly women and the penury experienced by some groups among them derive to a considerable extent from the operation of social and economic policies within male-dominated capitalism any major change in their status rests on the development of alternative policies. There is not space here to outline a full manifesto (see Bornatt *et al.*, 1985; Walker, 1986) but three fundamental sets of policies will be highlighted.

The practical implication of the analysis presented here is that the main determinants of the poverty of elderly women and the inequalities between them and elderly men have already been established long *before* retirement age. As in other spheres of women's lives, the key to their poverty and deprivation in old age is the socially-constructed relationship between gender and the labour market. The labour market is the primary source of the inequalities which are carried into retirement. Major changes are required in the structure and organisation of work to give women in general, and older women in particular, equal access to paid employment and, in addition, a genuine choice about retirement. The promotion of *work* for all, regardless of gender, throughout the economy is the only realistic way that choice can be provided for women and older workers. This means that *both* paid *and* unpaid labour must be assessed in terms of their contributions to society and rewarded commensurately.

A broad focus on work is necessary because the concentration of policy on access to paid employment is unlikely to overcome the sexual division of labour in the home and the restrictions it imposes on women's role in paid employment. Care must be taken, however, to ensure that a broader-based policy does not simply confirm the subordinate position of women as the primary domestic workers. Equality of access must be promoted in all forms of work, with the right not to take part in some roles being as strongly guarded as the right of access to others. Furthermore, flexible retirement, with a minimum pension age of 60 for both women and men, would provide opportunities for older people to choose when precisely to retire (Walker and Laczko, 1982).

Secondly, since many of the inequalities in pension provision derive from assumptions underlying the Beveridge social security system, an alternative approach is required if the poverty of elderly women is to be overcome. All pensioners have a need for income *regardless* of whether their previous employment was waged or unwaged. The priority is the provision of an adequate flat-rate pension regardless of history or gender. This means that the contribution or employment test, which discriminates against substantial numbers of women, should be abandoned. Pensions should be paid on an individual basis and at a level that enables elderly people to participate in the normal life of the community.

Thirdly, the special needs of the large proportion of very elderly people with disabilities, overwhelmingly women, must be recognised in the form of a disablement allowance paid *in addition* to the retirement pension. This would compensate for the extra costs and disadvantages of disability, and thereby help to reduce the disparity experienced by many elderly women between their needs and resources.

What chance is there that a start on such a package could be made in the near future? After all, the poverty of elderly people has been recognised by both official and independent research for over 100 years. Moreover, this account has demonstrated that social policies themselves reflect the paternalistic assumptions embedded in capitalist relations. The socially-constructed relationship between age, gender and the labour market has not only been the cause of poverty in old age, but has also formed the basis for the spread of a more general dependency among the elderly and ageism in many aspects of public policy and social attitudes. Elderly women are especially prone to ageist assumptions and comments. Despite their preponderance in the population they are usually ignored by the wider society and also to some extent by the women's movement (Peace, 1986). There are signs that this situation is changing slowly with, for example, the establishment of the Older Feminists Network in 1982 and the recent Age Concern/EOC joint initiative on incomes in old age. But Britain lags far behind developments in the USA, where older persons' organisations like the Gray Panthers are dominated by women and where the shared interests between women and elderly people are recognised more commonly. Men, both young and old, and the social institutions they have constructed in their image, have proved consistently impervious to the longstanding case for equality between the sexes in the distribution of power and resources. There are very few hopeful signs of change on that front. Men are unlikely to be divested of power and advantage without a struggle.

Perhaps the combination of the growing strength of the feminist movement in this country and the expanding numbers of elderly women over the next 20–40 years will provide the keys to political and social change. The women's movement in the USA has played a major role in exposing the similar processes which disadvantage women and older people and which are responsible for the creation of sexism and ageism (and, for that matter, racism). Moreover this broader focus has enabled elderly women to participate fully in the opposition to the twin evils of sex and age discrimination. Without a recognition of the common disadvantage experienced by women and older people there is always a danger that proposals to eliminate sexism in certain aspects of social policy may unwittingly condone ageism by arguing that there is actually a conflict of interest between women (as carers) and elderly people (see, for example, Finch, 1984). Until the potential political power of the 6.7 million women aged 60 and over is recognised and organised, policies to combat their poverty are not likely to be forthcoming. Unfortunately the very poverty that afflicts elderly women so deeply is a major factor in their political acquiescence.

10 Occupational Pension Provision and Women's Poverty in Old Age

Dulcie Groves

When in the 1960s poverty was 'rediscovered' in the UK, it became clear from research findings that those elderly people who had occupational retirement pensions derived from their previous employment were least likely to be living in poverty, as then defined. It also became clear that women were greatly under-represented among that minority of elderly people who had such occupational pensions. Furthermore, most female occupational pensioners were, in the language of the day, spinsters—mainly former teachers or civil servants. Few married women had occupational pensions derived from their own earnings. Surprisingly few widows had occupational pensions derived from their husbands' entitlements. Elderly non-married women were substantially over-represented among the poorest. 'Very elderly' women over 75 were among the poorest of all.

What are the links between female poverty in old age and access to occupational pension scheme benefits? Why was this early-1960s generation of older women, the youngest survivors of whom are, in the late 1980s, among the oldest within the current 'very elderly' female population, so under-represented among those with an employer's pension? How effective has occupational pension provision been in removing the present generation of 'young elderly' women, currently aged 60–75, from poverty? What are the prospects for the present generation of working age women (16–60) with regard to occupational pension entitlements when they themselves reach pensionable age?

Women's access to occupational pension benefits, particularly those derived from their own (not a husband's) paid work record, is a crucial issue in the light of the major changes to retirement pension provision proposed by the second Thatcher government. It is also important in the light of recent legal changes which have as their goal 'economic self-sufficiency' for divorced women. The aims of this chapter are, first, to explain why women now over pensionable age have benefited less than men from the existence of occupational pension provision, thus increasing their likelihood of being poor in old age. Secondly, it will comment on working-age women's access to membership of employers' pension schemes and the extent to which it appears that their risk of poverty in retirement may have lessened, both by increased access in their own right and through improved provision for widows. This critique, presented in an historical perspective, will focus both on women's opportunities to generate eventual occupational pension scheme benefits themselves via paid employment, and on issues relating to widows' benefits.

The modern 'occupational pension' (or employer's pension) derives from an early nineteenth-century civil service provision whereby elderly (or infirm) employees deemed to be suffering from physical or mental disabilities could be 'superannuated'; that is, 'retired' and awarded a replacement income or pension in an amount proportionate to the total number of years of service completed. By mid-century, a standard format had been devised which allowed a long-service civil servant to retire at a minimum age of 60 on a pension equal, at maximum, to two-thirds of his previous salary. The scheme was devised by men for men, since no women civil servants were at that time employed (Rhodes, 1965, Ch. 2).

These civil service pension arrangements were in due course copied, with modifications, by other public and private sector employers, though up to World War I it appears to have been a small minority of mainly the more prestigious employers who developed such formal occupational pension provision. Some schemes developed out of previous informal arrangements, characterised as ex-gratia pensions, whereby an employer would award a retirement pension to a particularly long-serving or otherwise 'deserving' employee—a paternalistic, 'one-off' arrangement which could fail if the employer later ceased trading. All such pensions came to be known, in common parlance, as 'private pensions', to distinguish them from the state pensions first introduced in 1908 for indigent elderly people over 70, followed later (1925) by contributory state retirement and widows' pension schemes (see Alan Walker's chapter in this volume).

Strictly speaking, all these 'occupational' or employers' pensions were either 'public sector' pensions derived from formal arrangements made for central or local government employees or 'private sector' pensions. The latter were derived from commercial, industrial or other employment within the 'private sector' of the labour market. Banks and insurance companies were early providers of formal occupational pension schemes during the second half of the nineteenth century. After World War I there was an expansion of such private sector provision. Employers who might previously have paid 'ex-gratia' pensions to favoured employees began to set up formal schemes arranged through insurance companies (Rhodes, 1965, p.87). The target beneficiary was the salaried 'family man' who, by reason of earning more than the £250 limit applied to non-manual workers, was excluded from participation in the new 1925 contributory state scheme, under which a retirement pension became payable at 65 and a modest pension became available to widows of any age (Groves, 1983, p.41).

These early developments in occupational pension provision pre-dated the later nineteenth-century trend towards the employment of women in 'white-collar' occupations. Women were not, for instance, recruited into the civil service until the 1870s. They came on the scene when the private telegraph companies were 'nationalised' and integrated into the Post Office, the women literally being taken on as a 'job lot' with their male colleagues. These and later women were brought into a civil service pension scheme designed, as noted, for men. The civil service, like the private telegraph companies, found its female employees to be competent, 'docile' workers, with the additional advantage of being cheaper to employ than men. Women did not qualify for a 'family wage' since it was assumed (erroneously in some cases) that they lived at home with parents or relatives and that they did not have dependents to support financially. The crunch came when it was realised that these competent women had a propensity to marry (Martindale, 1939).

The civil service 'efficiency experts' of the mid–1870s quickly worked out that the retention of married women would be 'inefficient' in managerial terms, since the longer that female employees remained in government service, the more they would cost because of the modest incremental salary progression within their low-paid 'women's grades'. Furthermore, there was a danger that they would stay in service long enough to qualify for a retirement pension— an even more expensive proposition. Swiftly a 'marriage bar' was introduced, though its application does not appear to have been universal in the civil service until 1894 when government typists (hitherto an 'unestablished' all-female grade) obtained permanent, pensionable 'established' status by agreeing to a rule requiring automatic resignation on marriage. It was agreed that in lieu of the pension forgone, such women would qualify for a 'marriage gratuity' on leaving—a lump-sum of a value relating to years of service not exceeding twelve (Martindale, 1939; Holcombe, 1973).

The 'marriage bar' became the rule in other forms of public sector employment and in many types of private sector employment, especially when unemployment rates were high between the two world wars. Thus up to the end of World War II (when the public sector marriage bar was abolished and young women retained paid jobs on marriage), in order to qualify for an occupational pension in old age derived from her own earnings a woman usually had to remain unmarried. The choice was marriage or career. Furthermore salaried men were not expected to have 'working wives'. The development of widows' provision in occupational pension schemes is a reflection of this bourgeois family form (see Hall, 1979).

Holcombe (1973) has pinpointed five major occupations entered by women, from choice and/or financial necessity, in the late nineteenth century—teaching, the civil service, nursing, clerical work and employment in the retail trades. Women's occupational 'choices' were limited and these five occupations predominated up to the time of World War II and well beyond it. Elementary school teachers had access to a national pension scheme from 1898 so that teaching, along with the civil service, came to be thought of as a 'secure' pensionable occupation—a 'good job' for a single woman. Nursing in public hospitals was also pensionable, while the more prestigious voluntary hospitals were early pension providers. The Royal National Pension Fund for Nurses (1887) is an early example of the personal 'portable' pension, which entailed taking out an insurance policy so as to purchase an annuity on retirement. However nurses were very badly paid which may in part account for a seemingly low take-up of non-compulsory pension scheme provision for nurses (Maggs, 1983, p.131).

In 1936 the Ministry of Labour carried out a pioneer survey of private sector employers' pension scheme membership, finding that women comprised about 20 per cent of the total membership of around 1.6 million persons. Nearly half the women were in the 'administration, clerical and sales' category, a minority being in sales. Private sector nurses were included and, indicative of an expansion of occupational pension provision into higher-status 'manual' employment during the inter-war period, just over half the women in private sector schemes were manual workers (Ministry of Labour, 1938). However, the 'progressive' employers who developed this form of occupational welfare, mainly after World War I (Jones, 1983), typically operated a 'marriage bar' and the 'women's pension scheme' doubled as a savings scheme which produced marriage gratuities.

The eventual pensions received by women who participated in these inter-war schemes would have reflected their low and unequal pay as well as conditions of service which typically required women to retire much earlier than men, especially in private sector employment. The Ministry of Labour survey showed that no fewer than 37 per cent of the 'adminstrative, clerical and sales' group were made to retire by 55 and a similar proportion by the age of 60, whereas 65 was the 'normal' retirement age for men (Ministry of Labour, 1938). Such practices reflect pre-war pension policies which, from the point at which women first began to enter white-collar employment, were clearly geared towards the recruitment of successive cohorts of low-paid young women for routine duties, a rapid turnover being ensured via the marriage bar. Employers were content to retain a cadre of single women who could supervise other women, though once into their fifties such women were at risk of being construed as 'too old'. Formal occupational pension provision was used 'in the managerial interest' to retire women early, a practice which could increase their risk of poverty in old age. Meanwhile, for men, such provision was a well-established device used to attract and retain competent male employees. Occupational pension scheme rules and related personnel policies helped to construct salaried men, in particular, as 'good providers', who typically served out a lengthy working life with one employer.

While occupational pension provision was originally intended as 'superannuation', it gradually came to incorporate provision for dependants, typically widows or dependent children including unmarried adult daughters. Again, 'ex-gratia' arrangements appear to have preceded the inauguration of formal schemes. The civil service in 1909 reduced the retirement pension from two-thirds to half salary in order to provide a lump-sum in addition. By this means a male pensioner could choose to provide for any dependents after his death (Rhodes, 1965, p.51). The police force was the first public sector occupation to achieve widows' pensions as such. By the mid-1930s male civil servants could choose to 'allocate' part of their pensions; that is, to opt for a lower pension on retirement, so that if they died first their wives would get a modest continuing pension (ibid., p.79). From 1937 male teachers could opt to take only one-third of the lump sum due to them on retirement so that an annuity would potentially be available to their widows (Gosden, 1972, p.148). By the mid-1930s such 'option' arrangements were characteristic of private sector provision also; it was for the male breadwinner alone to decide whether he would so provide for his dependants or take his full pension on retirement. The new insurance-based schemes adopted by the private sector between the wars offered the possibility of a lump-sum payment where a scheme member died in service (Owen, 1935, p.88).

In the two decades between the outbreak of World War II and the poverty studies of the early 1960s there were changes both in patterns of female economic activity and in the nature of occupational pension provision. The latter expanded under favourable tax arrangements begun during the war (Pilch and Wood, 1979). However, although in wartime married women were positively encouraged and in some cases required to re-enter or remain in the labour market, working in those very occupations from which they had previously been 'barred', such women were often categorised as temporary workers, or were employed part-time. There is no evidence to suggest that they made substantial wartime gains in terms of occupational pension entitlements.

Nor, once the war had ended and formal marriage bars were removed, did the increasing presence of married women in the labour force mean that efforts were made to extend female access to membership of occupational pension schemes. Far from it. It was still the case that a white-collar woman employee within the public sector (including, now, the nationalised industries) had reasonably good pension prospects provided that she completed a lengthy period of full-time service. However the early surveys of the Government Actuary's department show that in the private sector in 1956 there were only 34 per cent of 'salaried' women (71 per cent of men) and 23 per cent of 'waged' women (38 per cent of men) in schemes (Government Actuary, 1958, p.4). By 1963 somewhat comparable proportions were 40 per cent of 'non-manual' women in schemes (80 per cent of men) and 15 per cent of 'manual' women (55 per cent of men) (Government Actuary, 1966, p.12).

It was accepted practice for employers to admit women to schemes at older ages than men—30 was not uncommon. In the post-war decades, the majority of women had married and subsequently left paid work to have children by the age of 30 (see Rimmer, 1981). However, they increasingly returned to work in both the public and private sectors once their children were in school, but tended to do so part-time (see Manley and Sawbridge, 1980). Nor, even if full-time, did they typically do the same type or level of paid work as that performed by the men who were included in the employers' pension schemes. The post-war National Insurance arrangements made it an unattractive proposition for married women, typically low-waged, to opt for paying full National Insurance contributions when a much cheaper 'married woman's option' was available. This option gave a married woman the right to a dependent wife's retirement pension at 60 per cent of a full single person's rate, once her husband had retired. Furthermore, even if a woman paid in for a full pension she had to pass the 'half test'; that is, she had to work for at least half of her married life before she could count in her contributions both before and after marriage (Groves, 1983, pp.45–7). This rule resulted in only a small minority of married women becoming fully insured and helped to reinforce their financial dependence within marriage. It also helped to construct married women and, by extension, all young women, as employees who were 'not interested' in pensions, their wages typically being constructed as 'pin money'. The technical pensions literature of the early 1960s advised employers to leave women out of pension schemes and give 'ex-gratia' (unfunded) pensions to that dwindling minority of single women who did become long-serving employees (Pilch and Wood, 1960, p.80). Occupational pension providers were more interested in improving the benefits available to women as widows, rather than as scheme members in their own right. By 1960 widows' pensions were available in all public sector occupations apart from teaching, though they were still relatively uncommon in the private sector which continued to rely on 'allocation' options and lump sum provision (Government Actuary, 1958; 1966).

The above scenario helps to explain the part played by access to occupational pension scheme benefits in determining the income levels of the elderly women whose financial circumstances were studied between 1959 and 1965. Cole with Utting (1962, Ch. 5) estimated that 76 per cent of single and widowed women over pensionable age in Britain in 1959 were living in poverty (defined as less than £3.50 per week). Whereas 37 per cent of couples and 38 per cent of non-married men had an employer's pension, only 7 per cent of non-married women had one, including an even smaller percentage of widows. Likewise Townsend and Wedderburn (1965, Ch. 4), studying elderly people over 65 in Britain in 1962, found only 11 per cent of non-married women with occupational benefits—18 per cent of single women and 9 per cent of widows, the older women being the poorest. By 1965 it appeared that 48 per cent of retired men over 65, but only 24 per cent of single women over 60 and 11 per cent of widows over pensionable age had employers' pensions, younger women predominating among those women who had a pension in their own right (Ministry of Pensions and National Insurance, 1966, p.154). The single women had, on average, better pension levels than the men in all age groups, reflecting the levels of female employment in white-collar, public sector jobs. However Townsend and Wedderburn (1965, Ch. 5) make it clear that the low level of many occupational pension payments sometimes served merely to keep their recipients off National Assistance, though still on the margins of poverty. Indeed, while it is not the brief of this chapter to comment on state pension provision, it must be remarked that in the early 1960s, as subsequently, it was chiefly the low level of state provision which made the presence or absence of entitlement to occupational pension benefits so crucial to many household budgets, not least to lone female households.

The introduction in the early 1960s of the state 'graduated' pension scheme, an earnings-related second-tier provision for lower-income employees not in occupational pension schemes, opened up a growing gender gap in employee pension coverage. The lowest earners, seldom included in employers' pension provision and among whom women predominated, were excluded from the graduated scheme. Meanwhile employers continued to expand occupational provision for full-time salaried and some manual grades of staff, to the extent that full-time employment in the public sector became largely synonymous with access to occupational scheme membership. Employers, on the advice of specialists within the pensions 'industry', contracted out their better-paid grades of full-time staff from the new graduated scheme (Heclo, 1974, p.273). Hence the number of men in private sector schemes increased dramatically, by 3 million between 1956 and 1967, but women by only half a million (Government Actuary, 1981, p.6). From the late 1960s to the mid-1970s there was much political debate on pensions reform and two failed attempts at legislation before the Social Security Pensions Act 1975 was passed, becoming effective in 1978. The Labour Party favoured a major role for earnings-related state pension provision while the Conservatives wished for broad occupational coverage and a residual second-tier state pension, in which many employed women would have found themselves. The compromise was a system within which 'approved' occupational pension schemes were closely related to a new state earnings related pension scheme (SERPS). Employers could contract 'occupational groups' of employees out of SERPS and into employers' provision (see Groves, 1983).

Early results of a Government Actuary's 1983 survey show that, during the years since the 1975 survey, about half of all men in private sector employment had access to occupational pension provision. However, whereas in 1975 17 per cent of women had access, the proportion increased to 25 per cent in 1979 (Government Actuary, 1978, p.8;

1981, p.4). By 1983 35 per cent of full-time private sector women were covered but only 11 per cent of part-timers (Department of Employment, 1985b, p.495). Since 1967 the number of women in public sector schemes has nearly doubled from 1 to 2 million, while the number of women in private schemes has risen from 1.3 to 1.4 million. By contrast, male membership has dropped by more than 2 million, to 4.4 million (ibid., Table 1). Female numbers partially reflect a major increase in female labour force participation since 1967, while male numbers reflect, among other factors, a declining number of men in the British workforce.

It might be thought that the present generation of 'younger' retired women have, by virtue of improved access to occupational pension benefits, greatly reduced their risk of poverty in old age, which for women officially begins five years earlier than men at the 'pensionable age' of 60. However in 1982, only 40 per cent of lone (i.e. non-married) women aged 60–64 had their own and/or a widow's occupational pension and 25 per cent of that age group were drawing a supplementary (means-tested) state pension. Between the ages of 65 and 69, 37 per cent of lone women and 62 per cent of lone men had some sort of occupational pension. Only 20 per cent of the lone men drew supplementary pensions, along with 33 per cent of widows and 28 per cent of other lone women (DHSS, 1984, p.17, Table 4; p.19, Table 7). Married couples were most likely to have occupational pensions and least likely to have a supplementary pension. However Hunt (1978, p.28, Table 6.4.3) showed that employers' pensions were a very small component of elderly wives' incomes. The typically bimodal career followed by women in Britain over recent decades (leaving aside the marriage bar which affected older women) has meant that married women and mothers of any marital status do not fit into structures of occupational pension provision designed for male breadwinners. Both the current generation of 'young elderly' women and women now of working age have been profoundly affected by the following aspects of women's employment and employers' pension provision.

Occupational pension provision has always served best the interests of employees who have a life-long record of full-time employment in the better-paid occupations which offer an employer's pension as a fringe benefit. Outside public sector employment, which offers transferable pension rights, occupational pension benefits are maximised by minimal job changing or by an ability to compensate for any loss of pension rights on job change through a better remunerated new job. It is men rather than women who have, typically, been able to fulfil these requirements. Most women since World War II have had interrupted working lives. The Department of Employment's survey of women who were of working age in 1980 (Martin and Roberts, 1984) presents much evidence to explain why most women do not complete lengthy periods of pensionable service and why, where they have had access to occupational pension benefits, they tend to end up with lower weekly rates of pension and smaller lump sums than their male contemporaries. Most employers have required women to retire from their jobs at a 'normal' pensionable age of 60, whereas a much greater number of men are permitted to remain until 65, despite trends towards earlier retirement. While this practice has now been successfully challenged in the courts, its effects on pension scheme provision and older women's economic activity rates have yet to be seen (Dibben, 1986).

Women's limited access to employers' pension benefits are directly related to the traditional domestic division of labour which assigns the 'breadwinner' role to men, principally husbands, and the major responsibility for the unpaid work of the home (especially child-care) to women. Joshi and Owen (1981, pp.106–7) studied the labour force participation of successive cohorts of women in Britain from 1950 to 1974 and found that it was motherhood, rather than marriage, which determined the length of women's lives in paid work, with Ms Average withdrawing from the labour market for seven years. Younger women had higher economic activity rates. Martin and Roberts (1984, pp.11–12) found that older women, many of whom would not have been contributing to the state pension scheme in their own right, tended to leave the labour market in their mid-fifties. Caring for elderly relatives or an ailing husband is a common reason for such withdrawal (Finch and Groves, 1983).

A striking feature of women's economic activity (highlighted in the chapters by Susan Lonsdale and Heather Joshi in this volume) is the extent to which mothers and some childless women work part-time. This typically depresses their eventual income in old age. Only 12 per cent of part-time women workers (11 per cent of those in the private sector and 13 per cent of those in the public sector) were members of occupational pension schemes in 1983. Interestingly, though men work part-time far less commonly, 22 per cent of part-time men in both sectors were in employers' pension schemes (Department of Employment, 1985b, p.495).

In addition, employers are making increasing use of temporary and fixed-term 'short duration' contract staff. Meager (1986) has presented the findings of a 1984 study which showed that such employment strategies have been widely applied in relation to personal service, office and manual workers. They have also featured to some extent in the recruitment of managerial, technical and professional staff. Two-thirds of the 'short duration' workers identified in the sample were women in non-professional categories. Case studies showed that employers made savings arising 'mainly from temporary workers having less beneficial (or no) entitlement to holiday and sickness pay, and particularly to occupational pensions' (Meager, 1986, p.12). It was the larger employers of more than 200 workers who had greatly expanded their temporary recruitment since 1980. These are the very employers who, in the past, have been most likely to include their workers in occupational pension schemes (Government Actuary, 1958; 1966; 1968; 1972; 1978; 1981).

Women's work has always been highly segregated (Hakim, 1981), with important implications for female access to occupational pension benefits. The Social Security Pensions Act 1975 specifically allows employers to exclude workers from membership of occupational pension schemes by occupational category, thus facilitating the legal exclusion of women in vertically segregated occupational categories which are mainly or exclusively female. However even where, as in many public sector occupations, membership of an employer's pension scheme is automatic for permanent full-time staff, including women, horizontal segregation ensures that women, typically, end their working lives with lower pension benefits than their male colleagues. For instance in 1983, women constituted 77.5 per cent of the lowest civil service grade (clerical assistant), 9.9 per cent of the junior administrative grade (principal) and 3.7 per cent of the highest grade then occupied by women, the second-ranking Deputy Secretary grade (EOC, 1984, p.90).

Among women working full-time in the better paid jobs, there is a concentration of women in the lower grades of their particular type of employment. Martin and Roberts (1984, pp.151–2) and Heather Joshi's chapter here document the downward mobility experienced by women returning to paid work after a break, especially when returning to part-time work. Many full-timers have also had periods of part-time work or career breaks. Thus with their typically lower pay (see Susan Lonsdale's chapter in this volume) and lower lifetime earnings compared with men, the average woman ends up with a lower salary or wage on which to base her final salary for the purposes of working out occupational pension entitlements. Even if her scheme permits her to make additional pension contributions to make up for missing years of service, such payments will cost her more than would be the case for a man of the same age and salary status, since the arrangements assume that a woman will live longer and therefore claim benefits for longer than a man.

Study of the development of both state and occupational pension provision reveals arrangements which, especially until the 1975 legislation, endorsed the traditional domestic division of labour. It was difficult for married women to achieve a substantial basic retirement pension record within the state pension scheme and to gain access to an employer's pension scheme. The Social Security Pensions Act 1975 included an 'equal access' clause which entitles women to membership of an occupational scheme where this is available to men in the same category of employment. But as noted, this still leaves a substantial number of women with, over a working lifetime, limited access to occupational pension benefits in their own right. One way in which the 1975 legislation can be said to have further endorsed the domestic division of labour is by making provision of widows' pensions by occupational schemes one condition of approval by the Occupational Pensions Board. Indeed, the more recent history of pension provision shows more concern on the part of both governments and occupational pension providers to increase widows' benefits (themselves symbolic of the financial dependence of wives in marriage), than to help women build up their own occupational pension records. Some private sector occupational schemes are generous towards widows, especially if death occurs in service. Such provision can reduce a widow's risk of poverty in old age not least because, unlike public sector schemes, private sector schemes are increasingly permitting widows to keep their pensions on remarriage and operate no cohabitation rules.

The preoccupation with providing for widows is one outcome of the high marriage rate for women which has persisted in Britain since World War II. Single (never married) women now form a very small proportion of the older working-age groups and a far smaller proportion of the 'young elderly' female population (CSO, 1986, p.21, Table 1.5). However there are two groups of women whose marital status can put them at risk of poverty in old age because of their inability to qualify for dependants' benefits. An increasing number of couples are cohabiting, including older, previously married partners who in due course remarry. There is also an increasing number of women who have lost a potential occupational widow's pension, and associated benefits, on divorce.

If a man with occupational pension scheme entitlements

dies leaving a female partner with whom he is living, it will depend on the rules of his pension scheme and the discretion of the scheme trustees (or manager) as to whether the woman qualifies as a female dependant with regard to any pension and/or lump sum for which her partner may have nominated her. The trustees may refuse to accept her as a beneficiary or may require any benefits to be divided with other individuals. One route to female poverty in old age is therefore through financial dependence in a marriage-like relationship which fails to deliver the occupational benefits to which a wife would have been entitled (see McGoldrick, 1984, Ch. 5). Pension providers are currently being challenged in this way by the existence of new family forms.

Divorce is likewise raising complicated issues of entitlement to dependants' occupational benefits, since on divorce a woman loses her potential right to a widow's pension and/or benefits. Section 5 of the Matrimonial Causes Act 1973 allows a wife to oppose divorce after five years' separation on the grounds that dissolution of the marriage would cause 'grave financial or other hardship', but very few such cases have succeeded (see Cretney, 1984, pp.163–7). It is the older wife in a divorce case, who has no recent contact with the labour market or a poor earning capacity, who has sometimes much to lose through the ending of her marriage. Older women are less likely to remarry than younger women (Family Policy Studies Centre, 1983, p.12) and are consequently at risk of poverty in old age unless, unusually, they have been able to generate an adequate income through their own resources. Powell (1984, p.187) argues that in most divorce cases, insufficient account is taken of such potential benefits as an occupational widow's benefit or pension; nor is a proper actuarial value set upon such benefits. Arrangements for reallocation of property on divorce or a requirement that an ex-husband should take out life insurance do not necessarily compensate for the loss of an index-linked widow's pension in old age.

The Matrimonial and Family Proceedings Act 1984 has as one goal the promotion of economic self-sufficiency for both parties on divorce. Any benefits such as pensions, which the parties to the divorce will lose the chance of acquiring, must be taken into consideration. Pension schemes are required, under the terms of the Social Security Pensions Act 1975, to pay a legal widow a pension equal in amount to that which she would have received had her husband been contributing to SERPS. In 1985 the Lord Chancellor's Department circulated a consultation paper which proposed that while a legal widow must get her 'guaranteed minimum pension', the Court could order a pension scheme to pay any surplus to an ex-wife who remained unmarried or the pension scheme could be given powers to do this. No responses to these proposals have been published at the time of writing. Divorced women are not entitled to the dependants' benefits which can to some extent compensate both for lack of access to membership of an occupational pension scheme and for financial disadvantage due to the traditional domestic division of labour. Divorced women are among those most at risk of poverty in old age. Such risk can come directly from loss of occupational benefits.

As this chapter is being written, the Social Security Bill 1986 has moved through Parliament, with far-reaching implications for occupational pension provision. The government proposes to modify the SERPS scheme in ways which will make it a far less valuable means of compensating women for their disadvantages in the labour market and their consequent difficulties in generating their own second-tier pension provision for old age. Much is being made of the advantages to individuals of opting out of the traditional occupational pension scheme (and SERPS) by investing in a personal pension arranged commercially or through an employer. Such pensions are in fact 'money purchase' schemes, which connoisseurs of occupational pension provision will recognise as having been tried in the past and found wanting, since they do not stand up well to inflation (Occupational Pensions Board, 1981, p.25) and the eventual sum available for investment in an annuity is unpredictable. The Equal Opportunities Commission has argued (1985, pp.16–17) that with women's typically discontinuous employment, 'personal pensions' are liable to be a recipe for female poverty in old age. Lynes (1986) has argued that the much higher cost of annuities for women is a further major disadvantage. The government has in fact recommended 'unisex' actuarial calculations, to which the insurance industry is much opposed.

Women's access to occupational pension benefits would be improved if it became mandatory for part-time employees to contribute *pro rata*. There seems no good reason why occupational (and state) pension provision and all retirement benefits should not be subject to sex discrimination legislation. This would obviate practices such as employers excluding occupational categories typically filled by women, as the Social Security Act 1975 permits, or operating differential actuarial calculations for men and women. Nor will equality of access to occupational pension benefits come about without equality of pay. This said, it may be remarked that, especially outside the public sector, the occupational pension system is not well structured for anyone, male or female, with a discontinuous employment record or a history of multiple job changes. Indeed a really well-designed state pension scheme, not necessarily so closely tied to employment history, could probably do as well as occupational pension provision for most women, complete with lump sums if required.

Femininity has never been equated with financial self-sufficiency. On a practical level, women's greater share of unpaid domestic work has inhibited their ability to generate an adequate income for old age. In terms of the more distant future, the achievement of a more equal division of labour between men and women must be argued in the context of occupational pension provision, as in other areas. And while widows' pensions do compensate some more privileged women for the typical financial disabilities of marriage and motherhood, the goal of disaggregating resources might be preferable to the extension of dependants' benefits to widowers, not least in the light of increased divorce and the preference of some women not to marry. Meanwhile there is a real need to render women less invisible in debates on employers' pension provision; in statistics on such provision; and in places where decisions on occupational benefits are made. For the foreseeable future, occupational pension provision is likely to exist in some form. If women are to minimise their risk of poverty in old age, one way of doing so is to grasp their fair share of what is on offer in an admittedly inequitable sector of pension provision.

Employers' pension provision distributes its rewards unequally to both men and women, but it penalises women in particular for their typically disadvantaged labour market careers and reflects their major responsibility for the unpaid work of the home. Nor does the existence of occupational widows' benefits offer compensation to the majority of women for the limitations on their opportunities to defer earnings for old age. A widow's benefit itself reflects the vagaries of a husband's employment record and can be lost on divorce. Given the inadequate levels of state pension provision and the limited opportunities most women have to save or invest for old age, their limited access to the benefits of occupational pension scheme membership has been a major factor in the construction of female poverty in old age. Such poverty compounds the inequalities typically experienced by women over a lifetime and magnifies such inequalities in old age.

NOTE

Much material for this chapter is derived from a doctoral thesis on women and occupational pensions (Groves, 1986).

Part 4
Women, The Family and Poverty

11 Women's Poverty and Caring

Hilary Graham

This chapter examines women's poverty in the home, focusing on the economic circumstances of women caring for pre-school children. The chapter is concerned with the links between domestic poverty and domestic responsibilities; with the way in which caring for others shapes and is shaped by the access that carers have to household resources. As a dimension of family life (and the nation's health) which is private and difficult to see, it is one that has been neglected in the study both of poverty and health.

Recently, however, research has begun to look at the material conditions of informal caring and, in particular, at the distribution of such resources as money, food, time and leisure within households (Pahl, 1982; Murcott, 1982; Parker, 1985a; Charles and Kerr, 1985). Such research has pointed to the fact that, while sharing a common address, family members do not always share a common standard of living. As Jessie Bernard remarked over ten years ago, 'there are two marriages . . . in every union, his and hers' (1973, p.14).

This chapter does not provide a summary of current research on his and her living standards; this important task has been done elsewhere (Graham, 1984; Brannen and Wilson, forthcoming). Rather, it contributes to our knowledge by reporting on the findings of a recent study of 102 women caring for pre-school children (Graham, 1986).[1] It is through their experiences that the chapter seeks to understand more about women's economic position as the family health-keepers. The study was conducted in 1984 in a new town with a predominantly white population. Because of the study's setting, the sample is unlikely to capture the diversity of women's experiences of poverty in the home. However, research into women's position in the domestic economy currently relies heavily on such small and non-random samples. Studies based in different areas with different population profiles are therefore inevitably highlighting only some of the complex dimensions of domestic poverty.

The chapter begins with some preliminary observations about poverty and caring and about the contradictions faced by women who experience both simultaneously. The second section introduces the empirical study and describes the world of caring for pre-school children as experienced by the mothers in the sample. The third section looks at women's access to the material resources necessary for caring, focusing on their access to money. The fourth section examines how women cope with caring in poverty, describing how they attempt to reconcile their health-keeping and house-keeping responsibilities.

Questions about women's access to household resources have generally been raised and explored in relation to two-parent (or at least two-adult) households; the concept of 'household distribution' itself implies a flow between two (or more) members of a family unit. The study seeks to broaden this focus by including one-parent as well as two-parent households and considers the material context of caring in these different kinds of family unit. By comparing the experiences of mothers in one- and two-parent households, we can understand something of the ways in which the hidden and unrecorded poverty of marriage is similar to, and different from, the visible and recorded poverty of single parenthood. We can appreciate more how the economic dependencies of marriage and single parenthood differentially affect both the experiences of poverty for women with children and their strategies for coping with it.

POVERTY AND CARING

Poverty and caring are, for many women, two sides of the same coin. Caring is what they do; poverty describes the economic circumstances in which they do it. To understand the complex and often contradictory links between poverty and caring, we need to reflect briefly on what kinds of experience the two concepts embrace.

Studies of caring for children often appear to describe the obvious. Yet the very obviousness of our knowledge can make it difficult for us to appreciate its significance. Caring for young children is typically a full-time and unpaid job and most women withdraw from full-time paid work to do it. Less than 10 per cent of women with pre-school children are in full-time paid work, with West Indian women the largest sub-group among mothers in employment (OPCS, 1982; Brown, 1984). No longer earning, women with young children rely on others for the money they need to keep themselves and their families. Their main sources of income are the earnings of a partner (for over 90 per cent of two-parent families) or social security (for 50 per cent of one-parent families) (Popay *et al.*, 1983, p.47).

The economic dependency of mothers with pre-school children—so much part of our image of family life—takes a particular and unusual form. Unlike other family dependants—children, for example, or a frail parent or a disabled spouse—women are economically dependent not because they need care but because they give it. Women's economic dependency within the family is created not by their own physical dependency but through the physical dependency of others. For children and for men, it seems, economic dependency is the cost of being cared for; for women, economic dependency is the cost of caring (Graham, 1983).

Economic dependency is closely linked with poverty. It is their economic dependency which binds the elderly, the unemployed and the disabled together and into poverty. Again the position of mothers is somewhat different. For most mothers their dependent relationship is mediated not through the labour market or the welfare state but through marriage and cohabitation. They depend on the earning capacity of their partners, supplemented by their own part-time earnings (Popay *et al.*, 1983). While dependent, the majority of women living with a partner are in households whose total income is above the poverty line; about three-quarters of women and children in two-parent households officially live out of poverty (DHSS, 1986a). However, research warns us against uncritically concluding that living with a man protects all dependent women with children from poverty. Instead, it records the extent to which statistics based on household income can mask individual poverty (Pahl, 1985a). Homer, Leonard and Taylor's (1984) study of the economic circumstances of women entering the Cleveland Refuge provides a measure of the extent and scale of women's poverty in violent marriages. Nearly half (45 per cent) of the women were assessed to have been previously living in households whose income was on or below the supplementary benefit level. However, when the women's income was calculated in relation to the items of household expenditure for which they were responsible, 71 per cent of the women and children were classified as living on or below this poverty-line income.

The change from full-time waged labour to full-time caring brings with it a change in women's material needs as well as their economic position. Carers need to secure shelter and fuel, food and clothes, not only on their own behalf but also on behalf of those they care for. Yet while mothers require more after the birth of children, they can find themselves with less. Giving up paid work can release human resources—time, energy, attention and patience— which many regard as essential for children's development. Yet at the same time it can make it more difficult to secure the material resources for caring. Without the women's wages, household income is lower and, without independent means, women can find that their access to an income is reduced. In other words, caring full-time in order to care for one's children properly can, paradoxically, make it more difficult to care for them adequately.

Turning the spotlight from the concept of caring to the concept of poverty does little to resolve the contradictions women face in trying to care for health in poverty. Much of the conceptual debate in recent years has focused on the definition of poverty in absolute or relative terms (see Chapter 1). While relative definitions alert us to important questions of accepted life-styles and standards of 'decent living', of powerlessness and the distribution of wealth, they can obscure the relationship between poverty and health. The relationship is central both to absolute conceptions of poverty and to the idea of a poverty line; as Seebohm Rowntree notes, absolute poverty is an income below 'the minimum sums upon which families of different sizes could be maintained in a state of physical efficiency' (Rowntree, 1903, p.19; quoted in Viet-Wilson, 1986). This definition alerts us (if not Seebohm Rowntree) immediately to the position of those household members vested with responsibility for the physical efficiency of the family; if poverty is incompatible with the maintenance of health, then increasing poverty among Britain's carers has far-reaching effects not only on their own health but on the health of those they care for.

Before we explore the experience of such poverty, a final dimension needs to be introduced into this complex picture. In looking at the hidden poverty of caring, research has focused on households rather than families, and on two-adult units rather than single parent or multi-person units. It has been concerned primarily with how material resources like money and food are distributed among man-woman couples living at the same address and sharing a common system of housekeeping (see, for example, Pahl, 1982; Murcott, 1982; Charles and Kerr, 1985). The study of intra-*household* flows of resources has left intra-*family* flows, between family members in different households, less well researched. We therefore know less than we should about the way in which the economic support of relatives affects women's economic position. The narrow focus on intra-household resource flows also has an unacknowledged ethnic bias; the support of parents and children beyond the immediate household is more common among Afro-Caribbean families than white families. As Brown's research indicates, 40 per cent of West Indian households send money to relatives outside the home (principally parents); the proportion among white households is 5 per cent (Brown, 1984).

The kind of household as well as the kind of family in which women care for children can crucially affect their experience of poverty. As in other areas highlighted in this section, the effects are paradoxical. Single-parent households (in which Afro-Caribbean families are over-represented) have much lower incomes than two-parent households and the income gap is widening. Figures from the Family Expenditure Survey indicate that, between 1981 and 1982, the average gross weekly income of single-parent families fell by £11, while that of two-parent families rose by £18 (NCOPF, 1984, p.3). However, studies suggest that the economic position of women can improve in the shift from poverty within to poverty outside marriage. In Evason's study of 700 lone mothers in Northern Ireland, 70 per cent were found to be living in poverty (defined as up to 40 per cent above supplementary benefit levels), yet 48 per cent of the divorced and separated women felt that their living standards were the same or better than they had been while they were living with their husbands (Evason, 1980).

Not only may women feel economically better off as lone mothers, but they may also (and relatedly) find it easier to cope with their poverty. The evidence of the new town study described in the next section suggests that in finding ways to make ends meet, women look to items of expenditure which they control and which are, or can be treated as, individual. Within this framework, lone mothers appeared to find it easier to 'individualise' collective expenditure; to identify areas of family consumption, like food and fuel, where they could make cuts in their personal consumption. Further, the small savings made in this way were not absorbed by the expenses incurred by their partner. It is this paradoxical kind of economic power—the power more effectively to cut one's consumption—that emerges as a key dimension of being simultaneously poorer and better off as a single parent.

THE NEW TOWN STUDY OF FAMILIES WITH PRE-SCHOOL CHILDREN

The sample was drawn from households taking part in a larger survey conducted in the autumn of 1983 by the new town authority responsible for the development of the area in which the study was based. Since the aim was to understand more about the caring activities and coping strategies of mothers, only two-parent and female-headed one-parent households were selected. All the 102 households in the study contained at least one child under five. Further, to enable comparisons to be drawn between the experiences of mothers living in different economic and social circumstances, the sample was stratified according to household status (one-parent/two-parent) and according to household income (with a gross weekly household income of £105 marking the boundary line between 'low' and 'average' income households). The figure of £105 was derived from the poverty line represented by supplementary benefit, and was based on what a two-parent, two-child family would have needed to earn in order to achieve an income equivalent to supplementary benefit.[2] According to these two criteria of household status and household income, the sample contained 20 low-income two-parent families and 44 two-parent families whose household incomes lifted them above the low-income threshold. Among this two-parent group, gross weekly incomes ranged from £500 to £41 (excluding child benefit). The sample had 38 lone mothers, 37 of whom fell into the low-income group. Thus about half (56 per cent) of the women in the study lived in low-income households. In addition, a third of the mothers in households above the poverty line stated that their income was insufficient to meet their family's needs.

In some important respects, particularly as regards housing and ethnic background, the study is not representative of women caring for young children in poverty. For example, the 38 lone mothers lived on their own with their children and not, like about a quarter of one-parent households in Britain, in accommodation which they share with others (OPCS, 1982). Furthermore the quality of their housing, like that of the 64 mothers in two-parent households, was generally good. The majority of the sample was white. While the majority of parents nationally are also white, we know that the experience of single parenthood is more common among Afro-Caribbean households than among white or Asian households (Brown, 1984). The fact that all the mothers in the study had at least one child under five years old meant that the sample contained a larger proportion who were young and economically inactive and, among the lone mothers, at an earlier stage of their careers as single parents than in other studies; 70 per cent of the respondents were not in paid work, and the majority of the lone mothers had been living on their own for less than two years. In line with national statistics, the two-parent mothers typically relied on their partner's earnings for the resources that they needed to keep themselves and care for their families. While over 85 per cent of the two-parent households had earnings as their main source of income, three-quarters of the 38 lone parents in the study relied on state benefits and only one, a teacher, had a gross weekly income which lifted her and her children above the low-income threshold.

KEEPING THE FAMILY GOING: HEALTH-KEEPING AND HOUSE-KEEPING ON A LOW INCOME

Women, both in their own words and through the medium of research, have described a range of factors which shape their economic position as the family's health-keepers. They have described the financial arrangements operating in their marriages and marriage-like relationships (Todd and Jones, 1972; Pahl, 1982; 1985a), and how these are organised to secure the basic needs of housing, fuel and food (Burghes,

1980; Homer *et al.*, 1984). In exploring these areas, research has identified the importance of independent sources of income for mothers, to cope not only with the effects of family poverty but also with an inequitable distribution of family income (Todd and Jones, 1972; Pahl, 1982; 1985; Walsh and Lister, 1985). This section sets the experiences of the mothers in the new town study in the context of this wider literature on the economic position of women in the home.

In tackling the question of how money is organised in marriage and marriage-like relationships, research has identified a range of systems through which couples match (or fail to match) financial resources to household responsibilities. Crucial to these systems are the ways in which they negotiate the *control* of money (who makes the key decisions about how much money is made available to whom and for what) and the *management* of money (the day-to-day budgeting arrangements, the payment of bills and the purchase of goods). Along these two axes of control and management, a range of systems have been identified (Pahl, 1982), including:

the whole income system, in which one partner controls and manages the money;
the allowance system, in which control and management are split, with one partner controlling and one partner managing the money;
the shared management system, in which, in theory if not in practice, control and management are jointly shared.

Using this typology, the most common system adopted by the two-parent households in the survey was an allowance system (40 per cent), followed by a shared management system (31 per cent). Among the 20 low-income two-parent households, the whole income system was most common.

While a useful typology, its focus on what happens to the male wage obscures important factors, both within and beyond the household, which influence what women can spend on caring (Wilson, forthcoming). For example, the carer's responsibility for housekeeping, in its literal sense, places a priority on the payment of housing bills. Mothers in the study described a common budgeting cycle, in which the costs of housing and heating were met before they bought their family's food, clothes and other day-to-day items. Housing and heating, together with hire purchase commitments, were regarded as fixed costs, items where neither the timing nor the amount of payment could be controlled to any major extent by the family. Half (32) of the two-parent families paid these costs by a standing order from their bank account and another 20 per cent had their housing costs paid through the housing benefit system. Because of this pattern of meeting financial commitments to outside bodies first, spending on items more directly related to caring—including food, clothes, transport for women and children and playgroup expenses—were met from residual income. Independent of any controlling influence that the mother's partner might exert on her access to money, mothers found themselves drawing on the family income when it was at its most depleted. As two mothers living in low-income households explained:

'The bills [for rent, rates and hire purchase commitments] come first, they've got to, then the meters [for fuel] and then food and then any extra cash for any little bits and pieces.' (Mother with two children, living on supplementary benefit)

'As it see it, you get your bills in [for housing and fuel] for a certain amount and you've got to pay it. You can't sort of say—well, I know some people do—but I can't say that I won't pay that bill because I've got to buy some food. I put away the money to pay that bill and if I haven't got anything left over to buy food with, then we have to manage.' (Mother living with and caring for three children and an invalid father, on maintenance and single-parent allowances)

As these two comments indicate, women in poverty find themselves faced with the conflicting tasks of keeping the family healthy and keeping it out of debt. With food as the major item to be paid for with the family's residual income, the conflict between health-keeping and house-keeping is often experienced in an acute form:

'Food's the only place I find I can tighten up. The rest of it, they take it before you get your hands on it really. So it's the food. . . . The only thing I can cut down is food. . . . You've got to balance nutrition with a large amount of food which will keep them not hungry. I'd like to give them fresh fruit, whereas the good food has to be limited. Terrible isn't it, when you think about it?' (Lone mother with two children, living on supplementary benefit)

For mothers faced with the task of reconciling an inadequate income with the nutritional needs (and the hunger) of their children, small additional sources of income take on an importance disproportionate to their size. Where this additional money bypasses the family's financial management system, it provides not only a small but an independent source of income. The major source of independent income, available to all the mothers in the study, was child benefit (Walsh and Lister, 1985). The majority of mothers (58 per cent) in two-parent families received their benefit monthly, while most lone mothers (78 per cent) received it on a weekly basis. Most mothers were happy with the payment system they had; those receiving their benefit weekly preferred it this way and those receiving their benefit monthly preferred to be on monthly payments.

The reasons for these preferences lie in the different ways in which child benefit was integrated into the housekeeping budget. Mothers receiving their benefit weekly tended to pool their child benefit with their other income and devote it to food (including school dinners), to general household expenses and to playgroup fees, saving some where possible for their children's clothes and shoes. For those on lower incomes, it provided a vital mid-week stop-gap, tiding mothers over until their housekeeping allowance or supplementary benefit arrived. Mothers receiving their benefit on a monthly basis, on the other hand, were more likely to devote it to major items of expenditure. Those on lower incomes often spent it on 'the bills' for gas and electricity, again saving where possible for children's clothes and shoes. In the sample as a whole, the main item to which child benefit was put was housekeeping (40 per cent). A quarter (25 per cent) identified children's clothes and shoes as the main items on which they spent their child benefit and 16 per cent identified housing, fuel bills and general food bills. Eleven per cent identified *children's* food specifically.

Although recording broad patterns only, these statistics underline the complex ways in which child benefit, as an independent and reliable source of income, supports the mother's efforts to meet the health needs of her family. Where the mother's personal income was low, this was particularly apparent. However to appreciate the role played by child benefit, it had to be placed within the overarching structure of family finances, as the mothers did themselves. In the comments below three mothers, all living in two-parent households, explain where child benefit fits into this structure. The first two mothers identified themselves as operating a whole wage and an allowance system respectively; the third described what approximated to a joint management system:

'I get my supplementary benefit on a Saturday; £82 [for two weeks], then I just buy, or rather, try to buy in what I can. We don't run out of food in this house but we do run out of money. If you wanted a bit of bread or something, there should be some there, but the money doesn't last two weeks. They just give you enough for food, but that's all they give you. You can't put your fuel money away by the time you've been to the shop. And they don't allow you anything for your other debts you've got up yourself. I use my family allowance for a couple of my big bills and sometimes we do borrow off his grandma. His grandma does live around the corner and she is helpful that way. If we do run out, she will lend it and I give it back out of my family allowance.' (Mother in two-parent household with two children, living on supplementary benefit)

'I haven't the faintest idea what he earns, I really haven't. He's a managing director and if he pays his bills, I don't ask, I've no need to know. He gives it to me monthly, about £30–£40 a week it works out [for food, sweets, cigarettes, bus fares, presents] but I need my child benefit weekly. I wouldn't be able to budget otherwise. That's my children's money, they get their clothes and what they need out of that.' (Mother in a two-parent household with two children, married to the managing director of a local firm)

'We don't really organise our money, there is no organisation there. My husband pays the bills [for rent, rates and fuel] when they come whether we have the money or not. I pay for what we need by cheque or get money out [for food, school dinners, bus fares, sweets, cigarettes and children's clothes] thinking I've got the money which I haven't. But doesn't everybody? I spend my child benefit on children's clothes if they need them and also things for the house. I look on it as housekeeping money, children's clothes money, my money. He doesn't have it to spend on him, I have it to spend on us.' (Mother in an average-income two-parent household, with three children, married to a teacher)

The importance of an independent source of income for women was emphasised in other ways by the respondents. The two-parent household mothers discussed the issue in the context of disagreements about money. A third of this group identified money as a source of tension in their relationship, with their accounts suggesting that the issues of male control and female management mark out the areas of conflict. While women typically criticised their partners for the way they exercised financial control, their partners accused their wives of mismanagement:

'Sometimes we disagree about money, yes. He always says I spend too much. . . . His hobby is fishing and do-it-yourself things and he'll just go out and buy the tools and I think, "Oh that money, what I could have bought with that money." So I will budget and go around the markets and that, and find the best buys and he'll just go to the best shops because it is convenient, so yes, we do disagree about money.' (Mother in average-income, two-parent household, with three children)

'Yes. He won't give me enough. I used to see his money but now I never see it. He could walk out of this house with £90 in his pocket and I wouldn't know! He thinks I spend it on ridiculous things, but look at the house—you can see for yourself!' (Mother in average-income, two-parent household, with three children)

Lone parents, too, identified male control and female management as the dimensions on which disagreements over money had hinged. Two-thirds reported that money had been a source of tension between them. As other research has suggested, the woman's lack of access to resources appeared as a major factor in the final breakdown of their relationship (Evason, 1980; Homer *et al.*, 1984; Pahl, 1985a):

'Ronald didn't like me buying anything for the children. If I went out and bought them a pair of shoes and he wasn't with me, there was hell to pay when I got home. He just didn't like me spending money without his consent. If he wanted to go out and buy things, that was different. He was very keen on photography and he bought a lot of photographic equipment. What things he wanted to buy was O.K., but the basics and things I needed to get for the children, he thought were unreasonable.' (A divorced mother with two children, formerly married to a security officer)

For the mothers who were now living outside marriage, not only could such negotiations be avoided but the distinction between control and management was dissolved. With only one adult in the household, the separation of control and management did not arise. While the two-adult households devised a wide variety of systems to formalise economic power, the lone mothers in the sample all had the same system in which the money was both controlled and managed by women. The amount of money and the timing of its arrival were typically outside the mothers' control: maintenance payments, supplementary benefit levels and wages were externally fixed; they could change without warning; and they provided only a poverty line income. However, once the money had entered the family's economy, the mother had the power to organise it and spend it as she wished.

It was these two features—the poverty of lone motherhood and the control that it offered over the available resources—which appeared to provide the economic base of family life for the lone mothers in the study. It was in these terms that they described and assessed their financial situation. Over half (20) of the women stated that they were financially better off than they had been with their partners, four mothers said that they were neither better nor worse off and a third (14) felt that they were worse off as lone mothers:

'I'm much better off. Definitely. I know where I am now, because I get our money each week and I can control what I spend. Oh, he was earning more than I get but I was worse off than I am now. I am not so poor on £43 supplementary benefit a week for everything for me and two children as I was then. At least I know where the money's being spent and where it's not being spent. It might not last long but at least it's being put into provisions for the home.' (A separated mother with two children, living on supplementary benefit, formerly living with her husband, a carpenter)

'I'm better off, I think. Although I have less money, it's all mine to allocate where I want. It's made a difference to how I organise money because I have control now while before he used to control it. It's harder to make ends meet but I know where the money is going so it is easier for me.' (A separated mother with two children, living on supplementary benefit, formerly living with her husband, a shop manager)

'It's not easier or more difficult financially now. It's always been hard, now and when I was married, but for different reasons. I still owe money on the electricity and gas accounts. I only just have enough and I have to think "economise, economise!" all the time, but I feel better off because I have control of the money, even though I haven't got much. He spent too much on silly things like records and drink. Now I can budget for the bills.' (A separated mother with two children, living on supplementary benefit, formerly living with her husband, a taxi driver)

In identifying themselves as no worse off outside marriage than within it, the accounts suggest that lone mothers were balancing less money against more control. Single parenthood thus appeared to represent greater poverty within the context of greater economic power; fewer resources but increased access to them. It is this complex equation that appears to lie behind the mothers' assessment of themselves as 'better off poorer'.

However, it is not simply a question of control and access. The survey data suggest that we also need to understand how women in one- and two-parent families cope with poverty. We know that single parenthood involves additional expenses, particularly on child-care and that, deprived of economies of scale, a lone mother needs over three-quarters of the former family's total income to maintain the same standard of living after a separation (Finer, 1974; Chambers 1979). Yet at the same time it appears that single parenthood makes certain economies both possible and cost-effective in a way that they are not for mothers living with a partner. The survey can suggest only tentative interpretations of this complex and little-explored aspect of caring in poverty; these interpretations are offered in the section below.

COPING WITH POVERTY

Research, both historical and contemporary, has confirmed that, for the reasons discussed above, it is within the carer's budget that many families seek to contain their poverty. Further, we know from the testimonies of women in poverty that they cut first and cut most their own consumption (Women's Co-operative Guild, 1915; Spring Rice, 1939; Oren, 1974; Burghes, 1980). This personal sacrifice takes a particular form, obvious but easily overlooked. Coping with poverty involves women in cutting back on items of the family budget which they control. It also involves cutting back on items which are, or can be treated as, areas of personal rather than collective consumption. Items which are not within the women's jurisdiction to control (like the family car) or which provide benefits which are indivisible (like rent and rates) tend to be excluded from their economies.

The survey data illustrate these complex patterns of choice and compromise facing women in poverty. Among the 57 women on low incomes, a range of personal items—clothes, make-up, public transport, leisure—were no longer purchased. Second-hand clothes were provided by jumble sales and 'hand-me-downs', with birthdays and Christmas presents being the major and often only source of new clothes, most commonly given by parents. The women rarely went out socially without their children; as one mother noted, 'I don't really have a social life, not one where money is involved.'

The one major exception to this pattern of cutting personal expenditure was smoking. Half the mothers in the low income households smoked; for many it was the only item of personal expenditure they had. One lone mother caring for three young children explained:

'I think smoking stops me getting too irritable. I can cope with things better. If I was economising, I'd cut down on cigarettes, but I wouldn't give them up. I'd stop eating. That sounds terrible doesn't it? Food just isn't that important to me but having a cigarette is the only thing I do just for myself.'

With no further scope for cutbacks in personal expenditure, many mothers recognised that they had to turn to items of collective consumption that they could control. The most important, in terms of the money it consumes and its relation to child health, was food. Fuel and transport were also major items of collective consumption in which economies, potentially at least, could be made. In talking about the cutbacks they made in these areas, mothers again identified the scope for personal sacrifice. They cut down on what they ate, not what 'the family' ate. Among the low-income families, over half (32) of the mothers reported that they used their own diet as a way of making ends meet when money was short; among the higher-income families only a quarter did so.

Within these patterns are differences—small but suggestive—between the mothers in the one- and two-parent low-income families. Lone mothers were more likely to identify their diet as an area for cutbacks (68 per cent) than mothers in the 20 two-parent families (35 per cent). They were also more likely to be cutting down currently on what they ate—51 per cent compared with 7 per cent. Their accounts suggest that these differences reflect, at least in part, the fact that cutting down on their own food was easier for those women who were not also cooking for a partner. It also offered a more cost-effective strategy to lone mothers; women who were already committed to cooking 'a proper meal' for their partner could save little by not eating it themselves.

The 'individualising' of collective expenditure was apparent, too, in the areas of fuel and transport. Here again, the scope for such a strategy appeared greater for lone mothers and the economies that could be achieved were therefore more significant. The majority of women in low-income households reported that they were economising on fuel, with a higher proportion among lone mothers (86 per cent) than among the two-parent mothers (60 per cent). Reflecting these differences, the lone mothers used their heating more sparingly, both in terms of the length of time they used it and the number of rooms they heated. The comments of the two-parent mothers suggested that the presence of a partner made it more difficult for them both to control the family's fuel consumption and to make cutbacks in their own use of fuel. For example, two lone mothers described the scope for savings in personal fuel consumption in the following ways:

'I put the central heating on for one hour before the kids go to bed and one hour before they get up. I sit in a sleeping bag once they've gone to bed.'

'When the children are in bed, I turn the heating off and use a blanket or an extra cardigan.'

In contrast, two mothers in low-income two-parent households commented:

'I turn it off when I'm on my own and put a blanket on myself. Sometimes we both do in the evening but my husband doesn't like being cold and puts the heating back on.'

'If we're in, I'd turn the thermostat down if we need to economise and I turn the heating off if I'm the only one in.'

Women's use of transport suggests the same patterns were at work. One fifth of the lone mothers owned a car; the proportion of car-owners among the 20 low-income two-parent families was 75 per cent. Despite the apparent potential for saving, selling the car was rarely suggested by the two-parent mothers as a way of saving money. The car was not within their financial control but that of their partner. A mother could achieve savings in her and her children's use of transport by walking, but not by saving on 'his' car:

'I know he wouldn't give up his car. It's his car he says, and I don't think he'd be prepared to sell it unless we got into real financial difficulties. But if I could, *I'd* get rid of the car and give myself at least £5 more housekeeping. I don't drive, I walk everywhere.' (Low-income, two-parent respondent)

'He wouldn't sell the car so I suppose I'd have to give up smoking. I don't spend *any* money on clothes or make-up for myself so I couldn't save on that. Mostly, I think I'd give up cigarettes because I can't give up on my social life, on going out or anything, because we don't really go out.' (Low-income, two-parent respondent)

CONCLUSIONS

In tracing some of the complex links between domestic poverty and informal caring, this chapter has inevitably obscured others. It has deliberately focused on the issues of household structure and economic power; on the ways in which women's position as a single or second parent in the household affects their experiences of caring in poverty. With the small sample involved both the qualitative and the quantitative data need careful interpretation. Nevertheless they suggest a way of understanding a set of contradictory experiences: about caring for health on an income incompatible with its achievement; about the reduction in women's access to material resources as their need for them increases; about seeking simultaneously to secure family health and contain family poverty through the food one's family eats. While the particular contradictions which the chapter has highlighted may not prove to be pivotal ones, contradiction and compromise seem to form the central core of women's experiences of poverty in the home.

NOTES

1. The study was based at the Open University and financed by the Health Education Council.
2. The £105 cut-off point was based on the gross weekly income that a

two-parent family would have needed to earn in 1984 to achieve a net weekly income equivalent to supplementary benefit. While based on the gross earnings equivalent of a two-parent family, it was applied to all households in the study. It thus provides a more generous poverty line income for the 38 lone mothers in the study, since the supplementary benefit rate (and thus the gross earnings equivalent) is lower for one-parent families. Although this potentially inflates the numbers of lone mothers classified as poor, the application of the correct gross earnings equivalent to the single parent group did not affect the number actually classified as poor.

12 Making Ends Meet: Women, Credit and Debt

Gillian Parker[1]

In the long fine days of summer the little daughter of a working brick-maker used to order chops and other choice dainties of a butcher, saying, 'Please, sir, father don't care for the price just-a-now; but he must have his chops good; line-chops, sir, and tender, please—'cause he's a brick-maker'. In the winter, it was, 'O please, sir, here's a fourpenny bit, and you must send father something cheap. He don't care what it is, so long as it's cheap. It's winter and he hasn't no work, sir—'cause he's a brickmaker'. (Mayhew, *London Labour and the London Poor*, vol.II, 1862, p.368)

At the end of 1983, some £27,000 million was owed by UK residents on credit sale, hire purchase agreements and personal loans (Parker, 1986a). This represents some 15 per cent of all household expenditure excluding food during that year. Current estimates suggest that consumers will encounter difficulties paying at least 5 per cent of that amount and that at least 1 per cent will remain irrecoverable (NCC, 1980). The work of the County Courts shows clearly how the incidence of indebtedness has risen in recent years. In 1978 1.5 million proceedings were started; in 1983 this number had increased to 2.2 million (*Judicial Statistics*, 1985, Cmnd.9599). In addition to consumer default, debt has been growing in other areas. In September 1983 it was estimated that local authority (LA) housing arrears in England and Wales stood at around £240 million (a similar estimate in 1982 had judged this figure to be around £100 million) and that over one million LA tenants—about a quarter—were in arrears (Audit Commission, 1984). At the same time mortgage arrears have risen. One recent study found that around 2 per cent of one national building society's accounts were three or more months in arrears in 1983 and, by extrapolation, that the top ten national building societies might have around 100,000 borrowers owing more than three months' payments (Ford, 1985). The incidence of arrears among local authority mortgagors is even higher; approximately 3 per cent were at least six months in arrears at the end of March 1983 (Building Societies Association, 1985).

Fuel debt is also at a substantial level. In the 12 months to 30 June 1985 some 93,940 households in England and Wales had their electricity supply disconnected. Although this represents only 0.52 per cent of all electricity consumers, the figure is an increase of 2.6 per cent on the previous year. Beyond this there is a substantial 'hinterland' of householders who have difficulty paying their electricity bills but who do not suffer disconnection. It has been estimated (Parker, 1986a) that in all some 1.5 million consumers, including those who are eventually disconnected, experience some difficulty paying their electricity bills. This figure represents around 7.5 per cent of all domestic electricity consumers.

The position with regard to gas is only slightly better. In the 12 months to July 1985, 32,680 domestic consumers were disconnected—0.23 per cent of all such consumers. In all, around one million domestic gas consumers (6.5 per cent of the total) experienced some difficulty paying for their gas supply in the 12 months to June 1985.

Even if there were considerable overlap between households experiencing different forms of financial difficulty, it is clear that a substantial proportion of the inhabitants of England and Wales, and by extension the UK as a whole, experiences considerable financial distress.

To talk of 'households', of course, disguises the reality of where the burden of indebtedness lies. By virtue of the position they hold within two-partner households many women carry responsibility for budgeting (Pahl, 1980) and, thereby, for making ends meet in times of financial crisis. Further, by virtue of the position they hold in society women, though apparently equal users of credit with men (NCC, 1980), are likely to have unequal access to certain types of low-cost credit, including mortgages. As is so often the case, a legislative framework which appears to enshrine equality (in this instance the Consumer Credit Act 1974) is unable to redress those structural inequalities which actually determine access to resources. Finally, if the dissolution of marriage or a partnership brings with it a reduced income, women may be particularly susceptible to debt in their own right, including housing arrears, with the subsequent risk of losing their homes. They may also be left to carry responsibility for arrears and debts which were jointly incurred before the ending of the relationship.

This chapter will examine in turn, women's responsibility within the household for financial management (budgeting); women's access to consumer credit; and the impact and consequences of indebtedness for women. It will draw on historical accounts of women's lives as well as on empirical evidence, including a study of clients of the Birmingham Money Advice Centre (Parker, 1985b).

BUDGETING

Concern about the budgeting practices of the poor or 'labouring classes' has a long history, although it was not until Rowntree's study of families in York (Rowntree, 1901), and subsequent studies in other parts of the country (e.g. Lumsden, 1905; Rathbone, 1909) that any kind of objective or scientific approach was applied to this concern. Despite the best, and usually philanthropical, intentions of those who carried out these surveys their concentration on description rather than explanation led to a failure to examine household expenditure in its wider economic, social and cultural context. Most significantly, the constraints under which working-class women struggled to keep their families fed, clothed and housed were almost totally ignored.

These failings led the authors of budget studies to suggest remedies which were far removed from the realities of everyday life of those they sought to help. Perhaps the most glaring example of this misguided advice, and one which even now recurs every time debate on the adequacy of social security benefits is raised, was the reformers' obsession with porridge and pulses. For example, Lumsden (1905, p.141) claimed that 'a diet of a much higher nutritional value could be purchased for the money now spent, i.e. oatmeal porridge, beans, peas, lentils, etc.'. Rathbone (1909) raised some doubts about Rowntree's emphasis on the importance of 'farinaceous' foods, but it took the Fabian Women's Society's more detailed and involved examination of the lives of women budgeting on a pound a week to show why such foods played so little part in the diets of working people:

The visitors in this investigation hoped to carry with them a gospel of porridge to the hard-worked mothers of families in Lambeth. The women of Lambeth listened patiently, according to their way, agreed to all that was said, and did not begin to feed their families on porridge. Being there to watch and note rather than to teach and preach, the visitors waited to hear . . . what the objection was. It was not one reason, but many. Porridge needs long cooking; if on the gas, that means expense; if on an open fire, constant stirring and watching just when the mother is most busy getting the children up. Moreover, the fire is often not lit before breakfast. (Pember Reeves, 1913, p.57)

The visitors then pointed out that the porridge could be made the day previously and warmed up in the morning — still no porridge:

It seemed after further patient waiting on the part of the visitors, that the husbands and children could not abide porridge . . . Why? Well cooked the day before, and eaten with milk and sugar, all children liked porridge. But the mothers held up their hands. Milk! Who could give milk—or sugar either, for that matter. Of course, if you could give them milk and sugar, no wonder! They might eat it then even if it was a bit burnt. (ibid., pp.57–8).

The women pointed out that porridge quickly burnt in the old pots and pans they had available, and that porridge took the taste of whatever had been cooked last in the pan. To compound their difficulties these women were bound by the likes and dislikes of their husbands: 'One woman wound up a long and patient explanation of why she did not give her husband porridge with: 'An' besides, my young man 'e say, "Ef you gives me that stinkin' mess, I'll throw it at yer" ' (Pember Reeves, 1913, p.58).

This passage is worth quoting at length because it demonstrates so clearly how the lack of financial resources limited (and limits) not only the amount of any commodity that could be consumed but, more importantly, they type of commodity bought. Furthermore, the Lambeth investigation showed that while men might carry the outward, public burden of low wages it was women who carried the real and essentially hidden burden. Moreover this burden was hidden not just from public scrutiny but *within* the household itself. Women were driven to extraordinary shifts in order to stretch the available resources to meet the needs of their households and the whims of their husbands. Yet as Tebbut has indicated, even the most sympathetic of husbands was so far removed from the everyday reality of his wife's existence that he was 'at a loss to understand the shortsighted methods [his wife was] forced to employ just to get by'. ' . . . A woman's management of the family budget was a world entirely separate from that of her husband, necessity forcing it to encompass a thriving subculture of credit activities. Men were quite insulated from these strains' (Tebbut, 1983, pp. 38–9).

The rigid sexual division of labour within households made it the woman's responsibility to keep the household solvent, regardless of the inadequacy of the money she was 'allowed' by her husband and regardless of the personal deprivation that she might endure in doing so:

Poverty . . . increases the housewife's difficulties in relentless geometric progression and it is not surprising that she takes one comparatively easy way out by eating much less than any other member of her family. By saving the necessity to plan for herself, the difficulties of the budget are somewhat reduced. (Spring Rice, 1939, p.157)

Even in the 1930s when Spring Rice was writing, it was made clear that it was the woman's own fault if her family were not better fed:

'Very few of these women know how to make the best of their slender resources by the wise expenditure either of money or time . . . every opportunity, if not *compulsion* to learn her trade would immediately release her from much of her present bondage.' (ibid., p.107, my emphasis)

This compulsion to 'learn their trade' was to be inflicted on women on the basis that, by doing so, much could be done to relieve them 'even without dealing with the basic evil of poverty and without disintegrating the sacred edifice of the home . . .'! (ibid., p.106). One has to look very hard in any of these historical accounts for a similarly damning analysis of the women's husbands, who often retained substantial proportions of their earnings for their own use.

Time and social change have not materially altered the patterns of responsibility within households, especially where income is low. The meticulous, 'penny-pinching' budgeting required has been described in Edwardian households (Pember Reeves, 1913; Roberts, 1973); between the two world wars (Spring Rice, 1939; Hoggart, 1958); in the 1960s (Land, 1969; Marsden, 1973); and in the 1980s (Burghes, 1980). Most significantly, Jan Pahl's unpacking of the 'black box' of household income has demonstrated the persistence of women's burdens in financial management (Pahl, 1978; 1980; 1982; 1984). Despite the changes in women's position in the job market in recent years (Hunt, 1968; Martin and Roberts, 1984) in many two-partner households it is still the man who is the main wage-earner and the woman who assumes major responsibility for housekeeping. Within this framework various patterns for the allocation of money and domestic responsibilities are possible (Gray, 1976; Edwards, 1981; Pahl, 1982; 1984; see also Hilary Graham's chapter in this volume).

Some men pay all their wages to the woman for house-keeping and take no other part in family finances (the whole wage system). Others may pay all or some of the major commitments such as the rent or mortgage, rates or fuel bills and leave the remainder to the woman to be met out of his allowance to her and, where appropriate, her own income (allowance system). Yet other men may take a very active part in all aspects of housekeeping and budgeting, sharing decision-making and sometimes even the tasks equally, occasionally taking over completely (pooling system). More rarely some couples maintain independent financial arrangements, each taking responsibility for previously agreed commitments (independent management system).

These patterns of allocation and responsibility are determined by many factors; age, stage of the life-cycle, family size, income, cultural background, socio-economic class, and reliance on state benefits (Land, 1969; Gray, 1979; Edwards, 1981, Pahl, 1980; 1982). Among low-income and 'working-class' households the whole wage and allowance systems, which put the major burden on the woman, still predominate (University of Surrey, 1983). Although the whole wage system puts a considerable burden of responsibility on the woman (Pahl, 1980) it could be argued that in circumstances where resources are very limited it is more sensible for one person to have total financial control (Land, 1969). Evidence from a study of indebted households (Parker, 1985b) suggests, indeed, that patterns of financial management may be implicated in the genesis of debt. Of 56 households studied in depth, 30 consisted of two partners, with or without dependent children. Among these the allowance system was the most common pattern of allocating resources, used by just under a half. This was followed by the whole wage system, used by just under a third. Only a fifth used the pooling system. The pattern of allocation systems in this group was thus atypical, even compared with 'blue-collar' local authority tenants (University of Surrey, 1983). There was, in total, more reliance on the allowance and whole wage systems than would be expected. However, given the low income level of the households studied and their heavy reliance on state benefits, an even higher proportion of whole wage systems would have been anticipated (Land, 1969; Gray, 1979; Pahl, 1980; Edwards, 1981).

The relationships between the allocation system used, the proportion of the man's income used for the housekeeping allowance, and the number of major household expenses met by the man were also examined. In eight of the 14 two-partner households where the allowance system was used the man met none of the major household expenses (rent, fuel, food, clothing, hire-purchase). When major expenses were met out of the man's retentions these were usually electricity bills, rent or mortgage, or hire-purchase payments. Overall, the less responsibility the man took for meeting major expenses the more likely he was to devote more than 90 per cent of his income to the housekeeping allowance. However, the eight men who used the allowance system and met no major expenses out of their retentions were keeping 10 per cent or more of their income as personal spending money.

Even in households where considerable debts had been incurred, therefore, some men retained considerable portions of their own income, giving women housekeeping allowances which in some cases were quite inadequate. Beyond this, few men were closely involved in household financial management. This disengagement usually meant that men were less aware of the cost of running a home and thus less likely to update housekeeping allowances in line with price rises (NCC, 1975; Young, 1977). Women in such partnerships were left with all the decision-making and all the anxiety of making ends meet. If financial problems occurred they might remain concealed for a long time, causing considerable stress to the women as they struggled to keep their families fed and clothed while trying to fend off the consequences of indebtedness. Conversely, men who gave a housekeeping allowance but remained responsible for certain outgoings sometimes incurred debts without the women knowing of them.

From first principles it would seem sensible in indebted

households either to pool all resources and make joint decisions about expenditure or for one partner to take charge of all income and outgoings. Yet many in the study continued with the allowance system even when it was no longer (if it ever was) a sensible approach. Some men may have done this without fully realising the implications for their partners; others may have been hidebound by cultural and historical attitudes towards their role as breadwinner; yet others may have been mean or selfish or using the allocation of financial resources as a way of retaining power over their wives. Regardless of the reasons, it is highly likely that the mismatch between the needs of the household and the allocation pattern adopted contributed to the financial difficulties being experienced.

ACCESS TO CONSUMER CREDIT

Credit now finances approximately one third of all consumer spending in the UK. Only 15 per cent of the adult population has never used credit and, at any one time, 50 per cent have credit commitments of some sort (NCC, 1980). While the use of consumer credit has grown substantially since the 1950s, and particularly since the mid–1970s, and while the major proportion of the population now chooses credit as its preferred method of obtaining household and other goods, access to and use of credit is not evenly spread.

Contrary to what might be expected, those who make the most use of consumer credit are those whose jobs place them in the higher socio-economic groups. Moreover, consumers in these groups are likely to use a greater range of types of credit than are those in lower occupational groups. The use of bank loans, credit cards and budget accounts in stores are particularly associated with the professional and managerial classes. Skilled manual workers are likely to use finance company loans at some time while the use of shopping or trading checks seems to be restricted almost entirely to those in semi-skilled manual occupation (OFT/NOP, 1979; NCC, 1980).

While income and socio-economic status are of course closely linked, differences in the use of consumer credit between people at different income levels can be more marked than between people in different socio-economic groups. A low household income is likely to be associated with never having used consumer credit, although both variables are mediated by the age of the household head. Higher income groups have both greater and wider experience of credit use and are more likely to have current credit commitments than those with lower incomes. Similarly the type of credit used varies with income. Bank loans, credit cards, credit or budget accounts at stores and second mortgages for home improvements are most likely to be used by consumers with high incomes. Middle income group householders tend to have experience of hire purchase, mail order buying, loans from finance companies and credit sale. The lowest income groups, by contrast, rely on checks and vouchers and the tallyman (OFT/NOP, 1979; NCC, 1980).

Regardless of income, the heaviest users of credit tend to be young people, taking on credit commitments to furnish their homes at a time when other resources are tied up in child rearing.

Although the above account emphasises use of credit, it also essentially describes access to credit. This is not an area in which free choice operates, but is closely determined by income, occupation, tenure, sex, age, home address and culture (Baldwin, 1975; NCC, 1980). Further, these variables determine access to particular types of credit and thereby influence the cost of credit to different sections of the community. Paradoxically it is those groups who can least afford expensive credit who pay the most for it (Piachaud, 1974; Masey, 1977). Shopping checks and vouchers, small cash loans, clothing from warehouses and the tallyman currently attract interest rates of up to 97 per cent (*Which?*, January 1986). By contrast, bank personal loans cost around 22 per cent per annum and finance company loans vary between 24 per cent and 32 per cent.

It hardly needs to be pointed out that women are disadvantaged both in obtaining access to any credit, and in relation to the type and therefore the cost of the credit which they can obtain. Low income and occupational status, and the low incidence of owner-occupation among single, divorced or separated women in particular, ensure that bank loans, credit cards and other forms of 'cheap' credit are beyond their reach. Further, the arrangements made within two-partner households for financial control mean that many women have no option but to seek credit from those who provide weekly repayment arrangements. Inevitably, these are the most expensive forms of credit.

It seems, further, that the reasons for which credit is sought will vary between men and women. The Crowther Committee (1971) drew the distinction between credit for improvement (i.e. for the acquisition of consumer goods and services that would not otherwise have been obtained) and credit for adversity (i.e. when used to tide a household or individual over a financial crisis). This latter strategy is one employed in low-income households with few or no other resources to enable them to ride out a difficult time. Again, the combination of women's overall economic status and the burden which they often carry within the household will ensure that it is they who most often seek 'credit for adversity'.

This, of course, is not a new phenomenon. Women's role in keeping the family housed and fed in the nineteenth century led them to pawnbrokers and sometimes to the (usually illegal) moneylender. As Tebbut has suggested these women were even more bound by their class and culture than were their husbands. In the closely-knit communities beyond which women rarely travelled, the options for financial help at a time of crisis were friends and relatives, the pawnbroker and the moneylender. When not in straitened circumstances the tallyman or scotch draper, the burial club and the clothing club were the extent of most working-class women's credit activities. Familiarity with these 'credit and retail expedients . . . tended to mitigate the pull of more economical alternatives' (Tebbut, 1983, p.65).

Today women, particularly in working-class households,

still use forms of credit with which they are familiar, even when they might be able to obtain cheaper credit elsewhere (Parker, 1980). The weekly 'callers' from shopping check companies and small-scale moneylenders are often from well-established 'family' firms and this influences the way in which they are regarded by their customers. Women do business with the company that their mothers, and even grandmothers, used and the callers come to be seen as family friends. Inevitably, the personalisation of a business transaction makes it particularly difficult when customers become financially distressed. Women are often reluctant to reduce payments to their callers, even if the electricity is about to be disconnected or a notice to quit has been received, because by doing so they feel they would be 'letting down' the caller or getting him or her into trouble.

Further, some women are reluctant to cut themselves off from this source of credit by missing or reducing payments when no other form of credit may be available or acceptable. A shopping check or small money loan may be relatively expensive but it is at least legal; the alternative for increasing numbers is the extortionate and illegal loan secured on a child benefit or other benefit book (Crossley, 1984).

Credit as a form of insurance figured often in the responses of householders interviewed in the debt study (Parker, 1985b). The group as a whole were relatively isolated from family members or even friends and had little or no savings. With no safety barrier of informal sources of loans or nest-eggs, the credit trader or moneylender often formed the only line of defence against disconnection or eviction when times were hard. The fact that borrowing might only compound their difficulties was usually far from the front of respondents' minds when they took out loans in these circumstances. In this they were little different from the women of the nineteenth century, who were keen to keep in with their local pawnbroker for fear of losing a financial lifeline which might keep them and their families out of the workhouse (Tebbut, 1983).

GETTING INTO AND BEING IN DEBT

There appear to be two main ways by which households find themselves in debt. First, there are those households which have enjoyed an income adequate for their needs and which have taken on credit commitments for household and other goods in anticipation of their income continuing to be adequate. When this expectation fails, usually through loss of the main breadwinner's income, these commitments become burdensome. If outgoings on these commitments cannot be reduced then, sooner or later, other aspects of household finances—housing costs, fuel, food—will be put under pressure.

Secondly, there are those households which have chronically low incomes because they are dependent on low-paid work or on state benefits. Single parents in particular will be represented in this group. There will also be some in this group where the household is 'poor' because the main breadwinner retains a large proportion of his income for his own use. For such households the normal expectations of life as a late twentieth-century consumer cannot be sustained *other* than by recourse to credit or, occasionally, a single payment from the DHSS.

From information reviewed in earlier sections of this chapter it is clear that, whatever the initial cause of household indebtedness, women will be very involved in coping with it and may experience its effects more keenly than do men. Regardless of who takes out credit arrangements for household durables it is usually women who take responsibility for stretching the budget to meet these and other demands. If income falls it is women who bear the brunt of responsibility again. In households where income is chronically low, women will be involved in a daily battle not just to make money available for household durables but, more basically, to ensure that a roof is kept over the household's head, that fuel continues to be readily available and that adequate supplies of food are obtained. This struggle may lead women to become involved in clandestine credit activity, taking out loans from legal or illegal sources unknown to their partners in an attempt to tide them over financial crises.

At the lowest levels of income, distinctions between budgeting, access to credit and becoming indebted are blurred. Indeed the literature on low incomes and poverty, and studies of indebted households indicates a certain inevitability about debt, particularly in low-income households with dependent children (Parker, 1985b; 1986b). Land (1969) for example showed how buying clothes caused particular difficulties for large familes with low incomes. Unemployment, single parenthood and reliance on supplementary benefit have also been shown to be associated with difficulty in obtaining clothing and household durables and with getting into debt (Marsden, 1973; Daniel, 1974; Marsden and Duff, 1975; North Tyneside CDP, 1978; Clark; 1978; Burghes, 1980).

The debt study (Parker, 1985b) showed clearly how these budgeting pressures could easily develop into full-blown indebtedness. For example, respondents were twice as likely to mention using credit for their children's clothes and shoes as for their own. Women often found themselves having to buy their children new clothes and shoes at a time when their household budget could not sustain the expense outright. Using credit, especially in the form of shopping checks or mail order catalogues, allowed them to meet these needs fairly promptly. In contrast, adults waited until the cash was available (if ever) or found other, usually second-hand, sources. This was especially the case for women. Jumble sales, 'nearly new' shops and clothes passed on from friends and relatives figured prominently in these women's accounts of their own clothes-buying.

The presence of dependent children clearly put pressure in other ways on the households studied. Not only were households with children significantly more likely than others to have credit commitments for clothing, but they were also more likely to be repaying small cash loans. Such loans were obtained to pay fuel bills, to meet Christmas expenses, and in a few cases to meet everyday expenses.

Recourse to such loans often represented the thin end of the financial wedge.

Purchasing household goods also put a strain on the households studied. A fifth never bought new furniture or carpeting and the remainder relied very heavily on credit. Some households used credit for even relatively small goods such as pots and pans, bedding and curtains.

Once households on low incomes or reliant on state benefits begin to experience difficulty making repayments they have few options open to them which would enable them to recover solvency. Over a half of the households studied had incomes at or below 120 per cent of their supplementary benefit entitlement, and over two-thirds at or below 140 per cent. Thus few apparently had much scope for reducing expenditure but despite this some had attempted to do so, usually by cutting back on food. Opportunities for increasing income were also limited; out of 39 households with dependent children, seven single parents and five (female) spouses said that they could not increase their income because of lack of adequate child-care facilities.

This complex interrelationship of low income and debt, and its impact on women, can be highlighted by some examples from the debt study:

Mrs B. had first run into financial difficulties 16 months before she was interviewed, when her husband was receiving a very low wage and they moved into a new house. Before this they had always paid for fuel through pre-payement meters and had kept up with their rent. The combination of a higher rent, quarterly credit meters and the need for extra furnishings, albeit secondhand, made it increasingly difficult to cope. Soon after she had sought advice for her difficulties Mrs B.'s husband left home, leaving her in an even more difficult financial position and with all responsibility for their jointly incurred debts.

Mrs R. said that she had 'always' had money problems, not triggered by any particular event but rather as a result of long-term dependence on state benefits. Twelve years before being interviewed Mrs R.'s common-law husband had died leaving her with three young children. A subsequent relationship produced two more children before Mrs R.'s partner left to marry a younger woman. Mrs R. said that her financial position had always been precarious because she found it difficult to manage on state benefits. At one stage she had paid her rent through the direct payment system but had been removed from this when her rent arrears had been cleared. Mrs R. soon found herself in difficulties again when the pressure of feeding and clothing five children mounted. She might miss a rent payment to enable her to buy a pair of shoes but once one payment was missed she found it almost impossible to catch up.

Mrs E. had been experiencing financial problems for around three years when she was interviewed. Most of these problems had been caused by her husband's inability or reluctance to pay bills on time; Mr E. had originally assumed responsibility for paying the rent and fuel bills but had not always done so. In addition, he always kept Mrs E. very short of housekeeping money. Despite suffering from a serious stomach ailment Mrs E. had taken a part-time cleaning job to try to improve the household's financial position. This household's indebtedness was not caused by any apparent or objectively measured lack of money; Mrs E. had never known how much her husband earned but suspected with good reason that it was considerably more than he ever gave her. Neither were the debts caused by any 'inadequacy' or profligacy on Mrs E.'s part, yet it was she who had to deal with unpaid rent and fuel bills and she who had to seek help. Thus she took on public responsibility for a situation that was none of her making.

This one-sided shouldering of responsibility was evident in many two-partner households. Women in such households were more likely than men to report that their health, mental or physical, had been affected by their financial problems. For example, Mrs L. reported that her nerves were 'in a state' because she felt that she carried far more responsibility than did her husband.

Women were affected by the hopelessness as well as the drabness of a life spent always counting pennies and dreading the arrival of bills. Mrs G. said that she was more irritable than she had been because she had little to look forward to; she could no longer have her hair done or give her children a treat. Mrs W. felt that she had deteriorated 'in herself', losing interest in her appearance and feeling 'let down'. Mrs M., who had been deserted by her husband and had experienced considerable problems with the payment of benefits, had lost several stones in weight through stress and not being able to afford to eat as she had previously done. Her experiences, however, had also made her more tolerant and understanding of others. She felt she could now appreciate why some women turned to prostitution or why people committed suicide, because she had been tempted by both 'solutions' to her financial problems.

CONCLUSIONS

Despite the social and economic developments of the last 100 years the responsibility which women carry for household financial management remains essentially unchanged. Even in households where women now share control of financial matters the burden of management or budgeting is still with them. In more traditional household financial arrangements this responsibility remains where it has always lain.

The effects of this continuing imbalance in responsibility are at least twofold. First, in households where income is low the impact is transferred from the main breadwinner or claimant (i.e. the man) to the woman, who is responsible for making it stretch to meet household needs. Secondly, where income may be adequate but the main breadwinner retains a large proportion of it for his own use, household poverty is disguised. In either situation a sleight of hand is achieved which takes these issues out of the public domain.

Inability to cope on a low income or on an inadequate housekeeping allowance thus becomes a matter not of public policy but of private failure. By this process it becomes the housekeeper's (i.e. the woman's) fault that the household cannot pay the rent or meet the fuel bills or clothe the children. If women then turn to credit as an expedient to stretch inadequate resources they risk the disapprobation of those, both within and without the household, who observe their behaviour without understanding its root causes. Women experience further disadvantage in the type and cost of the credit they can obtain. This is not always a result of direct discrimination against women, but follows indirectly from their relative poverty, lack of secure employment and low levels of owner occupation. It is these characteristics which determine access to the increasingly important resource of cheap credit:

While the wealthy use credit as a clever expedient it remains an essential part of the lives of the poor, for whom the ability to borrow continues to offer an illusory freedom. Their only way of participating in the consumer society has been to buy goods on credit, but it is a second-class participation since the most advantageous forms remain closed to the unemployed, low paid and single parents. (Tebbut, 1983, p.201)

NOTES

1 This chapter is based, in part, on research carried out by the author at the Birmingham Money Advice Centre. The research was funded by the Esmee Fairburn Charitable Trust.

Postscript

Towards the Defeminisation Of Poverty

Jane Millar and Caroline Glendinning

The evidence presented by the contributors to this book should, we hope, have removed any lingering doubts that the 'feminisation of poverty' constitutes a new development. On the contrary, data from historical and contemporary sources, from large scale surveys and from small intensive interviews, from complex statistical analyses and from detailed ethnographic accounts, have consistently pointed to the enduring nature of women's poverty. Moreover the analysis and discussion which has underpinned these data has pointed clearly to the structural causes of women's poverty—to its roots in the sexual division of labour. This assigns to women a marginal economic role while grossly undervaluing the economic dimensions of the work they do undertake within and outside the home. Consequently systems of financial remuneration, whether in the labour market, in the private and occupational welfare sectors or in state welfare and social security provision are designed primarily for male breadwinners by male breadwinners. As the contributors to this book have described in a wide variety of different contexts, these systems place women at substantial disadvantage and increase the likelihood that poverty will be an enduring feature of women's adult lives.

Poverty has, therefore, always been a feminine issue. However there are two important features of women's poverty which are relatively new. The first, which we discussed at some length in Chapter 1, is the growing visibility of that poverty—a visibility towards which we hope that this book will have made some contribution. The second relatively new dimension is the development of employment and welfare policies which are likely actually to increase the extent and depth of women's poverty. Jane Lewis and David Piachaud alluded in Chapter 2 to this trend, not only in Great Britain but in other industrialised countries. Other contributors have described the likely impact of recent and proposed measures in the areas of, for example, employment protection, state and occupational pensions and access to income during unemployment.

Certainly over the last few years women (and men) have expended a great deal of time and energy in defending what few rights women already have which might protect them against poverty, or in pressing for very small, piecemeal gains. For example the 1986 Social Security Act, the culmination of 'the most substantial examination of the social security system since the Beveridge report 40 years ago' (DHSS, 1985a, vol. 1, para. 1.4) contains proposals which will have a severely detrimental effect on women's rights to income and on their consequent financial circumstances. As other contributors have already pointed out, young unemployed women, women in pregnancy and with young children, and, in particular, future generations of elderly women will be badly affected by the changes. In addition there has been no guarantee in the legislation that Child Benefit—often the only weekly income reliably available to non-earning women with children—will retain its real value. Indeed cuts in the value of Child Benefit have contributed towards the cost of the new means-tested Family Credit scheme, which has been designed to reduce wage demands from low paid men. In addition at least half a million children will lose their entitlement to free school meals, thereby both increasing the pressures on the household budget and also shifting the balance of their care further into the informal (domestic) sector (Land and Ward, 1986). Nevertheless, the situation could have been much worse. The Green Paper originally proposed the complete abolition of the state earnings related pension scheme, which would have been even more damaging for future generations of elderly women than the eventual modified retention of the scheme will be. An original proposal to pay Family Credit through the (male) wage-earner's pay packet rather than in the form of an order book to the (female) child carer was withdrawn during the final stages of the legislation's progress through Parliament. Child Benefit was not cut as dramatically as had originally been feared; and the threat of a defeat in the European Court finally pushed the government, in June 1986, to extend Invalid Care Allowance to married and cohabiting women, a measure which will direct some £55 millions (plus associated arrears of benefit) into the hands of an estimated 50,000 women carers of disabled or elderly people, who have no other source of independent income (*The Times*, 24 June 1986).

Real though these gains are, they are nevertheless minimal and may in the long run be far outweighed by other developments which will substantially increase women's poverty. For example, one of the main thrusts of present government policy (in line with a general commitment to privatisation) has been to shift responsibility for social security and income maintenance from the state to the private sector. Examples of this include the changes to SERPS and the moves to make employers responsible for paying benefits (unsuccessful in the case of family credit, but already in operation with statutory sick pay and due to be introduced in 1987 for maternity pay). The experience of statutory sick pay (Baloo *et al.*, 1986) shows the extent to which low-paid and part-time workers are likely to be adversely affected by this shift to the private sector, which is in any case both inherently structured to women's disadvantage and difficult to regulate adequately. Any immediate strategy for change must therefore involve the protection of whatever rights women currently have; but it is also clear, in view of the evidence and arguments presented in this book, that far more radical structural changes are needed. We would suggest that these changes lie in two main areas.

First, it is absolutely essential that the dimension of

gender is introduced into both the conceptualisation and the measurement of poverty. As both we and our contributors have argued, the failure to do so obscures not only the extent but also the specific *causes* of women's poverty—causes which are not on the whole experienced by men. In particular, we would argue that a considerable amount of work needs to be done to develop the concept of relative deprivation and to extend that concept to cover a wide range of material circumstances and behaviours. In particular the concept of poverty needs to be extended to encompass differential personal access to resources of all kinds, both material and non-material (including the important resource of time). Furthermore, as we argued in Chapter 1, the conceptualisation of poverty must take into account not simply the levels of the various resources to which individuals have access, but also the means by which those resources are obtained and, most importantly, the degree of autonomy and control which any individual is able to exercise over how those resources are disbursed. An important consequence of this reconceptualisation of poverty is that it challenges the hegemony of conventional economic theories which assign value and worth only to labour for which payment is received. It is clear from this book that the *unpaid* work which women do in servicing the home and caring for others can no longer be ignored as it is a major factor contributing to their poverty (and, conversely, to the physical and material wellbeing of men).

At a methodological level, it will be increasingly unacceptable and inappropriate to use levels of *household* income to measure poverty. Methods must be developed for identifying the income which is available to the individuals within these households, and for measuring their relative consumption of the goods and services which that income purchases. Quite simply it will no longer be acceptable for studies of poverty, whether carried out by governments or independent researchers, to assume in their calculations that women are financially dependent on men or that resources within households are shared and consumed equally. As we have shown in this book, these assumptions are themselves a major *cause* of women's poverty, in that women's real or presumed financial dependency structures their access to resources in the family, in the labour market and in the welfare state.

The second major area in which changes are clearly needed is in the policy and political arena. Here we would state our reservations about the effectiveness of strategies which seek to promote equal opportunities and equal rights. These 'liberal-reformist' strategies typically include the removal of overt discrimination against women; placing more women in positions of public power and in higher paid, prestigious jobs; and attempting to combat sex stereotyping in schools (Dale and Foster, 1986). The main problem with this approach (which is arguably the cause of its lack of effectiveness) is that it is based upon a fundamental assumption that it is possible, as well as desirable, to treat men and women equally. What such policies apparently fail to take account of are the structural differences in the patterns of and demands on women's lives which prevent their competing on 'equal' terms with men, however many new opportunities are made available. So, for example, 'it is no use talking about full employment if women cannot take on paid work because of their responsibilities for the care of dependants' (ibid., 1986, p. 135). Fundamentally, legislative and policy programmes for reform focus exclusively on promoting women's involvement in the public domain. They do not attempt to tackle the sexual division of labour which assigns to women major responsibility for (unpaid) domestic and caring work and which impedes and inhibits women from the start in taking advantage of whatever opportunities may be available. Furthermore such programmes also fail to address the fundamental inequalities experienced by women *within* the private domain of the home and family (although arguably a greater degree of economic and political activity by women outside the home would also shift the balance of power within the home more in their favour). Indeed, we would argue that such policies may actually increase the burdens experienced by women, by increasing the pressures on them to achieve in the occupational and public domains (against, it should be added, still substantial opposition and difficulty) but without any corresponding reduction in the responsibilities they carry for domestic and family affairs. The overall impact on women's experience of poverty is, therefore, likely to be very limited.

We would certainly argue that much remains to be done to improve women's continuing experience of inequality in the world of paid work. However the starting point for such changes needs to involve a radical reappraisal of the conventional assumption that men are the main (or sole) breadwinners. If, instead, men and women were to be regarded as breadwinners of equal status, a number of positive policies are immediately apparent. These include improving the training and labour market qualifications available to women; improving job opportunities by removing the current pervasive occupational segregation; and pursuing policies for equal pay far more aggressively than at present. It is important to recognise that action on these issues must come not only from government, both in enacting and enforcing regulatory legislation and as a major employer itself; but also from the organised labour movement which, with a few notable exceptions, has hitherto apparently been more concerned to defend and sustain male advantages in the labour market than to tackle the poverty and inequality experienced by women (Scott, 1984, pp. 86–7).

By tackling labour market inequalities, women are also likely in both the short and longer terms to derive greater benefits from those systems of state and occupational welfare which are tied closely to labour market participation and earnings. But in order for this to happen, major changes are also needed in these welfare systems to remove the disadvantage currently experienced by women. Feminist demands for the principle of disaggregation—for individuals rather than couples to be the basic unit for tax and social security assessments—have highlighted these disadvantages and brought them into the public arena (McIntosh, 1981). However there is a danger that, on its own, disaggregation might well further institutionalise both means-testing and the existing sexual division of labour (Lister, 1982; O'Kelly, 1985). What is needed therefore is a simultaneous assertion of women's right to an independent income of their own, combined with a vigorous challenge to the conventional sexual division of labour within the home. Only by relieving women of their present high levels of responsibility for domestic and caring work can they have any chance of participating 'equally' in the labour market and improving their present marginal position. This sharing of domestic responsibilities could be achieved by individual men taking on a bigger share of the unpaid labour involved in maintaining the households in which they live and in caring for their children and other dependants—as indeed some men already do. However as Janet Radcliffe Richards (1982, p.331) points out, 'we seem in no danger of being submerged in seas of recruits' to feminism. In order for this challenge to be mounted more effectively we would therefore argue that it is also essential for state policies to be developed which take a lead in lifting some of the burdens of responsibility for domestic work from women's shoulders. Such policies should ideally have both fiscal and service dimensions. For example, it is important that levels of social security benefits in general are raised and, in particular, that levels of income maintenance are considerably higher than at present for those women (and men) whose responsibility for the care of children or other dependants limit their labour market opportunities and earnings potential. Fiscal policies of this kind would help to make visible the currently invisible value of at least some of the work done in the home. More importantly such policies, combined with positive employment policies, would help to increase the sources of income to which women have *independent* access. This in its turn would help to increase women's financial autonomy and independence, and redress the financial inequality and powerlessness which women currently experience within marriage and the family.

State development of services is also an important plank in any set of policies aimed at alleviating women's poverty. In particular, services which help to share more broadly the responsibilities of caring for children and others would do much to combat the essentially private world of care. The development of such services would also help actively to promote an ideological and cultural environment in which care is legitimately viewed as a *collective* rather than a private responsibility. The call for the development of a 'social wage' has somewhat diminished over recent years; yet the notion of a 'social wage', which includes the provision of a comprehensive network of supportive health, education and welfare services, has at least as much to offer women as, say, straightforward campaigns for equal pay. Above all we need to challenge in our research, in our government policies and in our professional practice, the notion of women's financial dependency on men. This notion, as we have seen, both causes and perpetuates the poverty experienced by women.

What is required as an overall strategy is . . . policies . . . which treat men and women as equal breadwinners, by increasing their labour market qualifications and their job chances; by pursuing wage justice for women; by increasing income support and services for children; by increasing the adequacy of all social security payments—and by laying to rest forever the dangerous myth that dependency protects women. (Cass, 1985, p. 16)

Bibliography

Abbot, E. and Bompass, K. (1943) *The Woman Citizen and Social Security* (London: by the authors).

Abel-Smith, B. and Townsend, P. (1965) *The Poor and the Poorest* (London: Bell).

Abrahams, M. (1978) *Beyond Three Score Years and Ten* (Mitcham: Age Concern).

Ahmed, S. (1978) 'Asian girls and culture conflict', *Social Work Today* vol. 9, no. 47, pp. 14–16.

—— (1983) 'Blinkered by background', *Community Care* no. 483, 13 October.

Allen, S. and Wolkowitz, C. (1986) 'The control of women's labour: the case of homeworking', *Feminist Review* no. 22, Spring, pp. 25–51.

Anderson, A. (1981) *Redundancy Provisions Survey*, Manpower Commentary no. 13, Institute of Manpower Studies (Brighton: University of Sussex).

Anderson, M. (1983) 'What is new about the modern family: an historical perspective', British Society for Population Studies Conference Papers, *The Family* (London: OPCS).

—— (1985) 'The emergence of the modern life cycle in Britain', *Social History* vol. 10, no. 1, pp. 69–87.

Anwar, M. (1979) *The Myth of Return* (London: Heinemann).

Arnot, M. (1983) 'An analysis of the forms of transmission of class and gender relations' in S. Walker and L. Barton (eds), *Gender, Class and Education* (Sussex: Falmer Press).

—— (1986) 'State education policy and girls' educational experiences' in V. Beechey and E. Whitelegg (eds), *Women in Britain Today* (Milton Keynes: Open University Press).

Atchley, R. C. (1976) 'Selected social and psychological differences between men and women in later life', *Journal of Gerontology* vol. 31, no. 2, pp. 204–11.

Audit Commission (1984) *Bringing Council Tenants' Arrears under Control* (London: HMSO).

Austen, R. J. (1984) *Black Girls and the Youth Training Scheme*, Unpublished MSc. thesis in Race and Ethnic Relations, University of Aston.

Austerberry, H. and Watson, S. (1981) 'A woman's place: a feminist approach to housing in Britain', *Feminist Review* no. 8, Summer, pp. 49–62.

Ayers, P. and Lambertz, J. (1986) 'Marriage relations, money and domestic violence in working-class Liverpool, 1919–1939' in J. Lewis (ed.), *Labour and Love: Women's Experience of Home and Family* (Oxford: Blackwell).

Baldock, C. V. (1983) 'Public policies and the paid work of women' in C. V. Baldock and B. Cass (eds), *Women, Social Welfare and the State* (Sydney, Australia: Allen and Unwin).

Baldock, C. V. and Cass, B. (eds) (1983) *Women, Social Welfare and the State* (Sydney, Australia: Allen and Unwin).

Baldwin, S. (1975) 'Credit and class distinction' in K. Jones (ed.) *The Yearbook of Social Policy 1974* (London: Routledge and Kegan Paul).

Baldwin, S. and Glendinning, C. (1983) 'Employment, women and their disabled children' in J. Finch and D. Groves (eds), *A Labour of Love: Women, Work and Caring* (London: Routledge and Kegal Paul).

Baloo, S., McMaster, I., Sutton, K. (1986) *Statutory Sick Pay* (Leicester: Leicester Rights Centre and London: Disability Alliance).

de Beauvoir, S. (1977) *Old Age* (Harmondsworth: Penguin).

Becker, G. (1971) *The Economics of Discrimination* (Chicago: University of Chicago Press).

Beltram, G. (1984) *Testing the Safety Net*, Occasional Papers on Social Administration no. 74 (London; Bedford Square Press).

Bernard, J. (1973) *The Future of Marriage* (New York: Souvenir Press).

Berthoud, R. (1984) *The Reform of Supplementary Benefit; Working Papers* (London: Policy Studies Institute).

Beveridge, W. (1942) *Social Insurance and Allied Services*, Cmnd. 6404 (London: HMSO).

Bissett, L. and Huws, U. (1984) *Sweated Labour: Homeworking in Britain Today*, Low Pay Pamphlet no. 33 (London: Low Pay Unit).

Blair Bell W. (1931) 'Maternal disablement', *Lancet* 30 May, pp. 1171–7.

Booth, C. (1889) *London Life and Labour* vol. 1 (London: Williams and Norgate).

Booth, C. (1894) *The Aged Poor: Condition* (London: Macmillan).

Bornatt, J., Phillipson, C. and Ward, S. (1985) *A Manifesto for Old Age* (London: Pluto Press).

Bradshaw, J. and Piachaud, D. (1980) *Child Support in the European Community* (London: Bedford Square Press).

Braham, P., Rhodes, E. and Pearn, M. (eds) (1981) *Discrimination and Disadvantage in Employment* (London: The Open University Press and Harper and Row).

Brannen, J. and Wilson, G. (eds) (forthcoming) *Resources within Households* (provisional title) (London: Allen and Unwin).

Brion, M. and Tinker, A. (1980) *Women in Housing: Access and Influence* (London: Housing Centre Trust).

Brittan, A. and Maynard, M. C. (1984) *Sexism, Racism and Oppression* (Oxford: Blackwell).

Broad, R. and Fleming, S. (eds) (1983) *Nella Last's War* (London: Sphere).

Brown, C. (1984) *Black and White Britain* (London: Policy Studies Institute and Heinemann).

Brown, J. C. and Small, S. (1985) *Occupational Benefits as Social Security* (London: Policy Studies Institute).

Building Societies Association (1985) *Mortgage Repayment Difficulties: Report of a Working Group* (London: Building Societies Association).

Bulmer, M. (1986) *Neighbours: The Work of Phillip Abrams* (Cambridge: Cambridge University Press).

Burghes, L. (1980) *Living from Hand to Mouth: A Study of 65 Families Living on Supplementary Benefit*, Poverty Pamphlet no. 50 (London: Family Service Units and Child Poverty Action Group).

Burnell, I. and Wadsworth, J. (1982) 'Home truths', *One-Parent Times* no. 8, pp. 8–12.

—— (1984) 'Sponsoring and stereotyping in a working-class English secondary school' in S. Acker, J. Megarry, S. Nisbet and E. Hoyle (eds), *World Yearbook of Education 1984:*

Women and Education (London: Kogan Page and New York: Nichols).

—— (1985) 'Employment processes and youth training' in S. Walker and L. Barton (eds) *Youth, Unemployment and Schooling* (Milton Keynes: Open University Press).

Byran, B., Dadzie, S. and Scafe, S. (1985) *The Heart of the Race* (London: Virago).

Cadbury, E., Matheson, C. M. and Shann, G. (1906) *Women's Work and Wages* (London: T. Fisher Unwin).

Caine, B. (1982) 'Beatrice Webb and the Woman Question', *History Workshop Journal* no. 14, Autumn, pp. 23–43.

Callender, C. (1985a) 'Gender and social policy: women and the redundancy payments scheme', *Journal of Social Policy* vol. 14, no. 2, pp. 189–213.

—— (1985b) 'Unemployment: the case for women' in M. Brenton and C. Jones (eds), *The Yearbook of Social Policy 1984–5* (London: Routledge and Kegan Paul).

—— (1986a) 'Women seeking work' in S. Fineman (ed.), *Unemployment: Personal and Social Consequences* (London: Tavistock).

—— (1986b) 'Women and the redundancy process: a case study' in R. M. Lee (ed.), *Redundancy, Layoffs and Plant Closures: The Social Impact* (London: Croom Helm).

Campbell, B. (1984) *Wigan Pier Revisited: Poverty and Politics in the 1980s* (London: Virago).

Campling, J. (1981a) *Images of Ourselves* (London: Routledge and Kegan Paul).

—— (1981b) 'Women and disability' in A. Walker and P. Townsend (eds), *Disability in Britain* (Oxford: Martin Robertson).

Caradog Jones, D. (ed.) (1934) *Social Survey of Merseyside* (Liverpool: Liverpool University Press).

Carby, H. V. (1982) 'White women listen!: black feminism and the boundaries of sisterhood' in Centre for Contemporary Cultural Studies, *The Empire Strikes Back; Race and Racism in 70s Britain* (London: Hutchinson).

Cass, B. (1985) *Poverty in the 1980s: Causes, Effects and Policy Options*, Paper presented to ANZAAS Congress, Monash University, August 1985.

Catholic Commission for Racial Justice (1982) *Rastafarians in Jamaica and Britain*, Notes and Reports, January (London: CCRJ).

Central Statistical Office (1985a) *Annual Abstract of Statistics* no. 121 (London: HMSO).
—— (1985b) *Social Trends 15* 1985 edn (London: HMSO).
—— (1986) *Social Trends 16* 1986 edn (London: HMSO).
Chambers, D. (1979) *Making Fathers Pay: The Enforcement of Child Support* (Chicago: University of Chicago Press).
Charles, N. and Kerr, M. (1985) *Attitudes to the Feeding and Nutrition of Young Children* (London: Health Education Council).
Cheetham, J. (1981) 'Open your eyes to strength', *Community Care* no. 392, 24 December.
Child, J., Loveridge R., Harvey, J. and Spencer, A. (1985) 'The quality of employment in services' in T. Forrester (ed.), *The Information Technology Revolution* (Oxford: Blackwell).
Clark, M. (1978) 'The unemployed on supplementary benefit: living standards and making ends meet on a low income', *Journal of Social Policy* vol. 7, no. 4, pp. 385–410.
Cohen, R. and Lakhani, B. (1986) *National Welfare Benefits Handbook* (London: Child Poverty Action Group).
Cohen, S. (1981) *The Thin End of the White Wedge*, Immigration Handbook no. 5 (Manchester: Manchester Law Centre).
Cole, D. with Utting, J. (1962) *The Economic Circumstances of Old People* (Welwyn: Codicote Press).
Community Relations Commission (1975) *Who Minds?* (London: CRC).
Commission for Racial Equality (1984) *Race and Council Housing in Hackney—Report of a Formal Investigation* (London: CRE).
Commission on Industrial Relations (1974) *Retail Distribution*, Report no. 89 (London: HMSO).
Cooper, S. (1985) *Observation in Supplementary Benefit Offices* (London: Policy Studies Institute).
Coote, A. (1981) 'The AES: a new starting point?', *New Socialist* no. 2, November/December, pp. 4–7.
Coyle, A. (1985) 'Going private: the implications of privatisation for women's work', *Feminist Review*, no. 21, Winter, pp. 6–22.
—— (1984) *Redundant Women* (London: The Women's Press).
Cragg, A. and Dawson, T. (1981) *Qualitative Research Among Homeworkers*, Research Paper no. 21 (London: Department of Employment).
Cragg, A. and Dawson, T. (1984) *Unemployed Women: a Study of Attitudes and Experiences*, Research Paper no. 47 (London: Department of Employment).

Craig, C., Garnsey, E. and Rubery, J. (1985) *Payment Structures and Smaller Firms: Women's Employment in Segmented Labour Markets*, Research Paper no. 48 (London: Department of Employment).

Cretney, S. (1984) *Principles of Family Law* 4th edition (London: Sweet and Maxwell).

Crine, S. (1981) *The Pay and Conditions of Homeworkers*, Submission to the House of Commons Select Committee on Employment (London: Low Pay Unit).

Cross, M., Edmonds (now Cook), J. and Sergeant, R. (1983) *Ethnic Minorities: Their Experience on YOP* (Sheffield: Manpower Services Commission).

Crossley, M. (1984) 'Tackling the scandal of illegal money lenders', *Municipal Review* no. 647, p. 56.

Crowther, A. (1982) 'Family responsibility and state responsibility in Britain before the Welfare State', *Historical Journal* vol. 25, no. 2, pp. 131–45.

Crowther Committee (1971) *Report of the Committee on Consumer Credit*, Cmnd. 4596 (London: HMSO).

Curran, M. (1985) *Recruiting Gender Stereotypes for the Office*, EOC Research Bulletin no. 9, Spring (Manchester: Equal Opportunities Commission).

Dale, J. and Foster, P. (1986) *Feminists and State Welfare* (London: Routledge and Kegan Paul).

Daniel, W. W. (1974) *A National Survey of the Unemployed* vol. XL, Broadsheet no. 546 (London: Political and Economic Planning).

David, M. (1983) 'The new right, sex education and social policy: towards a new moral economy in Britain and the USA' in J. Lewis (ed.), *Women's Welfare, Women's Rights* (London: Croom Helm).

David, M. (1986) 'Morality and maternity: towards a better union than the moral right's family policy', *Critical Social Policy* vol. 6, no. 1, pp. 40–56.

David, M. and New, C. (1986) *For the Children's Sake* (London: Penguin).

Davidoff, L. (1978) 'The separation of home and work?' in S. Burman (ed.) *Fit Work for Women* (London: Croom Helm).

Davis, A. (1982) *Women, Race and Class* (London: The Women's Press).

Deem, R. (1978) *Women and Schooling* (London: Routledge and Kegan Paul).

Deem, R. (ed.) (1980) *Schooling for Women's Work* (London: Routledge and Kegan Paul).

Delphy, C. (1984) *Close to Home: A Materialist Analysis of Women's Oppression* (London: Hutchinson).

Department of Employment (1984a) *New Earnings Survey, 1984* (London: HMSO).

—— (1984b) *Redundancy Payments* (London: HMSO).

—— (1984c) *Employment Gazette* vol. 92, no. 12, p. 559.

—— (1985a) *New Earnings Survey 1985* (London: HMSO).

—— (1985b) 'Pension scheme membership in 1983', *Employment Gazette* vol. 93, no. 12, pp. 494–7.

—— (1986a) 'Industrial tribunals—discrimination cases', *Employment Gazette* vol. 94, no. 2, pp. 52–6.

—— (1986b) *Family Expenditure Survey 1984* (London: HMSO).

Department of Employment and Productivity (1971) *British Labour Statistics, Historical Abstract 1886–1968* (London: HMSO).

Department of Health and Social Security (1983) *Tables on Families with Low Incomes—1981* (London: DHSS).

—— (1984) *Population, Pension Costs and Pensioners' Incomes: Background Paper for the Inquiry into Provision for Retirement* (London: HMSO).

—— (1985a) *The Reform of Social Security* vols. 1–4, Cmnd. 9517–9520 (London: HMSO).

—— (1985b) *Reform of Social Security: Programme for Action*, Cmnd. 9691 (London: HMSO).

—— (1986a) *Low Income Families 1983* (London: HMSO).

—— (1986b) *Social Security Statistics 1985* (London: HMSO).

Dex, S. (1984) *Women's Work Histories: Analysis of the Women and Employment Survey*, Research Paper no. 46 (London: Department of Employment).

—— (1985) *The Sexual Division of Work* (Brighton: Wheatsheaf Books).

Dibben, M. (1986) 'The cost of women's right to work', *The Guardian* April 3.

Drake, B. (1920) *Women in Trade Unions* (London: Labour Research Department).

Dyhouse, C. (1977) 'Good wives and little mothers: social anxieties and schoolgirls' curriculum, 1880–1920', *Oxford Review of Education* vol. 3, no. 1, pp. 21–36.

—— (1981) *Girls Growing Up in Late Victorian and Edwardian England* (London: Routledge and Kegan Paul).

Economic Advisers Office (undated) *Lone Parents: On and Off Supplementary Benefit* (DHSS: mimeo).

Edmonds (now Cook), J. (1981) 'Asian girls, English assumptions,' *Youth in Society* no. 60, November.

Edmonds (now Cook), J. and Powell, D. (1985) 'Are you a racist too?', *Community Care* no. 580, 19 September.

Edwards, M. (1981) *Financial Arrangements Within Families* (Canberra, Australia: National Women's Advisory Council).

Eekelaar, J. and MacLean, M. (1986) *Maintenance After Divorce* (Oxford: Clarendon Press).

Elias, P. and Main, B. (1982) *Women's Working Lives: Evidence from the National Training Survey* (Institute for Employment Research, University of Warwick).

Equal Opportunities Commission (1979) *Health and Safety Legislation* (Manchester: Equal Opportunities Commission).

—— (1982) *Caring for the Elderly and Handicapped: Community Care Policies and Women's Lives* (Manchester: Equal Opportunities Commission).

—— (1984) *Eighth Annual Report: 1983* (London: HMSO).

—— (1985) *Reform of Social Security: Response of the EOC* (Manchester: Equal Opportunities Commission).

—— (1986a) *Social Security Bill*, EOC Briefing, March (Manchester: Equal Opportunities Commission).

—— (1986b) *Building Business . . . Not Barriers: Implications for Women of the White Paper Proposals Relating to Part-Time Workers and Maternity Rights*, EOC Briefing, July (Manchester: Equal Opportunities Commission).

Ermisch, J. (1983) *The Political Economy of Demographic Change* (London: Heinemann).

Evans, J. M. (1983) *Immigration Law*, 2nd edn (London: Sweet and Maxwell).

Evason, E. (1980) *Just Me and the Kids: A Study of Single Parent Families in Northern Ireland* (Belfast: Equal Opportunities Commission for Northern Ireland).

Fabian Women's Group (1911) *How the National Insurance Bill Affects Women* (London: Fabian Women's Group).

Family Policy Studies Centre (1983) *Divorce: 1983 Matrimonial and Family Proceedings Bill, Briefing Paper* (London: Family Policy Studies Centre).

Feinstein, C. F. (1972) *National Income, Expenditure and Output of the UK, 1855–1965* (Cambridge: Cambridge University Press).

Fenton, S., Davies, T., Means, R. and Burton, P. (1984) *Ethnic Minorities and The Youth Training Scheme* (Sheffield: Manpower Services Commission and University of Bristol).

Ferri, E. (1976) *Growing up in a One-Parent Family* (London: National Foundation for Educational Research).

Fiegehen, G. C., Lansley, P. S. and Smith, A. D. (1977) *Poverty and Progress in Britain 1953–1973* (Cambridge: Cambridge University Press).

Finch, J. (1984) 'Community Care: developing non-sexist alternatives', *Critical Social Policy* vol. 3, no. 3, pp. 6–19.

Finch, J. And Groves, D. (eds) (1983) *A Labour of Love: Women, Work and Caring* (London: Routledge and Kegan Paul).

Finer, M. (1974) *Report of the Committee on One-Parent Families*, Cmnd. 5629 (London: HMSO).

Foner, N. (1979) *Jamaica Farewell—Jamaican Migrants in London* (London: Routledge and Kegan Paul).

Ford, J. (1985) 'High short-term mortgage debts', *Roof* vol. 10, no. 3, p.6.

Freeman, C. (1982) 'The understanding employer' in J. West (ed.), *Work, Women and the Labour Market* (London: Routledge and Kegan Paul).

Gardiner, J. (1977) 'Women in the labour process and class structure' in A. Hunt (ed.), *Class and Class Structure* (London: Lawrence and Wishart).

GB (1909) *Report of the Royal Commission on the Poor Laws and the Relief of Distress*, Cmnd. 4499 (London: HMSO).

Glendinning, C. (1980) *After Working All These Years* (London: Disability Alliance).

Gordon, D. M., Edwards, R. and Reich, M. (1982) *Segmented Work, Divided Workers* (London: Cambridge University Press).

Gordon, P. (1984) *Deportations and Removals* (London: The Runnymede Trust).

Gordon, P. and Newnham, A. (1985) *Passports to Benefits? Racism in Social Security* (London: Child Poverty Action Group and the Runnymede Trust).

Gosden, P. H. J. H. (1972) *The Evolution of a Profession* (Oxford: Blackwell).

Government Actuary (1958) *Occupational Pension Schemes—a Survey (London: HMSO)*.

—— (1966) *Occupational Pension Schemes—a New Survey* (London: HMSO).

—— (1968) *Occupational Pension Schemes—Third Survey* (London: HMSO).

—— (1972) *Occupational Pension Schemes 1971—Fourth Survey* (London: HMSO).

—— (1978) *Occupational Pension Schemes 1975—Fifth Survey* (London: HMSO).

—— (1981) *Occupational Pension Schemes 1979—Sixth Survey* (London: HMSO).

—— (1986) *Occupational Pension Schemes 1983* (London: HMSO).

Graebner, N. (1980) *A History of Retirement* (New Haven: Yale University Press).

Graham, H. (1983) 'Caring: a labour of love' in J. Finch and D. Groves (eds), *A Labour of Love: Women, Work and Caring* (London: Routledge and Kegan Paul).

Graham, H. (1984) *Women, Health and Family* (Brighton: Wheatsheaf Books).

—— (1986) *Caring for the Family* (London: Health Education Council).

Grant, L. and Martin, I. (1982) *Immigration Law and Practice* (London: The Cobden Trust).

Gray, A. (1976) 'Family budgeting systems: some findings from studies in Edinburgh and Portsmouth' in N. Newman (ed.), *In Cash or Kind: The Place of Financial Assistance in Social Work*, 3rd edn (Edinburgh: Edinburgh University).

—— (1979) 'The working-class family as an economic unit' in C. Harris (ed.), *The Sociology of the Family*, Sociological Review Monograph no. 28 (Keele, Staffs: University of Keele).

Gregory, J. (1982) 'Equal Pay and Sex Discrimination: why women are giving up the fight?', *Feminist Review* no. 10, Spring, pp. 75–89.

Griffin, C. (1985) *Typical Girls?* (London: Routledge and Kegan Paul).

Groves, D. (1983) 'Members and survivors: women and retirement pensions legislation' in J. Lewis (ed.), *Women's Welfare, Women's Rights* (London: Croom Helm).

—— (1986) *Women and Occupational Pensions 1870–1983: An Exploratory Study*, Unpublished PhD thesis, University of London.

Groves, D. and Finch, J. (1983) 'Natural selection: perspectives on entitlement to the invalid care allowance' in D. Groves and

J. Finch (eds), *A Labour of Love: Women, Work and Caring* (London: Routledge and Kegan Paul).

Hakim, C. (1978) 'Sexual divisions within the labour force: occupational segregation', *Employment Gazette* vol. 86, no. 11, pp. 1264–8.

—— (1979) *Occupational Segregation*, Research Paper no. 9 (London: Department of Employment).

—— (1980) 'Homeworking: some new evidence', *Employment Gazette* vol. 88, no. 10, pp. 1105–10.

—— (1981) 'Job segregation: trends in the 1970s', *Employment Gazette* vol. 89, no. 12, pp. 521–9.

——(1984) 'Homework and outwork', *Employment Gazette* vol. 92, no. 1, pp. 7–12.

Hall, C. (1979) 'The early formation of Victorian domestic ideology' in S. Burman (ed.), *Fit Work for Women* (London: Croom Helm).

Hamill, L. (1978) *Wives as Sole and Joint Breadwinners*, Government Economic Service Working Paper no. 15 (London: HMSO).

Hanmer, J. and Leonard, D. (1984) 'Negotiating the problem: the DHSS and research on violence in marriage' in C. Bell and H. Roberts (eds), *Social Researching; Politics, Problems, Practice* (London: Routledge and Kegan Paul).

Harris, A. I., Cox, E. and Smith, C. R. W. (1971) *Handicapped and Impaired in Great Britain* Part 1 (London: HMSO).

Haskey, J. (1986) 'One-parent families in Britain', *Population Trends* no. 45, pp. 5–13.

Heclo, H. (1974) *Modern Social Politics in Britain and Sweden* (New Haven and London: Yale University Press).

Henwood, M. and Wicks, M. (1984) *The Forgotten Army: Family Care and Elderly People*, Briefing Paper (London: Family Policy Studies Centre).

Higgs, M. (1910) *Where Shall She Live? The Homelessness of the Working Woman* (London: P. S. King).

Hoel, B. (1982) 'Contemporary clothing "sweatshops", Asian female labour and collective organization' in J. West (ed.), *Work, Women and the Labour Market* (London: Routledge and Kegan Paul).

Hoggart, R. (1958) *The Uses of Literacy* (Harmondsworth: Penguin).

Holcombe, L. (1973) *Victorian Ladies at Work: Middle-Class*

Working Women in England and Wales, 1850–1914 (Newton Abbot, Devon: David and Charles).

Homer, M., Leonard, A. E. and Taylor, M. P. (1984) *Private Violence: Public Shame* (Cleveland: Cleveland Refuge Aid for Women and Children).

Houghton, H. (1973) *Separated Wives and Supplementary Benefit* (London: Department of Health and Social Security).

Howe, L. E. A. (1985) 'The "deserving" and the "undeserving": practice in an urban, local social security office', *Journal of Social Policy* vol. 14, no. 1, pp. 49–72.

Hunt, A. (1968) *A Survey of Women's Employment* (London: HMSO).

Hunt, A. (1978) *The Elderly at Home: A Study of People Aged Sixty-five and Over Living in the Community in England in 1976* (London: HMSO and OPCS).

Husband, C. (1978) 'Racism in social work', *Community Care* 29 November, no. 241.

Jamdagni, L. (1980) *Hamari Rangily Zindagi (Our Colourful Lives)* (Leicester: National Association of Youth Clubs).

James, C. (1984) *Occupational Pensions: The Failure of Private Welfare* (London: Fabian Society).

James, E. (1962) 'Women at work in twentieth-century Britain: the changing structure of female employment', *The Manchester School of Economic and Social Studies Quarterly* vol. XXX, no. 3, pp. 283–300.

Jones, H. (1983) 'Employers' welfare schemes and industrial relations in inter-war Britain', *Business History* vol. XXV, no. 1, pp. 61–75.

Joshi, H. (1984) *Women's Participation in Paid Work: Further Analysis of the Women and Employment Survey*, Research Paper no. 45 (London: Department of Employment) to be read, if possible, in conjunction with 'Research Paper no. 45: Author's note on an error' (Department of Employment 1985.)

—— (1986a) 'Participation in paid work: evidence from the Women and Employment Survey' in R. Blundell and I. Walker (eds), *Unemployment, Search and Labour Supply* (Cambridge: Cambridge University Press).

—— (1986b) 'Gender inequality in the labour market and the domestic division of labour' in P. Nolan and S. Paine (eds), *Rethinking Socialist Economics* (Cambridge: Polity Press in association with Basil Blackwell, London).

Joshi, H. and Owen, S. (1981) *Demographic Indicators of*

Women's Work Participation in Post-War Britain (London: Centre for Population Studies).

Joshi, H. and Newell, M. L. (1987a) *Pay Differences between Men and Women: Longitudinal Evidence from the Birth Cohort of 1946*, Discussion Paper 156, Centre for Economic Policy Research, London.

Joshi, H. and Newell, M. L. (1987b) *Family Responsibilities and Pay Differentials: Evidence from Men and Women Born in 1946*, Discussion Paper 157, Centre for Economic Policy Research, London.

Judicial Statistics (1985) *Annual Report 1984*, Cmnd. 9599 (London: HMSO).

Kaluzynska, E. (1980) 'Wiping the floor with theory—a survey of writings on housework', *Feminist Review* no. 6, pp. 27–54.

Khan, V. (1976) 'Purdah in the British situation' in D. Leonard Barker and S. Allen (eds), *Dependence and Exploitation in Work and Marriage* (Harlow: Longman).

Kidd, T. (1985) *Equal Treatment: A Study of Social Policy Implementation*, Unpublished paper (Worcester: Worcester College of Higher Education).

Knight, I. (1981) *Family Finances*, OPCS Occasional Paper no. 26 (London: HMSO).

Land H (1969) *Large Families in London*, Occasional Papers on Social Administration no. 32 (London: Bell).

—— (1978) 'Who cares for the family?', *Journal of Social Policy* vol. 7, no. 3, pp. 357–84.

—— (1980) 'The family wage', *Feminist Review* vol. 6, pp. 55–57.

—— (1983a) 'Who still cares for the family?' in J. Lewis (ed.), *Women's Welfare, Women's Rights* (London: Croom Helm).

—— (1983b) 'Poverty and gender: the distribution of resources within families' in M. Brown (ed.), *The Structure of Disadvantage* (London: Heinemann).

—— (1986) 'Women and children last: *reform* of social security?' in M. Brenton and C. Ungerson (eds), *The Yearbook of Social Policy in Britain, 1985–6* (London: Routledge and Kegan Paul).

Land, H. and Rose, H. (1985) 'Compulsory altruism for all or an altruistic society for some?' in P. Bean, J. Ferris and D. Whynes (eds), *In Defence of Welfare* (London: Tavistock).

Land, H. and Ward, S. (1986) *Women Won't Benefit* (London: National Council for Civil Liberties).

Layard, R., Piachaud, D. and Stewart, M. (1978) *The Causes of*

Poverty, Royal Commission on the Distribution of Income and Wealth, Background Paper no. 5 (London: HMSO).

Leete, R. (1978) 'One-parent families: numbers and characteristics', *Population Trends* no. 13, pp. 4–9.

Leicestershire Child Poverty Action Group (1983) *Poverty Pay* (Leicester: CPAG)

Leira, A. (ed.) (1983) *Work and Womanhood: Norwegian Studies* (Oslo: Institutt for samfunnsforskning).

Letts, P. (1983) *Double Struggle: Sex Discrimination and One-Parent Families* (London: National Council for One-Parent Families).

Levie, H., Gregory, D. and Callender, C. (1984) 'Redundancy pay: trick or treat' in H. Levie, D. Gregory and N. Lorentzen (eds), *Fighting Closures* (Nottingham: Spokesman).

Levitas, R. (1986) *The Ideology of the New Right* (Cambridge: Polity Press).

Lewis, J. (ed.) (1983) *Women's Welfare, Women's Rights* (London: Croom Helm).

Lewis, J. (1984) *Women in England, 1870–1940* (Brighton: Wheatsheaf Books).

Lewis, J. C. (1985) 'Technical change in retailing: its impact on employment and access', *Environment and Planning: Planning and Design* vol. 12, part A, pp. 165–91.

Lipsky, M. (1981) *Street Level Bureaucracy* (New York: Russell Sage Foundation).

Lister, R. (1982) *Beyond Disaggregation*, Unpublished paper for Rights of Women Conference on Beyond Marriage, London, October.

Littler, C. and Salaman, G. (1984) *Class at Work* (London: Batsford).

Llewellyn Davies, M. (1915) *Maternity: Letters From Working Women* (London: Bell).

Lonsdale, S. (1980) 'Sickness—who pays?', *Low Pay Review* no. 3 (London: Low Pay Unit).

—— (1985a) *Work and Inequality* (London: Longman).

—— (1985b) 'Extension of Statutory Sick Pay', *Industrial Law Journal* vol. 14, no. 4, pp. 263–8.

Lord Chancellor's Department (1985) *Occupational Pension Rights on Divorce: A Consultation Paper* (London: Lord Chancellor's Department).

Low Pay Unit (1983) *Who Needs the Wages Councils?* (London: Low Pay Unit).

Lumsden, D. (1905) *An Investigation into the Income and Expenditure of Seventeen Brewery Families and a Study of their Diets* (Dublin: Guinness & Son Ltd).

Lynes, T. (1986) 'Welfare watch', *New Society* vol. 75, no. 1207, p. 280.

Mack, J. and Lansley, S. (1985) *Poor Britain* (London: Allen and Unwin).

Mackie, L. and Patullo, P. (1977) *Women at Work* (London: Tavistock).

MacLennan, E. (1980) *Minimum Wages for Women* (London: Equal Opportunities Commission and the Low Pay Unit).

Maggs, C. (1983) *The Origins of General Nursing* (London: Croom Helm).

Main, B. (1986) *Women's Hourly Earnings over the Life Cycle*, Unpublished paper, Department of Economics, University of Edinburgh.

Manley, P. and Sawbridge, D. (1980) 'Women at work', *Lloyds Bank Review* no. 135, pp. 29–40.

Marks, P. (1976) 'Femininity in the classroom' in J. Mitchell and A. Oakley (eds), *The Rights and Wrongs of Women* (Harmondsworth: Penguin).

Marsden, D. (1973) *Mothers Alone: Poverty and the Fatherless Family*, revised edn, first published 1969 (Harmondsworth: Penguin).

Marsden, D. and Duff, E. (1975) *Workless* (Harmondsworth: Penguin).

Marshall, R. (1972) *Families Receiving Supplementary Benefit* (London: HMSO).

Marti, J. and Zeilinger, A. (1985) 'New technology in banking and shopping' in T. Forrester (ed.), *The Information Technology Revolution* (Oxford: Blackwell).

Martin, J. (1986) 'Returning to work after childbearing: evidence from the Women and Employment Survey', *Population Trends* no. 43, Spring, pp. 23–30.

Martin, J. and Roberts, C. (1984) *Women and Employment: a Lifetime Perspective. The Report of the 1980 DE/OPCS Women and Employment Survey* (London: HMSO).

Martin, R. (1983) *Women and Unemployment: Activities and Social Contact*, Paper given at SSRC Labour Markets Workshop, Manchester, December.

Martin, R. and Wallace, J. (1984) *Working Women in Recession:*

Employment, Redundancy and Unemployment (Oxford: Oxford University Press).

Martindale, H. (1939) *Women Servants of the State 1870–1938: A History of Women in the Civil Service* (London: Allen and Unwin).

Masey, A. (1977) 'Savings, insurance and credit' in F. Williams (ed.), *Why the Poor Pay More* (London: National Consumer Council/Macmillan).

Massey, D. (1983) 'The shape of things to come', *Marxism Today* vol. 27, no. 4, pp. 18–27.

Maynard, M. (1985) 'Houseworkers and their work' in R. Deem and G. Salaman (eds), *Work, Culture and Society* (Milton Keynes: Open University Press).

McGoldrick, A. (1984) *Equal Treatment in Occupational Pension Schemes: a Research Report* (Manchester: Equal Opportunities Commission).

McIntosh, M. (1981) 'Feminism and social policy', *Critical Social Policy* vol. 1, no. 1, pp. 32–42.

McKee, L. and Bell, C. (1985) 'His unemployment, her problem: the domestic and marital consequences of male unemployment' in S. Allen, K. Purcell, A. Waton and S. Wood (eds), *The Experience of Unemployment* (London: Macmillan).

Meager, N. (1986) 'Temporary work in Britain', *Employment Gazette* vol. 94, no. 1, pp. 7–15.

Ministry of Labour Gazette (1938) 'Schemes providing for pensions for employees on retirement from work' vol. XXX, no. 5, pp. 172–4.

Ministry of Pensions and National Insurance (1966) *Financial and Other Circumstances of Retired Pensioners* (London: HMSO).

Mitchell, J. (1971) *Women's Estate* (Harmondsworth: Penguin).

Morokvasic, M. (1983) 'Women in migration: beyond the reductionist outlook' in A. Phizaclea (ed.), *One Way Ticket* (London: Routledge and Kegan Paul).

Moynihan, D. P. (1965) *The Negro Family: The Case for Action* (Washington USA: Office of Planning and Research, US Department of Labour).

Murcott, A. (1982) ' "It's a pleasure to cook for him": food, mealtimes and gender in some South Wales households' in E. Gamarniker, D. Morgan, J. Purvis and D. Taylorson (eds), *The Public and the Private* (London: Heinemann).

Murray, N. (1983) 'A basically racist society', *Community Care* no. 456, 31 March.

—— (1984) 'A cure for colour blindness?', *Community Care* no. 525, 16 August.

Nathan, R. P. (1986) 'A welfare revolution', *Washington Post* 4 October.

National Consumer Council (1975) *For Richer for Poorer: Some Problems of Low Income Consumers* (London: HMSO).

—— (1980) *Consumers and Credit* (London: National Consumer Council).

—— (1984) *Of Benefit To All* (London: National Consumer Council).

National Council for One-Parent Families (1978) *Britain's One-Parent Families*, Information sheet no. 5, November (London: National Council for One-Parent Families).

—— (1982) *Great Britain's One-Parent Families*, Information sheet no. 35 (London: National Council for One-Parent Families).

—— (1984) *Survival or Security: Evidence to the Social Security Reviews* (London: National Council for One-Parent Families).

Nelson, B. (1984) 'Women's poverty and women's citizenship: some political consequences of economic marginality', *Signs* vol. 10, no. 2, pp. 209–31.

Nissel, M. and Bonnerjea, L. (1982) *Family Care of the Handicapped Elderly: Who Pays?* (London: Policy Studies Institute).

North Tyneside Community Development Project (1978) *In and Out of Work: A Study of Unemployment, Low Pay and Income Maintenance Services* (Newcastle: North Tyneside Community Development Project).

Oakley, A. (1982) *Subject Women* (London: Fontana).

Occupational Pensions Board (1981) *Improved Protection for the Occupational Pension Rights and Expectations of Early Leavers*, Cmnd, 8271 (London: HMSO).

O'Donnell, C. (1984) *The Basis of the Bargain* (London: Allen and Unwin).

O'Donovan, K. (1985) *Sexual Divisions in Law* (London: Weidenfeld and Nicolson).

Office of Fair Trading/NOP Surveys Ltd (1979) *Consumer Credit Survey 1977* (London: Office of Fair Trading).

Office of Population Censuses and Surveys (1982) *Labour Force Survey 1981* (London: HMSO).

—— (1983) *Census 1981, National Report, Great Britain, Part 1* (London: HMSO).

—— (1984a) *Population Census: Economic Activity Tables* (London: HMSO).

—— (1984b) *General Household Survey 1982* (London: HMSO).

—— (1985a) *Labour Force Survey 1984* (London: HMSO).

—— (1985b) *Labour Force Survey Monitors, LFS 85/1, LFS 85/2, PP1 85/3* (London: OPCS).

—— (1985c) *General Household Survey 1983* (London: HMSO).

—— (1985d) *General Household Survey Monitor 85/1* (London: HMSO).

O'Kelly, R. (1985) 'The principle of aggregation' in R. Silburn and P. Townsend (eds), *The Future of Social Security* (London: Fabian Society).

Oren, L. (1974) 'The welfare of women in labouring families: England 1860–1950' in M. Hartman and L. Banner (eds), *Clio's Consciousness Raised: New Perspectives on the History of Women* (London: Harper and Row).

Owen, A. P. K. (1935) 'Employers' retirement pensions in Great Britain', *International Labour Review* no. xxii, pp. 80–99.

Pahl, J. (1978) *A Refuge for Battered Women* (London: HMSO).

—— (1980) 'Patterns of money management within marriage', *Journal of Social Policy* vol. 9, no. 3, pp. 313–35.

—— (1982) *The Allocation of Money and the Structuring of Inequality within Marriage* (Canterbury: Health Services Research Unit, University of Kent).

—— (1983) 'The allocation of money and the structuring of inequality within marriage', *Sociological Review* vol. 31, no. 2, pp. 237–62.

—— (1984) 'The allocation of money within the household' in M. Freeman (ed.), *The State, the Law and the Family* (London: Tavistock).

—— (1985a) *Private Violence and Public Policy: The Needs of Battered Women and the Response of the Public Services* (London: Routledge and Kegan Paul).

—— (1985b) 'Who benefits from child benefit?', *New Society* vol. 72, no. 1165, pp. 117–19.

Parker, G. (1980) 'Birmingham Money Advice Centre clients' in *Consumers and Credit* (London: National Consumer Council).

—— (1985a) *With Due Care and Attention: A Review of Research on Informal Care*, Occasional Paper no. 2 (London: Family Policy Studies Centre).

—— (1985b) *Patterns and Causes of Indebtedness: A Study of*

Clients of the Birmingham Money Advice Centre, Unpublished PhD thesis, University of Birmingham.

—— (1986a) Background paper for National Consumer Council Conference on *Consumers in Debt*, London, National Consumer Council, January.

—— (1986b) 'Unemployment, low income and debt' in I. Ramsey (ed.), *Creditors and Debtors: A Socio-Legal Perspective* (London: Professional Books).

Parker, S. R. (1980) *Older Workers and Retirement* (London: OPCS/HMSO).

Parmar, P. (1982) 'Gender, race and class: Asian women in resistance' in Centre for Contemporary Cultural Studies, *The Empire Strikes Back* (London: Hutchinson).

Parson, T. and Bales, R. F. (1956) *Family, Socialisation and Interaction Process* (London: Routledge and Kegan Paul).

Peace, S. (1986) 'The forgotten female: social policy and older women' in C. Phillipson and A. Walker (eds), *Ageing and Social Policy* (London: Gower).

Pearce, B. and McAdoo, H. (1981) *Women and Children Alone in Poverty* (Washington, USA: National Advisory Council in Economic Opportunity).

Pember Reeves M. S. (1913) *Round About a Pound a Week* (London: Bell, reprinted by Virago 1979).

Perkins, T. (1983) 'A new form of employment: a case study of women's part-time work in Coventry' in M. Evans and C. Ungerson (eds), *Sexual Divisions: Patterns and Processes* (London: Tavistock).

Phillipson, C. (1982) *Capitalism and the Construction of Old Age* (London: Macmillan).

Phillipson, C. and Walker, A. (eds) (1986) *Ageing and Social Policy* (London: Gower).

Phizacklea, A. (1983b) 'In the front line' in A. Phizacklea (ed.), *One Way Ticket—Migration and Female Labour* (London: Routledge and Kegan Paul).

Piachaud, D. (1974) *Do the Poor Pay More?*, Poverty Research Series no. 3 (London: Child Poverty Action Group).

—— (1985) *Round About Fifty Hours a Week: The Time Costs of Children*, Poverty Pamphlet no. 64 (London: Child Poverty Action Group).

—— (forthcoming) 'Problems in the definition and measurement of poverty', *Journal of Social Policy*.

Pilch, M. and Wood, V. (1960) *Pension Schemes* (London: Hutchinson).

—— (1979) *Pension Schemes: A Guide to Principles and Practice* (Farnborough, Hants: Gower Press).

Popay, J., Rimmer, L. and Rossiter, C. (1983) *One Parent Families: Parents, Children and Public Policy*, Study Commission on the Family Occasional Paper no. 12 (London: Study Commission on the Family).

Powell, J. V. (1984) 'Pension considerations on marriage breakdown', *Family Law* vol. 14, pp. 187–9.

Prescod-Roberts, M. and Steele, N. (1980) *Black Women: Bringing it all Back Home* (Bristol: Falling Wall Press).

Purvis, J. (1981) 'The double burden of class and gender in the schooling of working-class girls in nineteenth-century England' in L. Barton and S. Walker (eds), *Schools, Teachers and Teaching* (Sussex: Falmer Press).

—— (1983) 'Towards a history of women's education in nineteenth century Britain' in J. Purvis and M. Hales (eds), *Achievement and Inequality in Education* (London: Routledge and Kegan Paul).

Quadagno, J. (1982) *Ageing in Early Industrial Society* (London: Academic Press).

Rathbone, E. (1909) *How the Casual Labourer Lives*, for the Liverpool Economic and Statistical Society (Liverpool: The Northern Publishing Company).

—— (1924) *The Disinherited Family* (London: Edward Arnold).

—— (1925) *Widows, Orphans and the Old Age Contributory Pensions Bill* (London: National Union of Societies for Equal Citizenship).

Rein, M. and Erie, S. (forthcoming) 'Women and the welfare state' in C. M. Mueller (ed.), *The Politics of the Gender Gap* vol. 2 (London: Sage).

Rex, J. and Moore, R. (1967) *Race, Community and Conflict* (London: Oxford University Press/Institute of Race Relations).

Rhodes, G. (1965) *Public Sector Pensions* (London: Allen and Unwin).

Richards, J. R. (1982) *The Sceptical Feminist* (Harmondsworth: Penguin).

Richardson, A. (1984) *Widows Benefit* (London: Policy Studies Institute).

Rimmer, L. (1981) *Families in Focus: Marriage, Divorce and Family Patterns* (London: Study Commission on the Family).

Ritchie, J. and Barrowclough, R. (1983) *Paying for Equalisation: A Survey of Pension Age Preferences and their Costs* (Manchester: Equal Opportunities Commission).

Roberts, C. (1981) *Women's Unemployment*, paper presented at SSRC/Department of Employment Workshop on Employment and Unemployment, London.

Roberts, E. (1984) *A Woman's Place* (Oxford: Blackwell).

Roberts, R. (1973) *The Classic Slum* (Harmondsworth: Penguin).

Robinson, J. (1975) *The Life and Times of Francie Nichol of South Shields* (London: Allen and Unwin).

Robinson, O. (1985) 'The changing labour market: the phenomenon of part-time employment in Britain', *National Westminster Bank Quarterly Review* November, pp. 19–29.

Robinson, O. and Wallace, J. (1984a) 'Growth and utilization of part-time labour in Great Britain', *Employment Gazette* vol. 92, no. 9, pp. 391–7.

—— (1984b) *Part-Time Employment and Sex Discrimination Legislation in Britain*, Research Paper no. 43 (London: Department of Employment).

Ross, E. (1982) ' "Fierce questions and taunts": married life in working-class London, 1870–1914', *Feminist Studies* vol. 8, Autumn, pp. 575–602.

Routh, G. (1980) *Occupation and Pay in Great Britain 1906–79*, 2nd edn (London: Macmillan).

Rowntree, B. S. (1902) *Poverty: A Study of Town Life*, 2nd edn (London: Macmillan).

—— (1903) *The Poverty Line: A Reply* (no publisher given).

—— (1941) *Poverty and Progress: A Second Social Survey of York* (London: Longman).

Rowntree, B. S. and Lavers, G. R. (1951) *Poverty and the Welfare State* (London: Longmans Green).

Rowntree, B. S. and Stuart, F. D. (1921) *The Responsibility of Women Workers for Dependants* (Oxford: Clarendon).

Runnymede Trust (1985) *Bulletin*, September (London: Runnymede Trust).

Scarman, Lord C. (1981) *The Brixton Disorders—A Report of An Enquiry* (London: HMSO).

Scott, H. (1984) *Working your Way to the Bottom: The Feminisation of Poverty* (London: Pandora Press).

Sinfield, A. (1978) 'Analyses in the social division of welfare', *Journal of Social Policy* vol. 7, no. 2, pp. 129–56.

Sivanandan, A. (1978) 'From immigration control to "induced repatriation" ', *Race and Class* vol. 20, no. 1, pp. 75–82.

Skrede, K. (1986) *The Welfare State and Women* (Oslo, Norway: Institute of Applied Social Research).

Smail, R. (1985) *Two Nations: Poverty Wages in the North*, Low Pay Unit Pamphlet no. 35 (London: Low Pay Unit).

Smart, C. (1984) *The Ties that Bind: Law, Marriage and the Reproduction of Patriarchal Relations* (London: Routledge and Kegan Paul).

Smith, D. J. (1977) *Racial Disadvantage in Britain* (Harmondsworth: Penguin).

—— (1981) *Unemployment and Racial Minorities* (London: Policy Studies Institute).

Smith, E. (1915) *Wage-Earning Women and their Dependants* (London: Fabian Women's Group).

Smith, P. (1985) ' "Who's fiddling?" Fraud and abuse' in S. Ward (ed.), *DHSS in Crisis* (London: Child Poverty Action Group).

Snell, K. D. M. and Miller, J. (1987) 'Lone-parent families and the welfare state: past and present', *Continuity and Change* vol. 2, part 3.

Spring-Rice, M. (1939) *Working Class Wives: their Health and Conditions* (reprinted 1981, London: Virago).

Stanworth, M. (1983) *Gender and Schooling: A Study of Sexual Divisions in the Classroom*, 2nd edn (London: Hutchinson).

Stone, K. (1983) 'Motherhood and waged work: West Indian, Asian and white mothers compared' in A. Phizacklea (ed.), *One Way Ticket* (London: Routledge and Kegan Paul).

Storey-Gibson, M. J. (1985) *Older Women Around the World* (Washington USA: International Federation On Ageing).

Tarpey, T. (1985) *Explaining the Increasing Dependence of Lone-Parent Families on Supplementary Benefit*, Unpublished MA thesis, University of York.

Taylor, R. and Ford, G. (1983) 'Inequalities in old age', *Ageing and Society* vol. 3, no. 2, pp. 183–208.

Tebbut, M. (1983) *Making Ends Meet: Pawnbroking and Working Class Credit* (Leicester: Leicester University Press/New York: St Martin's Press).

Thane, P. (1978) 'Women and the Poor Law in Victorian and Edwardian England', *History Workshop Journal* no. 6, pp. 29–51.

—— (1982) *The Foundations of the Welfare State* (London: Longman).

Titmuss, R. M. (1958) *Essays on the Welfare State* (London: Allen and Unwin).

Todd, J. and Jones, L. (1972) *Matrimonial Property*, Social Survey Division (London: HMSO).

Townsend, P. (1979) *Poverty in the United Kingdom* (Harmondsworth: Penguin).

—— (1981) 'Elderly people with disabilities' in A. Walker and P. Townsend (eds), *Disability in Britain* (Oxford: Martin Robertson).

Townsend, P. and Wedderburn, D. (1965) *The Aged in the Welfare State* (London: Bell).

Unemployment Unit (1986) *Unemployment Bulletin* no. 20 (London: Unemployment Unit).

Ungerson, C. (1983) 'Why do women care?' in J. Finch and D. Groves (eds), *A Labour of Love: Women, Work and Caring* (London: Routledge and Kegan Paul).

University of Surrey SRM Group (1983) *Patterns of Money Allocation in Marriage*, Paper given at Resources Within Households Research Workshop, Institute of Education, London, May.

Veit-Wilson, J. H. (1986) 'Paradigms of poverty: a rehabilitation of B S Rowntree', *Journal of Social Policy* vol. 15, no. 1, pp. 69–99.

Walker, A. (1980) 'The social creation of poverty and dependency in old age', *Journal of Social Policy* vol. 9, no. 1, pp. 49–75.

—— (1981) 'Towards a political economy of old age', *Ageing and Society* vol. 1, no. 1, pp. 73–94.

—— (1985a) 'Making the elderly pay', *New Society* 18th April, pp. 76–8.

—— (1985b) 'Early retirement: release or refuge from the labour market?', *The Quarterly Journal of Social Affairs* vol. 1, no. 3, pp. 211–29.

—— (1986) 'Pensions and the production of poverty in old age' in C. Phillipson and A. Walker (eds), *Ageing and Social Policy* (London: Gower).

Walker, A. and Laczko, F. (1982) 'Early retirement and flexible retirement', House of Commons Social Services Committee, *Age of Retirement*, HC26–II (London: HMSO).

Walker, A. and Townsend, P. (eds) (1981) *Disability in Britain* (Oxford: Martin Robertson).

Walsh, A. and Lister, R. (1985) *Mothers' Life-Line: A Survey of*

How Women Use and Value Child Benefit (London: Child Poverty Action Group).

Weale, A., Bradshaw, J., Maynard, A. and Piachaud, D. (1984) *Lone Mothers, Paid Work and Social Security* (London: Bedford Square Press).

Werneke, D. (1985) 'Women: the vulnerable group' in T. Forrester (ed.), *The Information Technology Revolution* (Oxford: Blackwell).

Westwood, S. (1984) *All Day Everyday: Factory and Family Life in the Making of Women's Lives* (London: Pluto).

Which (1986) January and May editions (London: Consumers Association).

Wilkinson, F. (1981) *The Dynamics of Labour Market Segmentation* (London: Academic Press).

Wilson, A. (1978) *Finding a Voice—Asian Women in Britain* (London: Virago).

Wilson, G. (forthcoming) 'Money: patterns of responsibility and irresponsibility' in J. Brannen and G. Wilson (eds), *Resources Within Households* (provisional title) (London: Allen and Unwin).

WING (Women against Immigration and Nationalisation Group) (1985) *Worlds Apart* (London: Pluto).

Women's Co-operative Guild (1915) *Maternity: Letters from Working Women* (Bell and Sons; reprinted 1978 London: Virago).

Women's Industrial Council (1911) *Memo on the National Insurance Bill as it Affects Women*, TS BLPES Library.

Young, M. (1977) 'Housekeeping money' in F. Williams (ed.), *Why the Poor Pay More* (London: Macmillan).

Youth Training (1984) no. 6, March (Sheffield: Manpower Services Commission).

Zabalza, A. and Tzannotos, Z. (1985) *Women and Equal Pay: The Effects of Legislation on Female Employment and Wages in Britain* (Cambridge: Cambridge University Press).

Index

293